Legend Tripping

THE INTERNATIONAL SOCIETY FOR CONTEMPORARY LEGEND RESEARCH SERIES

This volume is the first of a set of casebooks providing thorough and up-to-date studies that showcase a variety of scholarly approaches to contemporary legends, along with variants of legend texts, discussion questions, and projects for students.

Legend Tripping

A Contemporary Legend Casebook

Edited by
Lynne S. McNeill
Elizabeth Tucker

Utah State University Press
Logan

© 2018 by University Press of Colorado

Published by Utah State University Press
An imprint of University Press of Colorado
245 Century Circle, Suite 202
Louisville, Colorado 80027

All rights reserved

 The University Press of Colorado is a proud member of the Association of University Presses.

The University Press of Colorado is a cooperative publishing enterprise supported, in part, by Adams State University, Colorado State University, Fort Lewis College, Metropolitan State University of Denver, Regis University, University of Colorado, University of Northern Colorado, Utah State University, and Western State Colorado University.

ISBN: 978-1-60732-897-1 (cloth)
ISBN: 978-1-60732-807-0 (pbk.)
ISBN: 978-1-60732-808-7 (ebook)
DOI: https://doi.org/10.7330/9781607328087

Library of Congress Cataloging-in-Publication Data

Names: McNeill, Lynne S., author. | Tucker, Elizabeth, 1948– author.
Title: Legend tripping : a contemporary legend casebook / Lynne S. McNeill, Elizabeth Tucker.
Description: Logan : Utah State University Press, [2018] | Includes bibliographical references and index.
Identifiers: LCCN 2018031103| ISBN 9781607328971 (cloth) | ISBN 9781607328070 (pbk.) | ISBN 9781607328087 (ebook)
Subjects: LCSH: Urban folklore—United States. | Legends—United States. | Culture and tourism—United States. | Haunted places—United States. | Supernatural.
Classification: LCC GR105 .M44 2018 | DDC 398.2—dc23
LC record available at https://lccn.loc.gov/2018031103

Cover photo by Lynne McNeill.

This book is dedicated to our husbands, Geoffrey Gould and Stephen VanGeem; to our mentors, especially Linda Dégh and Jeannie Thomas; and to our editors, Michael Spooner and Rachael Levay.

Contents

Acknowledgments ix

Introduction
    Lynne S. McNeill
    and Elizabeth Tucker 3

1. Early Studies
    Elizabeth Tucker 31

2. Legend Tripping in Ohio: A Behavioral Survey
    Bill Ellis 61

3. Adolescent Legend Trips as Teenage Cultural Response: A Study of Lore in Context
    Patricia M. Meley 72

4. Legend Trips and Satanism: Adolescents' Ostensive Traditions as "Cult" Activity
    Bill Ellis 94

5. Playing with Fear: Interpreting the Adolescent Legend Trip
    S. Elizabeth Bird 112

6. "Shame Old Roads Can't Talk": Narrative, Experience, and Belief in the Framing of Legend Trips as Performance
    Tim Prizer 129

7. Ostensive Healing: Pilgrimage to the San Antonio Ghost Tracks
    Carl Lindahl 153

8. Contemporary Ghost Hunting and the Relationship between Proof and Experience
    Lynne S. McNeill 178

9. "There's an App for That": Ghost Hunting with Smartphones
    Elizabeth Tucker 192

10   Living Legends: Reflections on Liminality and Ostension
         Lynne S. McNeill   207

   Discussion Questions and Projects   211
   References   219
   About the Authors   231
   Index   233

Acknowledgments

THE EDITORS WOULD LIKE TO EXPRESS MANY THANKS to the contributors to this volume for their insightful and inspirational work on the subject of legend tripping. The authors whose essays appear in this volume are leaders in the field of legend-tripping scholarship, and we are thrilled to have their work compiled into a single volume. Editing, formatting, and prefacing the work of other scholars means gaining a deep familiarity with the details of their research and writing. We were consistently impressed with the quality of thought and prose from Linda Dégh, William M. Clements, Gary Hall, William E. Lightfoot, Kenneth A. Thigpen, Bill Ellis, Patricia M. Meley, S. Elizabeth Bird, Tim Prizer, and Carl Lindahl, Gary Hall, all of whom have contributed significantly to the development of scholarship on legend trips. Linda Dégh deserves special recognition for her seminal legend research and inspiration of legend scholars' efforts.

Deep gratitude goes to the great folklorist Alan Dundes, who generated the concept of folklore casebooks. We pay homage to his memory by applying this concept to the field of legends and legend-related behavior.

Many of the chapters in this book have appeared previously as articles or chapters in other works. The editors would like to thank the past and current editors of the *Journal of American Folklore*, *Western Folklore*, *Indiana Folklore*, *Children's Folklore Review*, Aldine de Gruyter, *Papers in Comparative Studies*, and, of course, *Contemporary Legend*, for their permission to reprint these pieces. A list of all the articles and chapters for which we received permission appears at the end of these acknowledgments.

Some of the photographs in this volume appeared in the original works; others are new. We thank Geoffrey Gould for his excellent photography and photo-editing skills. We also want to thank Lauren Pond and Jesse A. Fivecoate for their splendid photographs, which they took legend trips to obtain: a synthesis of technique with spirit.

Additional thanks are due to Michael Spooner and the rest of the staff at University of Colorado Press, without whose hard work and input this volume would not have come to fruition. It has been a joy to work with all of them.

Kind colleagues and friends have made our work as editors much more pleasant. Warm thanks go to Janet L. Langlois, Simon J. Bronner, Ronald Baker, Tom Blake, Cathy Preston, Andrea Kitta, and Trevor J. Blank. We would also like to thank the two anonymous reviewers who provided us with insightful feedback and suggestions to improve our initial drafts.

Particular thanks go to the board and membership of the International Society for Contemporary Legend Research, which approved the legend casebook series of which our book is the first. Thanks especially to our fellow editors of the casebook series: Elissa R. Henken, Diane Goldstein, Bill Ellis, John Laudun, and Jeffrey Tolbert.

Lynne would especially like to thank Libby for her astounding breadth of knowledge, her thoroughness as a writer and researcher, and her patience as a mentor and coeditor. Libby takes great pleasure in thanking Lynne for her creative inspiration, her amazing writing style, and her understanding of the complexities of book production, including advanced digital technology that is too hard for a digital immigrant of the baby boom generation to understand.

PERMISSIONS

S. Elizabeth Bird, "Playing with Fear: Interpreting the Adolescent Legend Trip," *Western Folklore* 53:3 (1994): 175–193. Used with permission of *Western Folklore*.

William M. Clements and William E. Lightfoot, "The Legend of Stepp Cemetery," *Indiana Folklore* 5:1 (1972): 92–135. Used with permission of *Indiana Folklore*.

Linda Dégh, "The Haunted Bridges Near Avon and Danville and Their Role in Legend Formation," *Indiana Folklore* 2:1 (1969): 77–81. Used with permission of *Indiana Folklore*.

Linda Dégh, "The House of Blue Lights," *Indiana Folklore* 2:2 (1969): 11–28. Used with permission of *Indiana Folklore*.

Bill Ellis, "Legend-Tripping in Ohio: A Behavioral Study," in *Papers in Comparative Studies* 2, ed. Daniel Barnes, Rosemary O. Joyce, and Steven Swann Jones, 61–73 (Columbus: Center for Comparative Studies in the Humanities, Ohio State University, 1982–1983), 61–73. Used with permission of the Center for Comparative Studies at Ohio State University.

Bill Ellis, "Legend-Trips and Satanism: Adolescents' Ostensive Traditions as 'Cult' Activity," in *New Perspectives in Contemporary Legend*, ed. Paul Smith and Gillian Bennett (1991; repr., New York: Garland, 1996), 167–186. Used with permission of Aldine de Gruyter.

Gary Hall, "The Big Tunnel," *Indiana Folklore* 6 (1973): 139–173. Used with permission of *Indiana Folklore*.

Carl Lindahl, "Ostensive Healing: Pilgrimage to the San Antonio Ghost Tracks," *Journal of American Folklore* 118:468 (2005): 164–185. From *Journal of American Folklore*. Copyright 2005 by the Board of Trustees of the University of Illinois. Used with permission of the University of Illinois Press.

Acknowledgments

Lynne S. McNeill, "Contemporary Ghost Hunting and the Relationship between Proof and Experience," *Contemporary Legend* 9 (2006): 96–110. Used with permission of *Contemporary Legend*.

Patricia M. Meley, "Adolescent Legend Trips as Teenage Cultural Response: A Study of the Lore in Context," *Children's Folklore Review* 14 (1991): 5–25. Used with permission of *Children's Folklore Review*.

Tim Prizer, "'Shame Old Roads Can't Talk': Narrative, Experience, and Belief in the Framing of Legend-Trips as Performance," *Contemporary Legend* n.s. 7 (2004): 67–97. Used with permission of *Contemporary Legend*.

Kenneth A. Thigpen, "Adolescent Legends in Brown County: A Survey," *Indiana Folklore* 4:2 (1971): 141–215. Used with permission of *Indiana Folklore*.

Elizabeth Tucker, "'There's an App for That': Ghost Hunting with Smartphones," *Children's Folklore Review* 38 (2016): 27–38. Used with permission of *Children's Folklore Review*.

Legend Tripping

Introduction

Lynne S. McNeill and Elizabeth Tucker

SIX TEENAGERS PILE INTO AN OLD BUICK to travel to a notorious haunted slaughterhouse late at night. How can they find this slaughterhouse? There is no mention of the place on any map or website about their town. On the way there, they argue about directions and tell stories about spooky things that have happened there before. After getting lost a couple of times, they finally arrive. Nervous but excited, they gather their equipment: smartphones with night-vision apps, a spirit box, and an electronic voice phenomena recorder. Furtively, because they know they're not supposed to be here, they push open the haunted slaughterhouse's door, which creaks in protest. Immediately they spot bloody buckets, old tools, and piles of other strange old stuff. Is this place really haunted? Eager to find out, they turn on their equipment and settle in for some serious exploration.

This scenario typifies teenagers' legend trips in the early twenty-first century. Carrying plenty of ghost-hunting equipment and steeling themselves to be brave no matter what happens, teens plunge into the realm of the supernatural. Their parents may raise hell if they find out where they've gone, and police may cause trouble if they notice the intrusion, but the kids accept these risks. Their trip is important; it helps them navigate the difficult passage from childhood to adulthood.

In a different part of the same middle-sized town, four men and one woman plan to visit an abandoned psychiatric hospital. Ranging in age from the mid-thirties to the late forties, they do different kinds of work but share one abiding passion: finding evidence that ghosts exist. Two of the men got to know each other as teenagers, when they loved to listen to legends about a green mist spreading through the historic psychiatric hospital on one of their hometown's highest hills. Later, through message boards online, they met the group's other three members. The five of them meet regularly at one another's homes, planning nocturnal adventures.

As they prepare for their trip to the abandoned hospital, the five adults check their equipment, much of which they purchased online. Tape

DOI: 10.7330/9781607328087.c000

recorders, video cameras, night-vision goggles, electromagnetic frequency meters, and a laser grid scope are all ready to go. Once they get to the hospital, they will have to be careful to avoid the old hospital's security guards. Hopefully they will succeed in making a video before anyone stops them. No matter what obstacles arise, they will take this trip, which probes the boundaries of life, death, and the afterlife.[1]

Not all legend trippers are teenagers; some are young or older adults. Legends can inspire trips at any stage of life, but trips taken by young people have captured more interest from scholars. This casebook includes studies of both young and older people's adventures. The book presents scholars' research in chronological order, tracing areas of interest, debates, and questions for the future.

LEGENDS

How can we define legends? The distinguished legend scholar Linda Dégh tells us, "Evidently, the legend touches upon the most sensitive areas of our existence, and its manifest forms cannot be isolated as simple and coherent stories. Rather, legends appear as products of conflicting opinions, expressed in conversation" (Dégh 2001, 2). Since 1973, when Dégh and her husband Andrew Vázsonyi published "The Dialectics of the Legend," folklorists have understood that legends arise from a complex dialogue involving believers, skeptics, and others in between. Although believers help keep legends alive, skeptics do too. It is in lively conversation with exchange of varying views that the "dialectic-polyphonic nature" of the legend comes forth (Dégh 2001, 2). While resolution as to the truth of a particular legend may never be reached, the emphasis on possibility makes this genre an important means of exploring the nature of reality.

When students tell legends about a haunted college residence hall, for example, some may express full belief, but others may scoff at the possibility of ghosts. "You think you saw a ghost in your mirror," one skeptic may say. "Don't you think you could have just seen your own face from a different angle?" Serious discussion of the time of day or night, the history of the building, and mirrors' association with magic ensues. No matter how the conversation ends, debate makes it meaningful.

Ever since the earliest days of legend definition, scholars have tended to define the legend by comparing it to another kind of narrative. Differences between the legend and the folktale, called the *Märchen* by Germans and the fairy tale by some English speakers, have especially interested folk narrative scholars. Jacob Grimm explains this distinction in his *Teutonic Mythology*, published in German in 1844: "The fairy-tale flies, the legend walks, knocks at your door; the one can draw freely out of the fullness of poetry, the other has almost the authority of history" (Grimm 1883, xv). Acknowledging the folktale's poetic beauty, Grimm emphasizes the legend's greater authority; moored in human history, it offers wisdom relevant to the course of our own lives. Although the Grimms' *Kinder- und Hausmärchen* (Children's and Household Tales, 1812–1814) have become more well known than their *Deutsche Sagen* (German Legends, 1816) (Grimm and Grimm 2006), it is clear that these foundational scholars valued both genres very highly.

Since the mid-nineteenth century, other scholars have tried to explain the legend's differences from the folktale. One of the most valuable articles is Max Lüthi's "Aspects of the Märchen and the Legend," which compares the folktale to a castle and the legend to a cave. In the folktale, Lüthi observes, angles are sharp and colors are bright; the hero goes forth to meet his challenge, and the reader or listener knows that the outcome will be successful. In contrast, the legend offers hazy outlines and muted colors; the hero, like any of us, has no guarantee of a victorious outcome in troubling situations. More specifically: The *Märchen* [folktale] considers man; the legend considers what happens to man. The *Märchen* outlines the narrow road of the hero walking through the world and does not dwell on the figures meeting him. But the legend looks fixedly at the inexplicable which confronts man. And because it is monstrous—war, pestilence, or landslide, and especially often a numinous power, be it nature, demons, or spirits of the dead—man becomes small and unsure before it (Lüthi 1976, 24). Note Lüthi's focus on a "numinous power": a mysterious, strongly spiritual quality that comes close to holiness. Some of the most intriguing legends involve this kind of power, but not all legends do. Legends about the numinous, more commonly known as the supernatural, are the ones most likely to inspire legend trips.

Besides the folktale, the saint's legend is another type of narrative that is often compared to the legend. The Latin term for saint's legend, *legenda*, means a story that people will read. In contrast, the German term for legend is *Sage*, something that people will say or tell. Linda Dégh notes that reading saint's legends is a religious duty, but the "folk legend does not tolerate such sectarian and social compulsion" (Dégh and Vázsonyi 1973, 3). Nonetheless, there is some similarity between the legend and the saint's legend. Although the saint's legend has a clearer didactic message and demands more dutiful attention, both kinds of narratives have the potential to teach people to live better, safer lives.

The influence of religion should be considered carefully. Lauri Honko devotes much attention to *homo religious*, religious man, whose beliefs have a major impact upon folk culture (Honko 1962, 120–125). Will-Erich Peuckert observes in his study of legends that people in his home village consider nonbelievers in spirits of the dead to be atheists (Peuckert 1965, 124). Similarly, Juha Pentikäinen explains that the most devoted churchgoers seem to be those who have the most run-ins with ghosts (Pentikäinen 1968, 153). Dégh reminds us that the Catholic Church supported belief in witches and devils for centuries and encouraged its congregations to believe in legends throughout much of the medieval period (Dégh 1973, 4). Today, many centuries later, we can still observe close connections between religion, folk belief, and legend in various cultural contexts.

Scholars have also developed distinctions between legends that explain the narrator's own experiences and legends that do not. In 1934 the influential Swedish folklorist Carl Wilhelm von Sydow (1948) published "Kategorien des Prosa-Volksdichtung" (Categories of Prose-Folk Poetry), which includes the terms *memorat* and *fabulat*: in English, memorate and fabulate. Memorates, narratives about personal experiences, may become fabulates—less subjective narratives—over time. For example, a farmer's narrative about a personal encounter with a ghost may lose its reference to him and become more generally identified with a folk group or culture area. Von Sydow's categories have made folklorists ask questions about the role of personal experience in legend telling. Is a legend derived from personal experience less of a full-fledged legend? Since the late twentieth century, folklorists have not worried much about this question. It has become common for people to tell legends from personal experience, so the kind of story that von Sydow calls a memorate has become increasingly normative.

Another change since the late twentieth century has been decrease in concern about distinguishing local legends from migratory legends. In 1958, Reidar Thoralf Christiansen (1958) published his well-known classificatory study *The Migratory Legends*. His list of legend types and detailed catalogue of Norwegian variants offer a fascinating glimpse of Norwegian legends that have migrated from one place to another over time. Titles of legend types include "The Black Book of Magic," "Trolls and Giants," "Witches and Witchcraft," and "Spirits of Rivers, Lakes and the Sea."

One of the most famous migratory legends around the world is "The Vanishing Hitchhiker," which puts traveling ghosts into a multitude of different cultural contexts. When Christiansen developed his type list and catalogue, legends traveled relatively slowly, both orally and in print, with some mass media involvement. Now the mass and new media are so dominant around the world that legends can migrate very quickly. With one push of a button on a computer or a smartphone, a legend can travel around the world. Some legends continue to be most meaningful in their own geographical area, as Trevor J. Blank and David J. Puglia demonstrate in *Maryland Legends* (Blank and Puglia 2014); Elizabeth Tucker's *Haunted Southern Tier* (Tucker 2011) and other books in the History Press's Haunted America series similarly explicate the appeal of local legends. All legends have the potential to migrate quickly, taking on new features and characteristics as they travel. This process, wherein legends adapt themselves to different cultural and social contexts, is known as ecotypification, a term borrowed from the study of botany, where it's used to describe the way that the same plant species will manifest differently in different places due to changes in the local environment. The fact that legends can adapt themselves to different settings and situations is one of the reasons that they're such a tenacious form of narrative.

Legend scholarship since the 1980s has increasingly reflected awareness of what Lutz Röhrich (1988, 8) calls "the cultural language of fear." Concerns about health scares, organ thefts, business scams, political conspiracies, out-of-control sex, and communication horrors have emerged in folklorists' books and articles. Many of these studies have come from American folklorists. Although the United States can certainly not claim to have more fear-generating situations than any other country, its folklore scholars have become leaders in explicating the dynamics of the modern legend, and of the legend trip specifically.

The American legend scholar Jan Harold Brunvand began his influential series of books in 1981 with *The Vanishing Hitchhiker*, making *urban legend* a familiar term. As his later books, including *The Choking Doberman* (Brunvand 1984), *The Mexican Pet* (Brunvand 1986), and *The Baby Train* (Brunvand 1993), were published, "urban legend" became a household phrase in the United States. Brunvand discusses legend texts and scholarly research in an engaging style that appeals to a broad range of readers. The term that he established appears on Barbara and David Mikkelson's Urban Legends Reference Pages, https://www.snopes.com, which provides an important information center for both folklorists and nonfolklorists.

Another term for urban legends, *contemporary legends*, emphasizes our current time period rather than urban or rural settings, and is the usage preferred by many legend scholars. This is the term used by the International Society for Contemporary Legend Research (ISCLR), which studies both current and historical legends and rumors. Some members of ISCLR present papers on ghost stories, while others discuss legends and rumors about the horrors of war, conspiracy theories, dangers to children, and other contemporary issues. Recent award-winning books by ISCLR presenters include Andrea Kitta's (2011) *Vaccination and Public Concern in History: Legend, Rumor and Risk Perception*, Eda Kalmre's (2013) *The Human Sausage Factory: A Study of Post-war Rumour in Tartu*, and Joel Best and Kathleen A. Bogle's *Kids Gone Wild: From Rainbow Parties to Sexting, Understanding the Hype over Teen Sex* (Best and Bogle 2014). As these examples suggest, the range of contemporary legend subjects is broad and intriguing.

To describe a legend as "contemporary" doesn't necessarily mean that it's modern or up to date; if that were the case, then the contemporary legends of today would cease to be contemporary legends twenty years from now. The word *contemporary* simply means that these legends are (or were) contemporary to the time in which they're actively being told and shared. Narrative scholar Henrik Lassen conducted a study of the "improved product" legend, in which an inventor creates a revolutionary new product and, rather than being championed for it, is killed by the powers that be, people who benefit from the status quo (Lassen 1995). This legend has been told in recent years about cars that run on water (with oil industry executives suggested as the bad guys), and yet it was also told in ancient Rome about unbreakable glass (with the emperor, whose riches were all in the familiar form of gold, dispatching the unfortunate inventor). This is a great example of how a legend adapts to remain *contemporary* to different times and cultures.

EARLY LEGEND-TRIP SCHOLARSHIP

Scholars have used several different terms to identify visits to places associated with legends. The most frequent term is *legend trip*, so that is our choice for this casebook. We should note, however, that *legend quest* has been gaining strength in recent years. Linda Dégh observed, "Most of the adolescent legends are quest stories" (Dégh 2001, 253). A number of other scholars have used the term *quest* to describe exploratory journeys (Lindahl 2005, 165; Tucker 2007, 182–210; Bronner 2012, 319–323; Gabbert 2015, 146–169). "Trip" means the whole journey, while "quest" stresses the journey's objective and the hero's striving. According to Bill Ellis, "The trip, not the legend, is the thing" (Ellis 2001, 190). For legend trippers and for many of us who study legends (and we should note that those categories overlap!), that statement holds true.

Before discussing legend-trip scholarship, we should define two other relevant terms: *pilgrimage* and *tourism*. "Pilgrimage" usually pertains to religious journeys but has been used more loosely since the twentieth century. Victor Turner suggests, "The plain truth is that pilgrimage does not ensure a major change in religious state—and seldom in secular status—though it may make one a better person, fortified by the graces merited by the hardships and self-sacrifices of the journey" (Turner 1992, 37). It is not unusual for travelers to describe their trips to highly meaningful, long-desired destinations such as Machu Picchu in Peru as pilgrimages. Takers of legend trips also have strong feelings about their experiences, but they follow a more specific sequence of events related to storytelling and ritual, and their trips may not require the same effort of planning or length of wait that a pilgrimage might.

Another kind of travel related to legend trips is tourism, discussed in detail by Diane E. Goldstein, Sylvia Ann Grider, and Jeannie Banks Thomas in *Haunting Experiences: Ghosts in Contemporary Folklore* (2007, 191–200). Goldstein, Grider, and Thomas discuss ghost tourism, organization of visits to allegedly haunted places that excite and intrigue people of varying ages. They refer to Thomas Blom's "morbid tourism," which "focuses on sudden violent death and which attracts large numbers of people" (Blom 2000, 32). Unlike ghost or morbid tourism, which operates for profit, legend trips do not entail money and usually involve small groups of friends.

Legend-trip scholarship began after Linda Dégh joined the Folklore Institute's faculty at Indiana University in 1964. Having done extensive fieldwork related to folktales in rural Hungary, Dégh wanted to learn about American rural narratives. According to Richard M. Dorson, the Folklore Institute's chair, American folk legends originated from local and national history (Dorson 1974). Rather than following this approach, Dégh examined legends about the supernatural. She undertook ambitious fieldwork projects and read all the legend material in the Folklore Institute's archives. In 1968 she founded the journal *Indiana Folklore*, which would publish significant articles about explorations of places related to legends.

Dégh's early articles show that young people's visits to haunted places constitute an important kind of initiation. In "The Haunted Bridges Near Avon and Danville and Their Role in Legend Formation" (Dégh 1969a), she observes that visitors to haunted bridges "perform a series of designated acts known to be effective to prompt the ghosts to appear," and that these acts comprise an initiation into adulthood (80–81). Another article, "The House of Blue Lights" (Dégh 1969b), shows how many legend variants a spooky house (this one in Indianapolis) can generate. It also eloquently demonstrates the role of print journalism in legend formation.

Folklorists in southern Indiana, including a number of Linda Dégh's students, published studies of young people's visits to haunted places in the late 1960s and early 1970s. "The Legend of Stepp Cemetery" by

William M. Clements and William E. Lightfoot discusses young people's attempts to spot a woman in black sitting on a stump in a cemetery near Bloomington (Clements and Lightfoot 1972). Gary Hall's 1973 "The Big Tunnel" documents hair-raising visits to a tunnel between Fort Ritner and Tunnelton that was famous among local teenagers; this is the first essay that uses the term *legend-trip*. Kenneth A. Thigpen's 1971 "Adolescent Legends in Brown County: A Survey" postulates a three-part structure for teenagers' visits to haunted places: storytelling on the way to the site, rituals such as headlight blinking and horn blowing to "cause the fulfillment of the legend" while there, and discussion of what happened at the site during the drive home (204–205). Studies from this time period in other parts of the United States show that the three-part structure is valid (Samuelson 1979; Harling 1971).

Bill Ellis's (1982–1983) "Legend-Tripping in Ohio: A Behavioral Survey" further clarifies the legend trip's structure and purpose, asking key questions. It confirms the trip's importance for young people as a form of initiation into adulthood and makes the important new point that the trip functions as a "ritual of rebellion" for the young. In addition, Ellis's article reinforces scholarly use of "legend trip." His study's influence can be seen in articles of the early 1990s such as Patricia M. Meley's (1991) "Adolescent Legend Trips as Teenage Cultural Response," which carefully examines legend trips by a group of teenaged friends over a six-month period.

Since many studies of legend trips have come from American scholars, is the legend trip intrinsically American? The typical American legend trip, according to scholars, involves a group of teenaged friends, a car, and a visit to an exciting place associated with violent crime and/or the supernatural. All of these components except for the car are known to have been important parts of legend trips in Europe as well. In *Lucifer Ascending*, Bill Ellis (2004, 112–141) discusses examples of legend trips several centuries ago in England, France, and Germany. Graveyards, churches, monuments, and castles have all inspired legend trips by adventurous walkers in Europe. Ellis suggests, "British legend-trips have not been collected as intensively as in the United States, where the teenage automobile culture may well have revitalized a tradition of visits originally made on foot and known only within a small radius" (116). We agree that the car is a crucial ingredient of the American legend trip; it provides an ideal setting for storytelling and socializing. However, automobile transportation is not the only way to take a legend trip. In Europe, Asia, and other parts of the world, legend trips continue. We hope that they will be studied more closely in the future.

Figure 0.1. The road to Stepp Cemetery in Morgan-Monroe Forest near Bloomington, Indiana. Photo by Jesse A. Fivecoate.

OSTENSION

For analysis of legend-trip behavior, the term *ostension* has become central. Derived from the Latin *ostendere*, "to show," this term comes from semiotics, which took it from Ludwig Wittgenstein and Bertrand Russell. Linda Dégh and Andrew Vázsonyi's article "Does the Word 'Dog' Bite? Ostensive Action: A Means of Legend-Telling" (Dégh and Vázsonyi 1983) introduces the term to folkloristics, defining it as "presentation as contrasted to representation" (6). The article also proposes three variations of ostension: pseudo-ostension, a hoax; proto-ostension, a narrator's appropriation of a legend as his or her own experience; and quasi-ostension, a misunderstanding of something that takes place (18–20). Since ostension can involve so many levels of perception and intent, these variations help to clarify its dynamics.

Bill Ellis applies Dégh and Vázsonyi's concepts of pseudo-ostension and quasi-ostension to his study of the Satanism scare of the 1980s in "Legend-Trips and Satanism: Adolescents' Ostensive Traditions as 'Cult' Activity" (Ellis 1991). His analysis of this moral panic, which troubled many people, demonstrates the expressive potential of ostension for society at times of uncertainty and fear. One of the most significant aspects of Ellis's study is his ability to look beyond fragmentary artifacts of so-called Satanic worship to identify patterns of behavior in youth culture. Verification of such patterns is understandably difficult to achieve, since teenagers do not want to get punished for rebellious behavior. Nonetheless, Ellis's article makes a very persuasive case.

Is ostension always disruptive and rebellious? In *Legend and Belief,* Dégh observes that ostension can be harmless, especially in connection with Halloween. Criminal ostension, however, can cause serious problems; examples include the Tylenol poisoning of 1982, in which seven people died from cyanide poison put in the pain reliever, and the Diet Pepsi tamperers of 1993 (Dégh 2001, 423–424, 428–434), who emulated reports of a syringe found in a Pepsi can by putting various objects in their own Pepsi cans and trying to pass them off as evidence of further tampering. She also notes that instances of Halloween ostension such as taking off the seat of an outhouse or putting a farm wagon on a roof can fall into the categories of "practical joke" or "prank" (423–424). This point reminds us that legends can be enacted in pranks, as studies of children at summer camps (e.g., Posen 1974) and students at college (e.g., Grider 1973; Bowman 1987; Tucker 2005: 93–96) have shown; both legends and pranks ask for some level of buy-in from participants. In this kind of context and others, there is a close connection between amusement and fright: pranks provide an outlet for stress caused by fear and make the pranksters feel powerful. Nonpranking legend trips can often function the same way.

MORE RECENT LEGEND-TRIP SCHOLARSHIP

Folklore articles about legend trips from the late 1980s to the early twenty-first century have given increasing attention to performance of legend-trip rituals. S. Elizabeth Bird's (1994) "Playing with Fear," for example, applies play theory and analysis of gender roles to legend-trip performance. Separately considering males and females as well as younger and older legend tellers, she suggests that young men and women learn gender-related lessons while performing their roles to the best of their ability. Another article, Tim Prizer's 2004 "Shame Old Roads Can't Talk: Narrative, Experience, and Belief in the Framing of Legend-Trips as Performance," applies Erving Goffman's frame analysis.

Some early twenty-first century studies of legend trips have examined religious or quasi-religious elements. In his article "Ostensive Healing: Pilgrimage to the San Antonio Ghost Tracks," Carl Lindahl (2005) suggests that "there is ample evidence that ostension can transcend horror and inspire a sense of wonder in those who bring legends to life" (165). He examines narratives about a school bus getting crushed on train tracks; the scene of the tragedy becomes a sacred place where the spirits of children linger. Having read more than 100 accounts of visits to the San Antonio train tracks by Hispanics, he finds that these narrators express a sense of wonder in telling their stories. His use of the term *pilgrimage* suggests a quasi-religious feeling of awe.

A related subject has been legend trips' facilitation of an altered state of consciousness. In her article about haunted bridges near Avon and Danville, Linda Dégh (1969a, 80) notes, "The bridge visitors condition themselves mentally for a vision they desire to have." Comparing accounts of visits to these haunted bridges on dark, moonless nights, she finds that the narrators are emotionally involved in their search for a good scare. Bill Ellis views such trips by teenagers as rituals of rebellion, finding that drinking, pot smoking, and visits to haunted places are "trips" in more ways than one: they are "deliberate escapes into altered states of being where conventional laws do not operate" and where an adolescent's status may be increased by seeing a ghost (Ellis 2001, 189). Further discussion appears in Michael Kinsella's (2011) *Legend Tripping Online*, which examines alternate states of consciousness in relation to certain Internet sites.

Recently some scholars have studied performances of ghost hunters who have used technological devices. Lynne S. McNeill's (2006) "Contemporary Ghost Hunting and the Relationship between Proof and Experience" examines both the tradition of belief and the tradition of disbelief, finding that ghost hunters discover "at least according to their standards, potentially satisfying proof" (109). Elizabeth Tucker's 2016 "'There's an App for That: Ghost Hunting with Smartphones" analyzes a student ghost-hunting team's search for ghosts in a college residence hall using the latest available smartphone technology. This article proposes a new term, *hypermodern ostension*, for the kind of ostension that is heavily influenced by technology. As technology continues to develop, it will be fascinating to see what kinds of ghost hunts will happen next.

OUR OWN EXPERIENCES

It seems only fair for the two of us, McNeill and Tucker, to share our own legend-trip experiences. We have been studying legends one way or another since we were teenagers: McNeill in the 1990s, Tucker in the 1960s. As folklorists we have taught classes about legends and encouraged students to collect them from friends and family members. Every year we have participated in meetings of the International Society for Contemporary Legend

Figure 0.2. "Weeping Woman" memorial in Logan City Cemetery, Logan, Utah. Photo by Lynne McNeill.

Research, which have usually included legend trips to cemeteries, murder sites, and other intriguing but slightly nerve-wracking places.

When Utah State University hosted the International Society for Contemporary Legend Research's annual meeting in 2006, both of us visited the famous Weeping Woman one sunny afternoon with a whole crowd of folklorists. Holding hands as we stood in a circle around the statue, we chanted, "Weep, lady, weep" and then "Cry, lady cry." Then we lifted Cathy Preston, the smallest, lightest folklorist in our group, up to the top of the statue's head to see whether the statue was crying. We had fun and bonded wonderfully with each other, but we did not feel scared. Why not? We knew that if the Weeping Woman really did cry, she wouldn't do it during the day.

Our experiences as teenagers were fairly similar, though thirty years apart. Tucker, cruising around Colorado Springs with her best girlfriend in

Figure 0.3. Elizabeth Tucker (*right*) as a teenager longing for adventure in the mountains of Colorado, with her sister Margaret (*left*) and dog Dixie.

an old red and white station wagon named Angela, longed to have an exciting adventure. Angela had the same colors as the bloodthirsty vehicle that Stephen King (1983) would name Christine but offered no thrills beyond driving around town. Up to the age of fifteen, the most adventurous things Tucker had managed to do were participate in a séance and sneak out to go to a football game she was forbidden to attend. That changed when she got a chance to spend a week at a church camp up in the mountains. Late one night at camp, a boy named Jim told a story about the ghost of a mean old man named Chas McGee. Jim led the group to the cemetery where Chas was buried. Suddenly he pulled Chas's tombstone out of the ground and started running. Lights flashed; could that be Chas's ghost? Everyone got punished the next morning, but Tucker didn't mind; at last, something amazing had happened. Ten years later, she would start studying folklore at Indiana University and learn that the Chas McGee story was a legend.

Thirty years after Tucker's adolescent adventures, growing up in the Bay Area in California, McNeill and her friends experimented with forms of play that function as non-travel-based legend trips: séances and hypnosis games. They didn't use a Ouija board—maybe those seemed too scary, or maybe none of the friends owned one. McNeill *loved* that stuff; she found it mysterious, calming, and eerie. Because she cared so much about this kind of experience, she hesitated to go out at night to see if something supernatural would happen. Maintaining a too-scared-to-try-it-for-real stance let her hold off from "knowing" and just enjoy the work of "believing" and "wondering."

As teenagers, both of us liked the idea of ghosts and hauntings, hoping to enter the "world within a world" of the supernatural. We both loved the *Chronicles of Narnia* by C. S. Lewis, in which four children discover a realm of magic by opening a wardrobe door. A generation apart, growing up in different parts of the United States, we intuited the importance of legends and wanted to learn how they worked. What better way to learn than to take and study legend trips?

LIMINAL LIFE STAGES

No matter where we grow up, we all go through transitions from one life stage to another. These transitions make us liminal (from the Latin *limen*, threshold): in between one clear state of being and another. While liminal states can be confusing, they also involve important discoveries. One way to make such discoveries is to go on a legend trip.

Many people think that legend trips belong to teenagers. Certainly most of the scholarship on legend trips, beginning with Linda Dégh's meticulous analyses of such excursions in southern Indiana, addresses young people's experiences. However, as we observed at the beginning of this introduction, teenagers are not the only people who take trips of this kind. Legend trips can happen at any age, although they serve an especially important initiatory purpose among the young.

The essence of the legend trip is the enactment of ambiguity, the experiential affirmation of the weird or the unexplainable. At times of transition, especially when moving from one age stage to another, people feel drawn to experiences that express how they feel. For teenagers, who are undergoing the major transition from childhood to adulthood, legend trips offer a chance to articulate feelings of ambiguity and to explore compelling issues. Sex, violence, racial injustice, gender inequality, and other complex

Figure 0.4. Lynne McNeill as a teenager in California.

subjects arise within exploration of the supernatural, which is inherently ambiguous and fascinating. This kind of exploration provides an exciting, sometimes chilling initiation into the mysterious world of adult concerns.

For those who have already made the transition to adulthood, legend trips still offer plenty of ambiguity. McNeill can offer an example from the early days of her career. Working as a professional folklorist, a career in which supernatural experimentation can double as research, she discovered ghost-hunting apps for cell phones and visited the Weeping Woman statue one Halloween night after giving a public talk about paranormal research. The shift from day to night, from student to professor, from low tech to high created a new opportunity for a legend trip in a familiar place. When the app suddenly changed from random sounds to a women's voice saying, "You all should go!" (heard by both people present), McNeill found a frightening new layer of potential belief in the tradition.

Some young and older adults enjoy planning legend trips for children and adolescents. At summer camp, a liminal place between home and the wilderness, a legend trip can be an important expression of ambiguity. Counselors at a number of camps in upstate New York organize trips to places associated with Cropsey, a maniac who supposedly kills campers each year in memory of his own children who died in a fire (Haring and Breslerman 1977). At the beginning of summer, counselors at a camp in

Figure 0.5. Close-up of the Weeping Woman memorial in Logan City Cemetery. Photo by Lynne McNeill.

Canada take new campers on a tour of a "coffin factory" that gives them a frightening preview of what their camp experience will offer them. Such trips serve as initiations in which young adults test campers' courage. If these campers return the following year, they may help to initiate the next group of campers.

One popular legend-trip destination for both young and older people is the home of Lizzie Borden in Fall River, Massachusetts. In 1892 Lizzie's parents, Andrew and Abby Borden, were murdered by someone wielding an ax. Lizzie was acquitted at her murder trial, but the killer was never identified. A journalist wrote a rhyme that children soon started to sing as they jumped rope: "Lizzie Borden took an ax /and gave her mother forty whacks. / When she saw what she had done, / she gave her father forty-one." Today the Borden family home is a bed-and-breakfast. People of varying ages stay there overnight, hoping to communicate with spirits of the dead. One of Tucker's students went to the Lizzie Borden B & B for her sixteenth birthday, accompanied by her mother and a few friends.

Figure 0.6. Gazing globe in a psychic medium's garden in Lily Dale, New York. Photo by Geoffrey Gould.

All of them enjoyed using a Ouija board to try to contact the Borden family's spirits.

Another well-known destination is Lily Dale in western New York, a Spiritualist assembly where psychics commune with spirits of the dead. Founded in 1879, three decades after Margaret and Kate Fox claimed to contact spirits in Hydesville, New York, Lily Dale has stimulated lively interest in Spiritualism. Students from nearby colleges enjoy traveling to Lily Dale, as do older adults from the United States, England, Germany, and other countries. In 2011 Home Box Office made a documentary, *No One Dies in Lily Dale*, which increased the assembly's fame. Since Lily Dale is well known as a place in which spirits of the dead are easy to reach, it has a special appeal for people who have lost relatives and close friends. For older adults who have suffered significant losses, the opportunity to talk with the spirits of loved ones through psychics may be particularly meaningful (Tucker 2015a).

EPIC AND LEGEND-TRIP HEROES

Both adolescents and adults enjoy epics, long narrative poems in which heroes dare to do something that seems impossible. Legend trips have their roots in these ancient poems. Epic heroes must accept a challenge that is so difficult they fear they may never get home. In accepting this challenge, they prove their courage as well as their willingness to try something that sounds a little crazy to most people. Epic heroes' quests involve vanquishing monsters, killing fierce animals, outwitting sorcerers, confronting supernatural forces, and entering realms where living people are not allowed to go. Legend trippers' quests may seem simpler and less soul-searing, but they involve similar risk taking and rule breaking.

Entering prohibited, horrifying places is an important part of what the epic hero achieves—and in our contemporary world, this kind of achievement also characterizes people who go on legend trips. Although visitors to haunted and notorious places are not as famous as epic heroes, they have a similar attitude that might, in contemporary slang, be called "badass": bold, disrespectful of boundaries, and ready for almost anything that may happen. In their transgression of boundaries, both epic heroes and legend trippers fit the pattern of tricksters who insist on doing whatever they want to do, demonstrating the strength of their life force (Hyde 1998).

Tricksters, by definition, are characters who break the rules and in doing so, help us to see why those rules (whether official or unofficial) are there in the first place. The emphasis on liminality in legend tripping—whether the liminality of the supernatural, of adolescence, or simply of the setting, such as camp—provides a natural context for turning societal expectations on their head. Being decidedly "betwixt and between" makes it seem easier to break rules and do things like trespass or even commit vandalism; engaging in this kind of rule breaking can serve as a release, making it easier to put up with society's restrictions the rest of the time.

Like tricksters, epic heroes dare to break rules and go places where no one is supposed to go. One of the earliest epics, *Gilgamesh*, dates from approximately 2100 BCE in Sumeria. Gilgamesh, king of Uruk, fights with Enkidu, a wild man created by the gods; afterward he and Enkidu become close friends. Together they defeat the giant Humbaba. After the gods condemn Enkidu to death, Gilgamesh travels to the land of death to try to save his close friend. Like Orpheus in the later Greek myth of Orpheus and Eurydice, he tries his best to bring a loved one back from the dead; tragically but predictably, he fails.

Another epic hero who attempts to break through to the kingdom of death is Aeneas, central character of the *Aeneid*, which Virgil wrote sometime between 29 and 19 BCE. Traveling from Troy to Italy after the Trojan War, Aeneas founds Rome and becomes the ancestor of the Romans. In the sixth book of this epic, Aeneas asks for help from the oracle known as the Cumaean Sibyl to descend into the underworld so that he can speak with his father's spirit. Succeeding in this quest, he has a vision of Rome's destiny. Cumae, near Naples, is the alleged location of the Cumaean Sibyl's entrance to the underworld; it is now a popular tourist destination. As they have always done, people continue to wonder about the realm of death and imagine what it would be like to go there as a visitor.

Homer's *Odyssey*, written toward the end of the eighth century BCE, presents the journey of another Trojan warrior who encounters supernatural forces. During his long voyage home, Odysseus struggles with a one-eyed Cyclops, a sorceress who turns his men into pigs, and dangerous Sirens whose enchanting songs threaten to cause a shipwreck. To prevent himself from succumbing to the Sirens, he orders his shipmates to lash him to the mast. Finally he returns home, where his last task is the recovery of his faithful wife, Penelope.

Yet another epic hero is the central character of the *Epic of King Gesar*, which circulates actively today in Mongolia, Tibet, and other parts of Central Asia (Chadwick and Zhirmunsky 2010). Dating from the twelfth century, this epic has many variants. King Gesar, whose name resembles that of the Roman emperor Caesar, kills demons and gigantic animals as he struggles to establish his kingdom. In some versions, he descends to the underworld to be initiated or to rescue his mother. Gesar's adventures continue to grow as singers sing new songs and folklorists record their performances.

We do not mean to suggest that the epic heroes of the past were the only legend trippers of their times. It's quite likely that even in ancient Sumeria, just as in our contemporary societies, ordinary teenagers would gather together and set out to investigate their local communities' legendary haunted spots. Unfortunately, most early historical and folkloristic documentation privileged the impressive and important over the mundane and minor; this means that we'll likely never know about many of the legend-tripping experiences of the common people of the past. But the journeys of epic heroes still apply here—they provide us with a sense of the symbolic power of embarking on a journey, whether big or small, that involves approaching the liminal, facing one's fears, and investigating the world around us.

EARLY LEGEND TRIPS

Most of the legend trips we examine in this casebook are specific to American and British youth culture from the mid-twentieth to the twenty-first century, but we do have some tantalizing records of legend trips that happened much earlier. Most of these records come from Europe, but some originate from Asia. Wherever legends have a strong connection to a particular place, there is potential for people to go on legend trips.

From medieval folklore we learn of supernatural legends from rural England that Gervase of Tilbury recorded in his *Otia Imperialia* about 1212. Gervase describes a tall mound in a wooded vale in Gloucester County, explaining that if you stand on that mound and say, "I thirst," a cheerful servant will offer you a "most pleasing drink" from a large bejeweled horn (Oman 1944, 7). He also tells of a "well-established tradition" in the Gogmagog or Wandlebury Hills: if a knight rides unattended into camp by moonlight, shouting, "Let a knight come against a knight," an adversary will magically appear. When a knight named Osbert FitzHugh shouted this challenge, he received a grievous wound that opened up every year on the anniversary of the conflict (Oman 1944, 8). Both of these accounts suggest the possibility of exciting, somewhat frightening legend trips. Although the story of the mound no longer circulates, the mystery of what happened in the Gogmagog Hills still entices tourists to travel there.

Records of German folklore from the nineteenth and earlier twentieth century show how many people visited legendary places. Even very small villages had their own churches, and each church had at least one legend associated with it. One church, for example, held the ghost of a priest who had baptized someone in the name of the devil. Another church, which sank into the ground because its priests and monks misbehaved, could be located by listening to the muffled pealing of its bells on Good Friday. Ghosts of knights and nuns would return to their churches at certain times, encouraging parishioners to risk viewing their spectral presences. Besides legends about churches, German folklore includes many legends about haunted bridges, houses, and other locations (Hoffmann-Krayer and Bächtold-Stäubli 1931–1932: 1402–1408).

One of the most engaging and moving records of an early legend trip appears in Lafcadio Hearn's 2012 *Glimpses of an Unfamiliar Japan*. A sensitive observer of Japanese culture, Hearn wrote in his first anthology about finding a statue of Jizô, a god who protects people's souls, in a Buddhist cemetery. He learned that there was another statue of Jizô in the "cave of the children's ghosts" on the Shimane Peninsula. Since children's spirits were too weak to cross the river between our world and the afterlife, they had to build towers of tiny stones in this seaside cave. Demons tried to knock the children's towers down, but visitors helped by building the towers back up. When he traveled to the cave, Hearn saw tiny footprints. He was participating in a legend trip that had existed for many years and can be found now on in Internet advertisements of boat rides for tourists, as Bill Ellis (2015, 211) notes in "The Haunted Asian Landscapes of Lafcadio Hearn."

LEGEND TRIPS IN LITERATURE, FILM, AND TELEVISION

To understand legend trips, especially in the United States and England, we need to consider certain classics of literature, film, and television that have influenced trippers' expectations. Ever since the rise of the Gothic novel in the middle of the eighteenth century, readers have viewed picturesque ruins, castles, and mansions as possible sources of supernatural stimulation. Horace Walpole's *The Castle of Otranto* (1764) was presented by its publisher as a found manuscript that was written in 1529 by the canon of the Church of Saint Nicholas. The novel begins with the son of Manfred, lord of the castle, getting crushed to death by a falling helmet. Fearing that this sudden death has resulted from an ancient prophecy, Manfred resolves to marry his son's fiancée, starting a series of intrigues and deceptions that will culminate in tragedy. There are many supernatural events, including three drops of blood falling from a statue's nose. The castle in Walpole's novel is the first of many large, mysterious buildings that readers explore as they move through the story; reading books of this kind whets the appetite for exploration of old castles and mansions.

The earliest American writer of Gothic literature was Edgar Allan Poe, who published his short story "The Fall of the House of Usher" in 1839. Worried about his friend Roderick Usher, who appears to be ill, the story's nameless narrator travels to Usher's house and immediately notices that it has a crack from its roof to its foundation. Roderick is obsessed with his house and has a morbid attachment to his twin sister Madeline, who falls into cataleptic trances and ends up being buried alive. Like the Usher twins, the house is ill; it is *alive* and wishes nobody well. This story marks the beginning of American horror stories and films about sentient houses of evil intent, which have complex symbolic meaning.

Another creepy house of early American literature is the one in Nathaniel Hawthorne's 1851 novel, *The House of the Seven Gables*. Based on a seventeenth-century gabled house owned by Hawthorne's cousin Susanna Ingersoll, the house in this novel has a tragic connection to the Salem witchcraft trials of 1692. Accused of being a witch, the character Matthew Maule curses his relative Colonel Pyncheon with the fateful words "God will give him blood to drink!" (1999, 3). Like the castle in Horace Walpole's Gothic novel, this house has a prophecy of doom derived from a difficult past. Today, as the House of the Seven Gables in Salem, the Ingersoll house draws many visitors.

As Sylvia Ann Grider (1999) explains in "The Haunted House in Literature, Popular Culture, and Tradition," the American haunted house is "the ugly stepsister of the enchanted castle" (193). Certain features show that the house is haunted: a "gambrel roof, turrets or towers, and broken or boarded-up windows with 'spooky' inhabitants peeking out" (181). Often located on a hill or in another isolated place, this house symbolizes unhealthful separation from other people, neglect, and openness to dangerous supernatural forces. Grider notes that the image of the American haunted house as a spooky mansion owes part of its genesis to funeral homes: large, imposing buildings that offer comfortable spaces for people to mourn their lost loved ones.

Since the early 1960s, visits to haunted houses have been vividly portrayed in horror films. *The Innocents* (1961), based on Henry James's novella *The Turn of the Screw* (1898), begins with a young governess's journey from London to Bly, a country house in Essex, where she will teach young Miles and Flora. Soon she learns that both the last governess, Miss Jessel, and a valet, Peter Quint, have recently died. Does the governess actually see the ghosts of Jessel and Quint, or is her mind disturbed by social alienation and repression? Literary critics have tended toward the second possibility, but horror fans have favored the first: the governess's and valet's ghosts haunt the house and its grounds, exerting an evil influence on anyone who dares to approach them.

Another classic horror film, Shirley Jackson's (1963) *The Haunting*, is based on her acclaimed novel *The Haunting of Hill House* (Jackson 1959). Two young women with a sensitivity to spirits, Eleanor and Theodora, travel to an eighty-year-old mansion at the behest of a scientist who hopes to prove that ghosts exist. The two women quickly discover that the house wants Eleanor to stay forever. Once Eleanor has decided to stay, she crashes her car into a tree. Like Poe's House of Usher, Hill House has a malevolent, seething presence. Like James's *The Turn of the Screw*, the narrative offers some ambiguity. Is Hill House truly haunted, or is Eleanor losing her mind? For viewers of the film who enjoy feeling scared, this is an easy choice; the house's evil influence explains everything that happens.

Like Hill House, the house that takes center stage in *The Amityville Horror* (1979) inspires a feeling of dread. This film was released shortly after the publication of Jay Anson's 1977 book of the same title, a narrative about sensational supernatural incidents that allegedly took place after Ronald DeFeo murdered six members of his family on November 13, 1974, at 112 Ocean Avenue in Amityville, New York. According to Anson, this supernatural activity had its genesis in the house having been built upon an Indian burial ground. Although this claim has no clear substantiation, it expresses the Gothic and horror film trope of a curse explaining horrific events. In the film, the house on Ocean Avenue looks like a demonic pumpkin with glowing yellow eyes; like Poe's House of Usher and Jackson's Hill House, it seems to have its own evil sentience. This house has become a popular destination for legend trips in spite of its owners' attempts to keep people away. Over time the house's owners have changed its façade, but teenagers have persisted in visiting, especially on Halloween (Tucker 2008).

In 1999 a shocking new film, *The Blair Witch Project*, brought legend trips into entertainment news. This film seemed disturbingly different from previous horror films, but its introduction resembled that of the first Gothic novel, *The Castle of Otranto*; *Blair Witch* was presented to the public as "found footage," just as *The Castle of Otranto* was said to be a found manuscript. The "found-footage" model of film making plays on the legend genre's qualities of belief and possibility, making it an ideal visual genre to use with legend-like stories. According to the legend created by the film's writers, Daniel Myrick and Edouardo Sanchez, three film students disappeared in the woods near Burkittsville, Maryland, while trying to learn about the Blair witch, who was executed in the eighteenth century. Part of the story described a hermit who claimed that the spirit of the Blair witch had forced him to kidnap and kill children. The release of a "mocumentary" on the SyFy Channel encouraged belief in this fabricated legend. Another reason for the movie's uncanny appeal was that its actors seemed genuinely scared. Later, moviegoers learned that the actors had been deprived of food while out in the woods and had not had any warning that certain scary things would happen during the night filming. Their screams were real! Since the directors placed the actors within the induced natural context of a legend trip, they succeeded in scaring both the actors and the film's eventual viewers.

Since the release of *Blair Witch*, it has become routine for viewers to see publicity driven variants of legend trips on television. Numerous TV shows have presented investigations of haunted places in which it seems likely that something terrifying will take place. Mikel J. Koven's (2008) *Film, Folklore, and Urban Legends* analyzes the convergence of folklore, belief, and the media in the wildly popular British reality TV show *Most Haunted*, which started in 2002. Koven finds that this show presents "a kind of televised 'legend trip'" in which the televisual text "functions like a traditional legend-teller, creating a complex, matrixlike relationship among the supernatural belief traditions, the television show, and those watching that show" (154, 153). Because of this relationship, Koven argues, *Most Haunted* is not just entertainment; it is "*ostensive* entertainment" (171). It certainly is, and so are the multitudinous other ghost-hunting reality TV shows that have appeared since then.

There are so many ghost-hunting reality shows on TV now that it is difficult to keep track of them all. One of the most popular is *Ghost Hunters*, which premiered on SyFy in 2004; its spin-off, *Ghost Hunters International*, began in 2008 and ended in 2012. Another extremely popular reality show, *Ghost Adventures*, began in 2008 on the Travel Channel with an intriguing variety of international locations: Romania, Jamaica, Ireland, France, and Canada, among others. *Ghost Lab*, on the Discovery Channel since 2009, stars two brothers, Brad and Barry Klinge, who travel around the United States in an enormous truck seeking evidence of the afterlife in haunted places. Tucker was Skyped in as a guest speaker on *Ghost Lab* when the Klinge brothers came to New York. *Ghost Mine* premiered on the SyFy Channel in 2013 and lasted for two seasons; *Ghost Asylum* premiered in 2014 on Destination America, featuring the Tennessee Wraith Chasers, and is still going strong. With so many ghost-hunting teams out making TV shows, it might seem that there are no more new places to visit—but there are always more.

DIGITAL LEGEND TRIPS

While it may seem a strange kind of "place," the Internet is a growing setting for a number of contemporary legend-trip experiences. We're in an age where the distinction between being "online" and being "offline" is less and less clear; most of us have phones or other portable devices that let us take the Internet, in all its connective, informative power, with us in our pockets. This has affected our experience of legends trips just as much as it has affected so many other aspects of our lives. Michael Kinsella (2011), in *Legend-Tripping Online*, talks about the familiar ways that legend trips are mediated, even in entirely offline situations, such as through the use of a Ouija board or electronic voice phenomena recorder. He then moves to look at situations of technological mediation: the ways that computers, cell phones, and the Internet can further mediate our ostensive experiences.

Given that the Internet allows people to interact with each other and with narratives without the requirement of physical presence, we find opportunities online that don't exist offline. We can observe and even "go along" with someone's legend trip to a haunted location that might be hundreds of miles from where we are, if they've posted a video of their adventure to social media. We can copy and paste a chain letter warning about a girl who died after being bullied in the hopes that our forwarding the message will help us avoid her wrath. We can watch filmed experiments with events like séances and the game "light as a feather, stiff as a board" and compare them to our own ritual attempts, without ever meeting the people who made the video.

Taking the idea of legend tripping further, toward a more purposefully constructed, commercial experience, we have alternate reality games (McNeill 2012), experiences that play on many of the same ideas as legend trips and found-footage movies: blurring the line between what's known to be real and what's suspected to be fiction. Alternate reality games often serve as viral marketing—in anticipation of a film or video game release, companies will begin planting clues for fans, such as phone numbers to call or websites to visit, in existing media. Fans then can break through the fictional barrier between the real world and that of the film or game, and can find themselves following trails that lead to increasingly strange additional clues, taking them to places in the real world they might otherwise never visit. Even when the end result is revealed to be commercial, participants often feel as though they've participated in something quite "folk," and may pursue more traditional legend trips and legendary explorations in response.

As Kinsella says, things like digital legend tripping and alternate reality games become "world-making venues" that invite participants to "perform belief in worlds of plausibility to which the community gives breadth, coherence, and a sense of the real" (2011, 63). The world-making nature of the Internet makes it a perfect medium through which to explore the legend's inherent qualities of possibility and doubt. The ability to form a community online, without the need for like-minded people to live nearby, also makes the Internet a great place to share ideas about things like hauntings, aliens, cryptids, and ESP. Discussion forums abound where people share their own memorates, compare details of experiences, and pose questions about the veracity of various accounts. A local legend that doesn't get much attention locally may find a new life online.

Legend trips online can merge the virtual and physical worlds. Offline legend trips can be filmed and posted online, acting as a guide or model for others to follow. A search for "Bloody Mary" on *YouTube* brings up hundreds of thousands of results, ranging from shaky video footage taken on a cell phone to near-professional-quality amateur short films. Some legend trips are *expected* to be filmed and posted to social media; the #CharlieCharlieChallenge, a divination ritual that uses two crossed pencils to communicate with a spirit named Charlie, shows up far more often online than it does offline (as indicated by its popular hashtag).

The Internet isn't limited to serving as a showcase for offline legend tripping, either. There are entirely digital forms of legendry and legend tripping, too. The emergent genre of "creepypasta" is one way that legends and legend tripping manifest digitally. Derived from the slang term *copypasta*, which emerged in 2007 to describe traditional copied and pasted digital texts, creepypasta refers to similarly shared content, but marked with an ominous or eerie tone. The most (in)famous example of creepypasta is the Slender Man, an Internet horror figure who burst onto the scene in 2009 and who has intrigued, frightened, and baffled Internet users ever since. In 2015, the journal *Contemporary Legend* published a special issue about Slender Man, with articles addressing questions of belief, play, and ostension, among other topics. The editors explain, "The Slender Man phenomenon is greatly indicative of folklore in the digital age, where media convergence and hybridized cultural communication outlets afford individuals greater access to (and dissemination of) information, operational autonomy, and the provision of infinite choice while exploring a vast array of creative avenues" (Blank and McNeill 2015, 9). The description of the Internet as a "hybrid" space is an important development of recent digital folklore studies; scholars have noted that in digital spaces, folk culture and institutional or commercial culture are often blended or combined (Blank 2013, 2015, 2016; Bronner 2009; Howard 2008). "User-generated" content (the more folk elements of digital content) often appears framed by commercial or official elements (such as a social media company's site).

As discussed in the *Contemporary Legend* special issue, the fact that Slender Man can be proven to be fictional—created in response to a web forum challenge to "create a paranormal image"—does not stop the spread of belief in him as a real legend, if not always as a real creature (though that's a popular outcome, too!). Folklorist Andrea Kitta, in her contribution to the special issue, takes on the question of belief directly, noting that Slender Man exists offline in children's games, oral storytelling, and belief. As she explains, "A person's experience reading a Slender Man narrative or watching a video can *feel* just as real as having an actual experience with Slender Man" (Kitta 2015, 64). Elizabeth Tucker's article on Slender Man and dark play similarly highlights the ways that folk culture brings Slender Man offline and confuses the question of his possible reality (Tucker 2015b, 124–129).

The Internet community at large has done such a good job filling in a folkloresque (Foster 2015) backstory for this creature that an online search about the creature's origins can lead to results that confuse rather than answer the question of whether or not the Slender Man is a "real" legend from antiquity. Jeff Tolbert (2013), in his article "'The Sort of Story That Has You Covering Your Mirrors': The Case of Slender Man," refers to this process of communal creation as "reverse ostension." As he explains, "If ostension involves the privileging of experience over representation (e.g., acting out the content of a legend text, rather than simply listening to the recitation of a traditional story), Slender Man's creators are effectively reversing this process by weaving together diverse strands of 'experience' (in the form of personal encounters with the creature, documentary and photographic evidence, and other material) into a more or less coherent body of narratives" (3). Of course, folklore that is born digital rarely stays that way. Already there are many accounts of people seeing (or sensing) Slender Man offline, including the horrific stabbing of a young girl in Wisconsin by her two friends, who claimed that the Slender Man told them to do it. If Slender Man was initially brought into being through reverse ostension, the process has now come full circle, and ostensive actions (and crimes, unfortunately) are now growing from the legend.

HOW TO USE THIS CASEBOOK

Like Alan Dundes's folklore casebooks, which began in the 1980s (e.g., Dundes 1988), this casebook intends to fill the need for an up-to-date, thorough study of a subject that matters to folklorists. Since *Legend Tripping: A Contemporary Legend Casebook* presents major essays on this subject in chronological order, with prefaces written by the two of us, it should be useful as a reference book and as a text in college folklore courses. With support from the International Society for Contemporary Legend Research, we have prepared a book that professional folklorists, especially legend scholars, can use in doing research. The book should also be useful for scholars in other fields, including anthropology and sociology. Up to this point, no one book has presented all of the materials we include here. We have enjoyed putting our book together and hope that our fellow folklorists, scholars in related disciplines, and their students will enjoy it too.

We hope to go beyond an academic audience to appeal to contemporary readers. With roots in ancient epics and connections to popular novels and films, legend trips explore the boundary between life and death; they also open the door to marvelous understanding from a numinous source. Those of us who have gone on legend trips ponder what took place and wonder if we can go on another trip sometime. Of course we can! As our book shows, legend trips are not just for teenagers; they are for anyone with a lively curiosity who wants to have an amazing experience.

The "Discussion Questions and Projects" section at the end of the book is not just for professors and students; it is for anyone who wants to engage in dialogue about legends and legend trips. Some of the questions and projects have a connection to digital technology. As digital technology grows and changes, we will probably see new modes of legend tripping develop. Currently we can buy ghost-hunting apps for $1 or less. Although we don't know what kind of legend tripping will happen next, we can be sure that it will be well worth studying.

NOTE

1. The descriptions of the two legend trips discussed here are based on interaction with members of two groups of people in Binghamton, New York, between 2009 and 2015.

1

Early Studies

Elizabeth Tucker

WHEN LINDA DÉGH STARTED TEACHING at Indiana University in the mid-1960s, she wanted to learn what kinds of stories people told in the rural area around Bloomington. Having worked closely with narrators of folktales in rural Hungary, she had developed highly effective fieldwork methods. As she got to know students in Indiana University's Introduction to Folklore class, she realized that many of them knew significant folk legends and would enjoy collecting more from friends and family members. Dégh inspired her graduate students to collect and study legends of rural Indiana and other areas. With the help of graduate assistants, she founded the journal *Indiana Folklore*, published from 1968 to 1980. Although *Indiana Folklore* (Dégh 1980b) published a variety of material, it became a treasure trove of legends and legend analyses, some of which examined young people's visits to haunted places. In addition to these publications, other studies by Dégh's students addressed visits that would eventually be called legend trips: most by young people but some by older adults.

HAUNTED BRIDGES

One of Dégh's first articles about Indiana folk legends, "The Haunted Bridges near Avon and Danville" (Dégh 1969a), appeared in the journal's second volume. This article presents nineteen-year-old Gary E. Brown's collection of haunted bridge legends and Dégh's analysis of the meaning of visits to the bridges: the first analysis of this kind. Gary Brown collected haunted bridge legends as part of his work in Introduction to Folklore. The legend complex represented in Brown's paper is loosely based upon Ernest Baughman's Motif E266.2(a), "Ghost of laborer on bridge who fell and was killed during construction of bridge leads people to commit suicide." Based on the ancient concept of human sacrifice to ensure that a newly constructed edifice will be safe, these legends about bridges near Avon and Danville suggest that spirits within the bridges appear or make noises if visitors disturb them. Visitors may see a ghostly form or hear chains rattling. Some legends about the bridges' construction concern a worker who died and was thrown into fresh concrete; others tell of a baby thrown in by a young mother.

Here is an excerpt of Brown's transcript of his interview with his friend Scott about the haunted bridge near Avon:

GARY: Did you ever go in the bridge?
SCOTT: Yeah, the first time I went out there it was real cold and in the winter time. We had to jump across a 5 foot jump to get there.
GARY: Did anything unusual happen?
SCOTT: Well, you had to crawl and there were these big chambers, and the guys in front would hide and scare the living —— out of you when you went into the chamber.
GARY: Did you take any girls, Scott?
SCOTT: No, hell, I live in the country; I don't have to drive 40 miles to a country road.
GARY: Scott, did you ever hear any stories about the haunted bridge?
SCOTT: Well, this guy takes a girl out parking under the bridge and they were listening to the radio. There was a news bulletin that an escaped convict was in that area. He was highly dangerous because he had a steel hooked arm. After some time the boy and girl heard a noise outside the car. They were so scared they didn't look up, they just drove on. The guy was so shook up he pulled into the first filling station that they came to, and when the guy opened his door the steel hook that was on the mad man's arm fell off.
GARY: Scott, where did you hear this story and who told you?
SCOTT: We were sitting under the bridge and those two stories were told while we were sitting there by Charlie Sheppard. (Dégh 1969a, 61–62)

As the above excerpt shows, expeditions to visit the haunted bridges near Avon and Danville could be exciting and perilous, involving jumps and climbs into inner chambers. Friends in the front of the line would scare friends who were still making their way into the chambers. Once they all made it inside, the young people would share legends. Scott tells a variant

Early Studies

Figure 1.1. The haunted bridge near Avon, Indiana. Photo by Jesse A. Fivecoate.

of the famous legend "The Hook." This is just one of many legends associated with the haunted bridges, including stories about a woman in white and a creature called the Mud Man. Brown's paper demonstrates the richness and variety of legends told by young people visiting places that are known to be haunted.

The most important part of this early article by Linda Dégh is her analysis of what happens when young people go to notorious haunted locations:

> The stories in the bridge legend cluster, as many of the modern legends popular among young people . . . have two distinct parts. The first part recounts a supernatural (or extraordinary) event that occurred in the past and that serves as an explanation of a present phenomenon attributed to it. The scene featured by the tellers is appropriate for the common basis of all stories telling about violent death caused by suicide, murder, execution, car or train accidents. All of them happen in the dark of the night and the narrators suggest that the tragic event is being re-enacted at certain nights, appropriate for the revenants to return. The account of the tragedy is usually brief and sober; it simply states the facts of people meeting their untimely death at the appointed place, without going into details in search of the background of human tragedies. Also, the statement on the haunt is quite matter-of-fact.

Not so is the second part of the narratives, which relates the personal experience of the teller as he explores the phenomenon. Although it hardly contains real narrative motifs, this part reflects the emotional involvement of the narrator. In the bridge haunt stories, as well as in many similar modern American legends, the latter part of the legend becomes extremely important as it includes an account of the active and real physical participation on the part of the narrator and his associates.

This dichotomous structure of both form and content of the folk legend is rarely elaborated in full. Variants of the individual tellers are usually incomplete and uneven, depending on their personal interest. Under the emotional impact of the experience, informants might feel more strongly affected by they have witnessed during their visit to the place than by the narratives passed onto them. Because of the personal involvement of the tellers, their variable attitudes are directly related to the formulation of the texts and, therefore, are of major interest to the folklorist.

As is commonly known, the formal imperfection of the traditional legend genre is due to the reason for its telling: the communication of a message—a warning and/or advice of some kind. To make this message of considerable importance more effective, the narrator poses as an eyewitness to the legend action, testifying to its veracity. Nevertheless, the type of modern American folk legend group under discussion polarizes the constituent elements, making a clear distinction between (1) the legend proper and (2) the explorations of the teller. The experience that induces the teller to speak up is in our particular case not a passive one that happened unexpectedly to the guileless narrator. The narrator of a traditional folk legend would use his encounter with the bridge ghost as a point of departure: "There is a spook on this bridge" or "My grandfather tells about a ghost he saw on the bridge" or "When I came home around midnight I heard a scream on the bridge" and so on. He also would repeat this evidence as a conclusion of the story, ending with the spelling out of the advice.

> Our raconteur . . . is eager to challenge danger and step forward to claim his share in the experience. He expects to be scared by what he is prepared to meet and is most active to induce the apparition to give himself a good scare. The participant narrator is not an accidental visitor to the haunted place; he shows a remarkable familiarity with ghost lore. The scene itself, as described in all variants, suggests the horror to be met. Old and side-road bridges qualify as the site of haunts, like deserted old houses or cemeteries, way out in the country, overgrown with weed, hedges and trees in a deep valley or on a hilltop. A dangerous curve on a dirt road, leading to the bridge sets up the "general scary conditions" necessary for the experience.

Figure 1.2. Close-up of the inner compartments of the haunted bridge near Avon, where legend trippers have shared stories. Photo by Jesse A. Fivecoate.

Dark, foggy, moonless nights or nights when the moon is full and moving shadows reflect the windblown trees are equally fitting to the occasion. At this point, reaching the second part of his story, the narrator switches to the first person in his account. However, he is not alone on his dare; what he tells about is the collective experience of a group—two or three carloads of young people. What they want is to sense the chill of fear, and conversely, to prove defiance of fear. In spite of the group solidarity in the endeavor, the challengers break up and have to meet the danger individually. They explore the inside and the environs of the bridge, ready for the scare. They might even play cool in taking written notes on individual experiences or in checking whether the rumors concerning the haunt were true or not.

All the above implies that the bridge-visitors condition themselves mentally for a vision they desire to have. They also perform a series of designated acts known to be effective to prompt the ghosts to appear. The hour and the weather conditions should be carefully selected; there is an indication that Halloween night might be the appropriate time for an effective visit. (Halloween as the time of haunt is mentioned in Indiana legends; however, the scarce number of references do not yet allow us to assume what seems to be likely: that visits to haunted places belong to Halloween customs). The rituals bridge visitors perform include walking under the bridge, climbing into the chambers, reciting ghost stories, etc. The parked car seems to be an adequate shelter from which the explorers might urge the ghost to appear: they roll up the windows, honk the horn three times or shine the lights three times.

In view of the active interest in the supernatural so typical of young people in their teens and early twenties, one is tempted to infer that there is a profound belief that maintains the popularity of the haunt legends. The frank statements of the informants, however, indicate that the quality of belief is immeasurable as a factor in legend maintenance. Almost all respondents said: there might be a grain of truth in the stories but all they saw might have been just an illusion. Many informants noted that haunt stories are favorite subjects of general conversation within their group and what they heard often influenced them in what they have seen. They really were not sure whether they heard or experienced the facts of their version. They probably never considered seriously the question of their own belief and if their mental attitude ere important at this conjecture; routine folklore interviews would certainly not reveal adequate information. The point is: belief or disbelief, the visit to the haunted bridge, is a kind of test, one of the initiation rituals among the many young males have to pass as they leave childhood and make their way toward adulthood. The exploit is not only a dare but also very enjoyable fun. Feeling the chill of a "good scare" is definitely welcome to youths in this civilized, comfortable and rather uneventful affluent world. To escape boredom and enjoy adulthood, what could be more exciting than to make use of a brand new operator's license and drive out at night to visit the haunts of the region? Although our informants were of both sexes, we believe that the active dare is more a male than a female exploit, whereas the telling of the stories belongs to both boy and girl get-togethers. (Dégh 1969a, 77–81)

Dégh's suggestion that driving out at night to visit haunted places is "more a male than a female exploit" fits the legend collections available at that time as well as American popular culture's focus on male daredevils during the 1950s and early to mid-1960s. During the years since then, female daredevils have joined their male counterparts, and folklorists have documented young and older women's legend trips. One notable study ten years after the publication of Dégh's article is Sue Samuelson's (1979) "The White Witch: An Analysis of an Adolescent Legend."

HOUSE OF BLUE LIGHTS

Like her article about haunted bridges, Dégh's article about the notorious House of Blue Lights in Indianapolis (1969b) addresses a kind of haunting that appeals greatly to readers and listeners. Just as many towns have bridges with a reputation for being haunted, many have houses known

Figure 1.3. Sign that gives the haunted bridge the "Seal of the Town of Avon." Photo by Jesse A. Fivecoate.

as the "haunted house" of the community. Because they are community-based, some haunted house legends never become known in a broader geographical area, but because the House of Blue Lights has such fascinating details, it has transcended its local boundaries.

First, some background about the house, which was first described by Magnús Einarsson-Mullarky (1968) in his article "The House of Blue Lights" in the inaugural issue of *Indiana Folklore*. Large, somewhat isolated, and equipped with a swimming pool and other special features, the house fascinated Indianapolis residents, especially teenagers. Skiles E. Test, the house's owner, died in the spring of 1964. The son of an affluent and influential Indianapolis family, he lived on a farm, where he raised Saint Bernard dogs and took care of stray dogs and cats. He lived alone after being married and divorced twice. According to an article in the *Indianapolis Star* quoted in Dégh's article, an auction held after Test's death drew about 30,000 people; by midafternoon, most of Test's "enormous stockpile of aspirin tablets, catsup, office equipment, artwork and household furnishings" had been taken away, The newspaper article also explained that the house had taken its name from blue lights that Mr. Test enjoyed putting up during the Christmas season (Dégh 1969b, 13). Except for the Christmas decorations, which appear on numerous American homes during the winter holiday season, these details suggest that Test was an eccentric, aberrant person who did not fit community norms. Like Roderick in Edgar Allan Poe's "Fall of the House of Usher," he found little comfort in his inherited wealth, and his large house seemed strange and sinister to others.

Dégh presents twelve legend variants that show how the house became a magnet for young visitors:

1

A long time ago, around the 1930s, Mr. Test's wife died. To keep himself from being lonely, he kept her in an open coffin in one of the tower rooms. The room itself was filled with flowers and were kept fresh. In the summer time, he used to move the coffin into the garden. That's why blue lights were seen outside as well as in. He used blue lights so that she would rest more peacefully.

Informant: John Earl, of Indianapolis; collected by Diana Dean, Indianapolis, July 18, 1967. FA IU:1274.

2

The wife of Mr. Test had been a very beautiful woman. When she died, he was very saddened and completely withdrew from the world. He decided to keep her near him always, so he had her placed in a glass coffin and kept it in the living room. Blue had been her favorite color, so he surrounded the coffin with blue lights—and then eventually the whole house. He would sit for hours just staring at the coffin.

Told by Steve Koers of Indianapolis; collected by Diana Dean, Indianapolis, July 18, 1967. FA IU:1272.

3

It's a house on Fall Creek, the "House of the Blue Lights" situated on a woody hill. It's on the corner of Fall Creek and Road 100. The man's wife died supposedly a long time ago and instead of burying her he put her into a big glass coffin and put blue lights all around her and keeps her in the house with him. A glass casket. You can see the blue lights through the house.

Told by Russ Jens, 19, of Indianapolis; heard when attended North Central High School. He had gone to this house. Collected by Stephen M. Dickhous. FA IU:1718.

4

The legend that I most vividly recall was the story of "The House of Blue Lights" in the Geist Reservoir area in Indianapolis, Indiana. I heard the story while on camping trip in the area with fellow Boy Scouts at the age of sixteen.

After drinking a few beers that someone managed to sneak past the scoutmaster we began to tell stories about the surrounding area. Most of us were sixteen and had recently received our driver's licenses. We were therefore eager to learn of good places to park with our dates. The story telling settled down to "serious business" when the subject of the "House of Blue Lights" was mentioned.

So the legend went, an old man in a very exclusive neighborhood near our campsite was said to have the body of his wife displayed in a glass-enclosed casket. The casket was supposed to have been surrounded by eerie blue lights that were visible from the yard of the home. Young people on dates often were asked to leave the neighborhood by security police who assured them that there was no lady in a glass coffin. The eerie mood set by the storytelling on a date was always effective in evoking the proper mood for love-making when we later (after learning the story), took our dates into the area to park.

It was disappointing to many young people in the Indianapolis area when Skiles Test died; his was the "House of Blue Lights." When the house was inspected after Mr. Test's death it was found that there was no glass coffin surrounded by a bank of blue lights. However it was odd that there was found numerous cat graves in the yard, boxes of shoes, food, etc. The eccentric old man evidently bought everything in bulk, and did indeed exhibit some strange habits.

Written report of Edward S. Marcus, student from Indianapolis, 1969. The camping trip took place in 1964.

5

On the northwest side of Indianapolis there is an old mansion built in the thirties. The owner's wife died about fifteen years ago. The rumor was that on the sunporch he had her casket. The only lights on the porch were blue lights which were visible from the garden, about fifty yards away and during the colder months when there weren't any leaves on the trees you could see the lights from a country road. It was a great fad of teenagers to get to the porch or rather to try to get to the porch. They were usually hampered by four big dogs. I almost got there but the dogs got too close. Recently the house was sold. While it was being advertised in the papers it was billed as the "House of Blue Lights." I first heard this story in 1955 or 1956.

Told by Richard L. Mills of Indianapolis to Kathy Mills in Bloomington, July 15, 1966.

6

This is a story which is frequently told around the high school groups in Indianapolis, Indiana. There is a big estate in town owned by a millionaire who died a few years ago. The house is up a long drive and is surrounded by a tall fence. Inside the fence were dogs . . . which were to keep out strangers. The fence had blue lights around it, and many times [for] the initiation into clubs or just to see inside the house kids would climb the fence and try to look into the living room which was lit up with blue lights. The owner was suppose to have put his wife in a glass casket after she died so he could look at her. He was to have had the casket surrounded with blue lights. He was supposedly to have had her there for several years. I heard after he died that he had been a little crazy, no doubt, and that he thought there was going to be another war; so he had bought several items in large quantities like nails and canned foods etc., preparing for the war. The place was to have had several hundred cats around too, and I heard that he had a special cemetery for them and buried each one in its own casket. I don't know how much of the story is actually true but I believe parts of it are true and could be traced back through newspapers; like the last part of the story preparing for a war and other things. I couldn't say for sure though on the part about his wife, but the story has been widely spread in Indianapolis.

Collected by Phillip Harping of Bloomington Campus, I.U., submitted May 5, 1968. FA IU:69/172.

7

Mr. Test kept the house closely guarded at all times to keep people from seeing his wife in her coffin. There were pits dug all over the grounds to trap anyone that wandered around there. Vicious dogs attacked any prowlers, and Mr. Test was known to have taken shots at people. He could be seen wandering through his house carrying a blue light with him all the time. His wife was kept in a closed casket above the ground in the garden. The dogs were kept in huge pens most of the time, but if anyone fell into the pits, he released them to attack.

Told by Rick Haberman of Indianapolis to Diana Dean, July 18, 1967. FA IU:1273.

8

There was an eccentric, old, rich man who had a farm and it is a wooded farm. He has blue lights all around the farm and the fence surrounding it. He has blue lights in his house and blue lights in a big swimming pool outside and a blue flood light in his backyard. The real story is, that he had killed his wife at some time, whether by accident or intent and keeps her body in a casket in the bottom of the swimming pool.

Told by Denny Miller, 19, student from Indianapolis; collected by Tommy Prinz at Foster Quadrangle, IU, Bloomington, May 8, 1968.

9

The story goes that there is an old man who lives on the northeast half of Indianapolis, Indiana. When the old man was younger he was given a bad deal with the firm with whom he was associated. As he lived to grow older he became more and more like a hermit. After his wife died he put her in a glass coffin and surrounded it with blue lights.

Told by Mike Jordan, 20, Indianapolis to Raymond E. Clift, 198. FA IU:1743.

10

The reason for the blue lights was for the orchids that Mr. Test grew in a green house on his property. He had been a very wealthy man and had hidden his money throughout the house. After his death, the lawyers found it hidden in all sorts of pockets throughout the house. Perhaps some of the money is still there, but the general public has lost interest in the house. His wife is definitely buried in Crown Hill Cemetery, complete with large tombstone. The lawyers, though, found an empty coffin sitting in one of the tower rooms, empty and dusty, never used.

Told by Jeff Salberg to Diana Dean, both of Indianapolis, July 18, 1967. FA IU: 1271.

11

"The House of Blue Lights" refers to a large estate on the north side of Indianapolis. Guards were said to take care of the place but they were never seen. The guy who lived there would buy things by the case. People disappeared periodically from the area so police were posted to watch it. Then the man living there disappeared too. Four years later a policeman was found shot in the head on the road near the property. It finally got to a point where no one would go near the house. They finally found him dead and arranged to auction off his furniture. About 200,000 people showed up. It was the largest turnout ever at an auction. The strange happenings at the house attracted many curious people.

Told by Keep Morse, 24, from Indianapolis to Dorothy Deal at IU dormitory lounge, December 19, 1967. FA IU:68/138.

12

There was a house in Indianapolis years ago. There was an old man who lived all by himself. When he died they found all kinds of junk and garbage and things in his garage and basement. He had a high fence there and it was lit with lights to keep people away. After he died and the electric power was turned off many of the children in Indianapolis would go back to this house that looked [like a] "haunted" house and even now they say that when they try to climb over this fence, blue lights would come on.

Told by Rita Jackson, 20, who heard it from schoolmates while attending school in Indianapolis. Collector: Stephen Joseph Daily, Kokomo, December 23, 1968. (Dégh 1969b, 18–23)

Dégh's analysis of the twelve variants of this legend explains in detail why the house became such a popular destination for teenagers:

In the light of the historical factors behind the legend, the first thing one is struck by is the accurate retention of the facts found most outstanding by all those who described the personality and household of the late Skiles Test. Both who furnished background and folklore information, elaborated with the same details: the blue lights, the swimming pool, the dogs, the cats, the animal cemetery, the fence and the iron gate, the household goods stored in large quantity as they were on display at the auction. All these facts combined show the eccentric personality of the man. What the common talker found worthwhile to remember when voicing the judgment of his society concerning actual points of interest, the folklore informant deemed also worthwhile to pass on.

The prosperous Test family, the deeds, the fate of individual family members was—no doubt—a point of interest to Indianapolis society. As a rule, not only local gossips spread the latest events about people in the limelight; no social evening can pass without some entertaining story about prominent people. Skiles Test was certainly interesting enough to talk about at different stages of his life. After his death the auction opened new insight into his personality, when finally the "secrets" of his farmhouse, the topic of tea party talk, became public. Fifty thousand visitors, of whom very few were professional antique dealers or buyers, came to inspect the place. Most of the visitors came to get some curio of no value as proof of their visit to the premises and to refreshen their data on the subject for social get togethers. This far, Skiles Test's personality was cast as that of a withdrawn eccentric who preferred the company of animals to that of people, who kept his privacy secure by fences and gates, who did not like to waste, bought on sales and kept goods in quantity even if they were of no further use to him. How did his public image evolve underscored by the typical colors of folklore?

The 12 variants that correspond to those analyzed by Mullarky change greatly the features of the owner of the House of Blue Lights. In most of the versions [(1), (2), (3), (4), (5), (6), (7), (9)], he is characterized by his tender love for his wife, whom he did not want to part with when she died. He dedicated his whole life to her, setting up a permanent catafalque where her glass casket is being placed. He sits by her keeping vigil over her eternal dream. The beloved one is surrounded by flowers (1), and by blue lights, blue being her favorite color (2). As far as color symbolism goes, in addition to the references given by Mullarky (84–85), one might include love magic: the touching of blue cloth in order to induce the sweetheart to appear (Brown Collection 6: items 4203 and 4275). The bier is placed in the "tower room" (1), in the living room (2, 6), on the sunporch (5), above the ground in the garden (7); the coffin is even moved to the garden in summertime (1). In this pattern it seems natural that the house owner, who loved his wife that much, lost contact with the outside world and became a hermit, displaying strange habits. He withdrew from the world when his beautiful wife died (2), and in his bereavement became a maniac (7).

Is it in accordance with this dramatic story that he became violent when prowlers tried to spy on him? The old man protected his beloved wife by keeping four watchdogs (5), by building a fence with posts illuminated by blue floodlights, surrounding the fence with mean dogs (6), and even trapping intruders and shooting at people (7). The versions in which the man killed his wife seem to be a negative replica of the main pattern. Although no malice is shown in the killing [the woman went crazy in Mullarky's version E and (8)], it was "neither by accident nor intent"; in our version, the man does not display the body but hides it under the swimming pool. This corresponds also to Mullarky's "Related text": it is obvious in both stories why the killer wants to keep out visitors. This is a complete and very logically structured legend in itself.

However, there are other, rather discordant elements in the story. Some of them appear at random, others de-emphasize the main story and eventually discard it. In one (6), for example, another story is included about a crazy man who bought large quantities of everything because of the fear of another pending war. Another variant (9) tells principally of the reason the old man became a hermit. It seems that his keeping the dead wife in a glass coffin is a consequence of his disappointment with the outside world.

The last three variants are rather distinct in their content and aim. Although they contain most of the usual details, what they really have in common is the mysterious house with blue light fixtures. One variant (10), explains that the lights come from a greenhouse, where sensitive plants are grown. But this explanation is only a side remark, as is the mention of the wife buried in the cemetery—it really means that the informant had heard about the glass casket, but suspects otherwise. This is the story of a miser, who hid his money, a hoarder who even bought his coffin. There is also a note for treasure hunters: it is worthwhile to search the place; the lawyers might not have found everything.

The House of Blue Lights of variant (11) is a real mystery house, where weird things were going on. It was guarded but the guards were never seen. People had disappeared near the property and a policeman was once found shot. The owner of the house disappeared too, but was later found dead. No one dared [come] near the house until the auction. The mystery—crime? supernatural?—is left open to conjecture.

There is only one ghost story among the versions (12). The weird old man who was a hoarder (his possessions turned out to be "junk and garbage" after his death) used blue lights to keep people away. The lights (as in HDA 2:1395) would come up after his death if someone would enter. This haunt corresponds to variants C and (12) in Mullarky's article.

The application of the blue light motif shows diversity. Most commonly they surround the glass casket (1), (2), (3), (4), (5), (6), (9); otherwise in (6) and in (12) the fence is lighted; in (7), the man carries the light; in (10), the greenhouse, in (8) the fence, the house, the swimming pool and the backyard; only (11) does not specify. It seems to be certain that the once existing blue lights around the farmhouse were the principal reason to suggest a mystery house to the fertile imagination of young people; these blue lights remained the central motif of the legend.

As far as the form of the legend is concerned, it remains imperfect and fragmentary, as already stated in the above. The variants are closer to the memorate than to the more elaborate fabulate; they often stay on the rumor-level. There are two reasons to account for this and for the lack of development into a lengthier narrative, despite the fact that stories about the House of Blue Lights had been reported since the mid-thirties.

First, the facts originated too close in time to let fantasy develop freely. The folklore-generating facts of the story did not penetrate folklore at the same time, as the historical events occurred at different times over a lengthy period of time. These facts are so different in their quality and value as folk narrative elements that they keep the story rather incoherent—although they could have been easily shaped into different stories. Consequently, in this case, the period of 30 to 35 years was too short to develop a legend because the real facts kept accumulating until the last two years.

Second, the story enjoyed a steady popularity among Indianapolis high school students for over 30 years, concurrently as it entered adult society in and outside of the city. From the Folklore Archives at Purdue University Jo Ann Stephens Parochetti quotes versions in her "Scary Stories from Purdue" [Keystone Folklore Quarterly 10 (1965): 49–54] from Indianapolis and one from Franklin, 20 miles south of Indianapolis. The folk legend material was both reaffirmed and watered down by historical factors known about the "House of Blue Lights." Among the generations of high school students, the farmhouse became one of the mystery houses so typical in the life of American adolescents. In the Indianapolis area this house became the object of a maturation test, a part of an initiation ritual. In possession of a new operator's license, the aspirant could drive to this "scary," desolate place, challenge the danger, enjoy the fear and the frustration of imagined horrors and vicariously gain the ritual related to this legend (3), (4), (5), (6), (8), (11); others yielded information only by specific questioning. Function left its imprint on the form of the story: it consists of two parts, the story of the strange occurrences in the blue light house and the account of personal experience of the teller (or his acquaintance) visiting the house. Since both story and visit are common knowledge to all respondents, relation does not need much elaboration. The telling in itself is also being utilized as a ritual, to rouse fear at specific get-togethers. Also its function in dating, to make girls draw closer to the protective male, preparing the atmosphere for love-making, is noted by an informant (4). (Dégh 1969b, 23–28)

As Dégh explains, the House of Blue Lights enchants Indianapolis residents through the strangeness of its illumination and the eccentricity of its owner. Legends portray the affluent Mr. Test as a miser and a hoarder who stockpiles ridiculous amounts of household supplies; he even keeps a coffin so that he will be prepared for his own death. Characterizing this unusual residence as a "mystery house," Dégh documents its fascination for teenagers, finding that six out of twelve of the legend variants mention visits. Since the teenagers must overcome their fear of entering this scary, isolated place, these visits help them become initiated into adulthood.

At this early point in her research in southern Indiana, Dégh was not studying the influence of the mass media. We can add two mass media–related observations to her analysis of the "House of Blue Lights" legend: one about a beloved movie and another about a popular song. It seems likely that this legend's emphasis on a glass coffin is related to the sparkling glass coffin presented in the Disney movie *Snow White*, released in 1937. Rereleased in 1944, 1952, and 1958, this movie delighted many child viewers for generations. There is also an apparent connection to Chuck Miller's rockabilly song "The House of Blue Lights," which became a teen hit in 1955; its original recorders, in 1946, were Ella Mae Morse and Freddie Slack. Describing an exciting house on the edge of town where people can dance and eat all the chicken they want, this song creates a party atmosphere. Its popularity, along with the description of Mr. Test's choice of Christmas light colors, probably gave this local legend its name.

ADOLESCENT LEGEND PERFORMANCE

Three years after the publication of Dégh's "House of Blue Lights" article, Kenneth A. Thigpen published "Adolescent Legends in Brown County: A Survey" (1971). This article categorizes seventy-three legends told by Brown County adolescents. The legends' subjects range from haunted houses and bridges to "The Watcher," "The Lady in the Graveyard," "The Hook," and "Heavenly Messages." Finding that most of these legends have local origins, Thigpen suggests, "The influence of the mass media on the body of legends collected from adolescents in Brown County seems to be slight" (210). In relation to the prevalence of stories about the supernatural, however, he recognizes the impact of TV shows such as *Night Gallery* (211).

Recognizing Dégh's analysis of the dichotomous structure of legends that includes an experiential component, Thigpen suggests that the experience has its own three-part structure: introduction to the phenomenon, enactment of what is supposed to happen, and discussion of results:

> While the narrative texts of modern experience legends may be analyzed on the basis of a dichotomous structure (Dégh 1969a), the performance of these legends should be analyzed on a different basis. Roger

Abrahams has suggested that the aspect of structure on which the analysis of the legend, as well as myth and tale, should be based is the structure of the context (Abrahams 1969: 109–10). It should also be considered that the performance of the dichotomous modern legend is dependent upon the experience itself. This experience, if it is an initiation ritual as Dégh (1969a: 77–88) suggests, not only functions for adolescent males, since girls and even adults are found to participate. The ritual more importantly functions to introduce the uninitiated to the realm of the supernatural. The performance of this ritual, in which the legend assumes a dramatic form (it is acted out), can be perceived as having a three part structure.[1]

The first part is introduction to the plausibility of the phenomenon. This includes relating the past event and describing the current phenomenon. This must be done by an initiate, one who has already had the experience. The introduction takes place before arriving at the scene. During this time, the legend is told in a manner that will heighten the anticipation of uninitiated and initiated alike, thus enhancing the receptive psychological state of all involved, so that they will be more likely to perceive the "supernatural" occurrence. At this point the legend retains its narrative form.

At the scene of the phenomenon, however, the participants act out the specified requirements to cause the fulfillment of the legend. This may involve blinking the lights three times, blowing the horn, parking in the middle of a bridge, or merely being at a certain place at a certain time. This is the most crucial part of the legend performance. During this, the second, part of the performance, participants are attempting to merge the supernatural realm described in the first part with reality. Whether the words of the legend are spoken or not, the awareness of all present centers on its message. During this time the phenomenon is perceived to appear. If the legend has no further prophecy concerning the fate of the participants, including the supernatural ones, then the second part ends. If there are warnings in the legend that harm may come to the participants if they stay, or that the supernatural will disappear as a result of unseemly disturbance, then further action may be predicated on this knowledge.

The third part of the performance takes place in retrospect. The initial part of the legend narrative, which tells of the past event, is diminished in this part of the performance. The participants compare and discuss their own experiences. These may also be told as memorates to the uninitiated and thus be added to the basic legend complex to be told as the first part of the performance. (Thigpen 1971, 204–205).

Thigpen's three-part sequence provides an outline for understanding legend trips, and the legends that he analyzes provide important information about the oral tradition of southern Indiana. The "Lady in the Graveyard" legends pertain to the Stepp Cemetery legend complex, an especially significant and well-developed set of legends to which we now turn.

Early Studies 47

Figure 1.4. Sign at the entrance to Stepp Cemetery. Photo by Jesse A. Fivecoate.

STEPP CEMETERY

Deep within Morgan-Monroe State Forest but only fifteen miles from Bloomington, Indiana, Stepp Cemetery has inspired legends since the early twentieth century. This venerable cemetery's graves date back to the 1850s. The only way to find it is to look for the "Property closed at 11 p.m." sign on the main road. Visitors must park and walk down a dirt road for a few minutes to get to the cemetery. At night, when it is hard to see where you are going, it can be difficult to find the right path.

In their article "The Legend of Stepp Cemetery," William M. Clements and William E. Lightfoot (1972) present twenty-seven legend variants. The texts' collector was Billie Champlin, a student in an introductory folklore class at Indiana University in the spring of 1971 who grew up in the local area. Carefully examining all twenty-seven stories, Clements and Lightfoot propose a classification system for Stepp Cemetery legend variants:

> In a generalized abstract, the legend of Stepp Cemetery goes as follows: (1) a woman, witch, or female ghost dressed in black frequents the grave of her husband, daughter, son, infant of unspecified sex, or any combination of these relatives; (2) the woman appears seated on a stump—sometimes called the "Warlock Seat"—near the entrance to the cemetery; (3) a person who sits on this stump, usually at a certain hour or on a certain day, often

Figure 1.5. Stone that marks the entrance to Stepp Cemetery. Photo by Jesse A. Fivecoate.

meets death or other misfortune within a stated period of time; and (4) several deaths and mutilations—the most frequent being that of a German shepherd dog—may be cited as proof of the stump's potency. Within, and often outside of, the narrative framework, extreme variation has taken place.

The diversity of the texts has presented some problems in developing a meaningful typology of the material. However, by thinking of the legend in terms of three major themes: (A) the woman in black; (B) the stump's curse; and (C) the mutilated carcass of the dog, some order can be imposed to facilitate our discussion. Since there is also extensive variation within those texts which deal primarily with the woman in black, Group A has been sub-divided into four further categories: (I) texts in which the woman in black is considered to be a living being; (II) those in which she appears as a disfigured living being; (III) stories in which she is thought to be a witch; and (IV) texts in which she appears as a ghost or revenant. (Clements and Lightfoot 1972, 96)

Since the "Woman in Black" is the crux of the Stepp Cemetery legend for most visitors, Clements and Lightfoot present characteristic examples of each of the four categories regarding her identity:

AI, The Woman as a Living Being
My first experience with this legend began on an October evening in 1964. I was a Freshman pledging a fraternity here on the Bloomington Campus. Some of the "actives" in the fraternity had been daring some of us pledges

to do some things that they hadn't had the nerve to do themselves. The subject centered around various acts against sororities and the University. Suddenly, one of the active's eyes lit up and he exclaimed that he knew something that none of us would do. He began his tale concerning "The Death Chair." He told us that forty years ago a woman in the area of the Morgan-Monroe State Forest had a child that was hit by a car and killed. She buried her child in a cemetery located in the State Forest. This woman also had the tree next to her child's grave cut down and had the stump shaped into a chair so that she might sit in it and guard her child against any strangers that entered the cemetery. When she was not in the chair it is said she had put a curse on it to protect the grave. It is said that if anyone sits in the chair or even touches it when she is not in it, that person will die one year to the day that he touched the chair.

Everyone in the room laughed off the legend when it was related to us but I am sure each person felt more seriously about it than anyone let on.

None of us visited the cemetery, but some of the other brothers in the house did and confirmed that the chair was there; but apparently none of them sat in it.

IUFA: Legends: 70:132, collected by Indiana University student Stephen D. Pickett on 24 September 1969 from himself. (Clements and Lightfoot 1972, 96–99)

AII, THE WOMAN AS A DISFIGURED LIVING BEING

One morning before classes started at Bloomington High School, several of my friends and I were standing in the hallway talking. One of my friends, named Steve Crandal, started telling a story. Steve was a very humorous person—he was constantly telling jokes and funny stories, so he had no trouble in getting our attention. However, this time he was telling a different type of story. The story was about a small cemetery in Morgan-Monroe State Forest named Stepp Cemetery. Steve said that he had heard (I do not know where he heard the story) there was a lady dressed in black who was lurking near the cemetery every night. The story was that the lady was protecting the grave of her young child who was dead and buried at Stepp. The "Lady in Black" would sit on a tree stump that was near the cemetery, or she would wander about making weird noises in the woods near the cemetery. One of her hands was a hook, and if she ever caught anyone near the cemetery, she would do something terrible to them.

IUFA: Legends: 70:90, collected by David King from Steve Crandal in 1967. The item was submitted in 1970. (Clements and Lightfoot 1972, 109)

AIII, THE WOMAN AS A WITCH

On a Saturday night, last spring, a fraternity brother and I went out with two girls who were familiar with the Bloomington area and Stepp Cemetery in Morgan-Monroe State Forest.

Figure 1.6. The "Warlock's Seat" on which cemetery visitors dare each other to sit. Photo by Jesse A. Fivecoate.

> We happened along a very dark and "spooky" looking road and conversation naturally became of ghosts and haunted houses. Then, one of the girls got the idea to take us to Stepp Cemetery. As we headed toward this place she told us the story . . .
> There is a small lonely cemetery situated in the middle of Morgan-Monroe, and every night there is an old witch with long grey hair, dressed in a long black dress (who she claims to have seen there on a different occasion). She sits on a small chair cut out of an old tree stump (which I saw to exist) guarding the grave of her dead baby (a grave of a baby is near the stump) from vandals destroying the gravestones there (reported as true). She puts flowers on her baby's grave every night (I saw flowers on this grave) and when visitors come in the night she slowly turns her head towards you and soon disappears into the forest. They say if you sit in her tree-stump chair you will soon die. (There was no special name given for the chair and the time of death was not mentioned). One additional observation I made was that there is grass covering every grave except that of her baby.
> This was the legend as it was told to me. The girls then joked about how my friend and I were too scared to go to the cemetery, so it became a challenge for us to see this graveyard.
> When we arrived it proved to be as "spooky" as your mind might imagine it to be. We had to hop over a single wire-fence to the entrance to

the graveyard and once inside proceeded very slowly toward the stump-chair. We took about four more steps and all of a sudden a wolf-type howl blared out in the woods and I turned and ran to the car with the others behind me. I returned a week later during the daylight and observed the various other things mentioned in the legend to be true.

> IUFA: Legends: 70:131, collected 25 August 1969 by nineteen-year-old Indiana University student Richard Feldman from eighteen-year-old I.U. student Roxanne Sparks. (Clements and Lightfoot 1972, 111–112)

AIV, The Woman as a Ghost or Revenant

As Tom told me, the legend is that an old lady, supposedly dead, dressed in black, haunts the cemetery and watches over husband and son who are buried there. She is supposed to have died a horrible death, but no one knows what it was. In front of the cemetery there is a tree stump that is in the form of a chair. It is said that the only time you can see the "black lady" is when it is dark and you are sitting in the chair. If you do see her, you are supposed to die the same death that she did that same day one year later.

IUFA: Legends: 71:85, collected by Lynn Stoia from Tom Hinkle during the summer of 1968. Lynn Stoia reported another story connected with the cemetery in which the woman has a hook in place of one of her hands and carries out the role assigned to the escaped maniac in most versions of "The Hook" (see Group AH). Motif E334.2, "Ghost haunts burial spot." (Clements and Lightfoot 1972, 119)

In their analysis, Clements and Lightfoot note that the legend of Stepp Cemetery "is not *one* legend but a complex network of oral narratives which interact both with each other and with other sets of legends" (128). Clements and Lightfoot apply functional analysis to the Stepp Cemetery legend complex, concluding that it has educative, compensatory/cathartic, integrative, and validative functions. The last two functions are most applicable to legend-trip study. The integrative function pertains to promotion of group solidarity and "expression of in-group affiliation," while the validative function "provides teen-agers and college students in the area with valid reasons for driving several miles in the middle of the night" and "justifies the ritual of sitting in, or going to great lengths to *avoid* sitting in, a chair-shaped stump located there." Behaviors related to the legend complex include "dancing around, throwing beer cans at, and shining automobile lights on the stump, mutilating dogs near the site, and overturning gravestones in the cemetery" (130). Following Linda Dégh's approach, Clements and Lightfoot find that this legend site "provide[s] an opportunity for young males to test their courage, thus initiating themselves into adulthood" (130).

Although legends of Stepp Cemetery have many variations, they tend to emphasize the possibility of dire consequences if a person dares to sit upon the Warlock Seat. The concept of a curse is well established in American oral and written literature, including Nathaniel Hawthorne's *The House of the Seven Gables* (1851) and Shirley Jackson's *The Haunting of Hill House* (1959). To sit or not to sit? Sitting means passing the test of bravery but possibly dying in the throes of a terrible curse, while not sitting means safety but humiliation. There is no easy answer for an adolescent who takes this challenge seriously.

THE "BIG TUNNEL"

Another frightening challenge is the subject of Gary Hall's "The Big Tunnel" (1973), which introduces the term *legend-trip*. Dark, spooky, and long, this railroad tunnel between Fort Ritner and Tunnelton, Indiana, has a reputation for being haunted by a murdered watchman carrying a lantern; a man was murdered in the tunnel around 1908 (Hall 1973, 145). Citing earlier legend theory and comparing variants of "Big Tunnel" legends, Hall discusses "influences of the legend-trip context on the process of legend-telling" (139).

Hall's vivid description of typical trips to the Big Tunnel by teenagers shows how terrifying such experiences can be:

> A trip might begin on a summer evening, or after a party, as a carload or two of young people decide to drive to the Big Tunnel. Most everyone in the car has been there before; in fact, a few have driven to the Tunnel as often as once a week during the summer months. Usually boys and girls ride in the same car, but seldom as couples. Someone might have a few cans of beer to pass around, but most often no one gets drunk.
>
> The night drive from Bedford to the Big Tunnel will take about 30 minutes. The winding road will take the teenagers through southern Indiana countryside shrouded almost invariably in dense fog. Once the car has left Bedford and turned onto the country road, someone mentions the Tunnel and the teens review its legendary history. Both individually and cooperatively they re-tell the five or six stories about the Tunnel that nearly everyone knows. They match other "scary" stories, each trying to tell the "scariest"; they tell local legends, modern migratory legends, horror stories from literature or movies and on occasion someone invents a new story. By the time the group is within a few miles of the Tunnel, many of the young people begin to feel the atmosphere of fear which their receptivity to these "scary" stories has generated. The last few miles along the narrow dark road "set" this atmosphere.[2]

To the right of the dirt road that leads the last mile or so to the Tunnel are five or six ramshackle buildings elevated six to eight feet on concrete stilts. Only a short distance away, the White River ensures that these dark buildings are obscured in fog. The weird outlines of these buildings are, the visitors say, a portent of evil. After crossing a small bridge, they stop near a roadside trash pile. A weather-beaten, over-stuffed chair stands beside the footpath leading up the thickly forested hill to the Tunnel. Someone will mention that this is the "Bum's Chair" where hoboes who lurk in the area sit waiting for Tunnel visitors. By now the darkness and almost palpable atmosphere of fear becomes too much for some of the young people. They may refuse to go further or might even insist everyone return to Bedford immediately. Usually, however, almost everyone musters up enough courage to take the footpath up the hill to the railroad and the overwhelming arch of the Tunnel.

The entrance dwarfs the visitors. Its total blackness makes the night seem light by comparison. Without lights, the teenagers—sometimes with hands joined—walk into the Tunnel and feel their way along the right wall. At intervals their hands slip and the wall seems to disappear; manholes, recesses about five feet high and two feet deep built as places of refuge from passing trains, are spaced throughout the Tunnel and are disquieting breaks in the solidity of the wall. To walk through the Tunnel is to walk through the haunts of headless watchmen, ghosts, and ogres, any of whom might be hidden in one of the manholes. Potential dangers are magnified by perceptual distortions inside the Tunnel. The air is chill and damp; the darkness is so complete that vision seems to fail (visitors most often mention this total darkness in their descriptions of the Tunnel); the walls amplify even the slightest sound—dripping water echoes through the Tunnel.

While some groups leave after their walk through the cavern, others try to time their trip so they will be inside at about 10 or 12 o'clock. It is then that night freight trains speed through the Tunnel. To stay inside, crowded in the manholes, while a train rushes through is the high point of the trip. One visitor notes:

All the kids go there. They usually go about the time a train is supposed to go through. They get inside holes in the wall and wait for the train to go through. You are not with it until you go to the Tunnel and stay in it while the train is going through it.[3] (Hall 1973, 147–150)

Crouching in the tight space, hearing the train roar past them, adolescents pray that they won't become the Tunnel's next victims. If they prove themselves to be "with it" by not running away, they pass an important fear test.

STEPP CEMETERY WITH A TWIST: EXORCISM

Although Stepp Cemetery has been a well-known legend-trip destination and party spot for adolescents, as noted by Clements and Lightfoot, it has also inspired legend trips by adults. Folklorists have particularly enjoyed visiting this historic and intriguing place. One especially meaningful adult legend trip occurred in the spring of 1975. As Dégh explains in *Legend and Belief* (Dégh 2001, 247–248), she got to know a middle-aged Spiritualist named BarBara Lee (a pseudonym), who identified herself as an exorcist. Passionately eager to help troubled souls go to heaven, BarBara sought legends that would help her understand the history of the Bloomington area. When Dégh told her the legend of Stepp Cemetery, BarBara expressed a desire to go there. She did not, however, want to go at night, so Dégh and Vázsonyi planned an excursion to Morgan-Monroe Forest the afternoon of May 17, 1975.

The following excerpt from a paper that I wrote for Folklore 404 (1974), taught by Roger D. Abrahams, analyzes BarBara Lee's presentation as a performance. An account of the Stepp Cemetery exorcism appears in Dégh's *Legend and Belief* (Dégh 2001: 247–290). At Dégh's request, I transcribed the audiotape of the Stepp Cemetery exorcism. In the paper, I refer to BarBara Lee as "BarBara," since that was her preferred name as a practitioner of exorcism. I refer to Linda Dégh as "Dr. Dégh," since that was the term of address that her other students and I used. An excerpt of the paper follows:

> I met BarBara Lee May 17, 1975, when Dr. Linda Dégh told our folktale seminar that an exorcism would be performed at Stepp Cemetery in Morgan Monroe Forest, near Bloomington. Delighted at the prospect of such an event occurring on the fringes of our academic community, I asked to join the party. It included two other folklore graduate students (Sylvia Grider and Sharon Sherman), two student/photographers (John Bunch and Martin Haltai), Dr. Dégh with her husband, Andrew Vázsonyi, and, of course, BarBara Lee.
>
> One could hardly imagine an exorcist less like the gaunt, priestly figures dressed in black who appear in the horror film The Exorcist (1974), which was released the year before this exorcism took place. A smiling, middle-aged lady dressed in white, BarBara radiates friendliness and is willing, even eager, to talk about her experiences with exorcism. At the time of the Stepp Cemetery performance, she wore a long, white dress and a silver crucifix. It was obvious that her brand of exorcism differed considerably from that of The Exorcist; I was eager to learn more about it.
>
> Before the day of the exorcism, BarBara had read "The Legend of Stepp Cemetery" by William M. Clements and William E. Lightfoot (Clements and Lightfoot 1972). Having told Linda Dégh that she wanted to learn about local legends, BarBara was very pleased to receive a copy of

this article, and she read it carefully. Somewhat nervous about visiting the cemetery after dark, she asked to go when the sun was shining.

During several interviews, informal conversations, and transcription of interviews conducted by Dr. Dégh and Sylvia Grider, I was able to gain some insight into BarBara Lee's self-presentation as a performer. Before the advent of The Exorcist, she said, she "de-possessed"; now, she "exorcises" (Lee 1975a). Interestingly enough, BarBara has never seen The Exorcist, finding it to be a "filthy" and "shocking" movie; nevertheless, she believes in its potential for exerting a good influence: "I think that movie was directly from heaven. I think God knew that. Because there were other movies that nobody cared about, but they had to be shocked" (Lee 1975a). Since The Exorcist has had such a wide impact, BarBara has found that the name "exorcist" requires no further explanation. Her calling cards say "BarBara Lee, Exorcist," and she hastens to correct anyone who refers to her work as "healing" or "witchcraft." She has found it especially hard to be called a "witch" and a "sorceress" by Christian ministers in Gosport, where she has lived since she left her husband and grown children in Cleveland.

As a child, BarBara heard voices, got to know a medium named Lisa, and learned that she could heal stomach ulcers and other ailments. When she was older, she was possessed by the spirit of Alva Tisch, a fashion editor who had committed suicide in the late 1930s (Davis 1975, 13). During early experiences with healing and possession, she became aware of the gravity of her choice to make use of her special powers: "People that I thought would help me said, 'Leave it alone, BarBara.' You know, it's dangerous" (Lee 1975b). Her Christian family, afraid that she might go to hell, also opposed her inclinations. Nevertheless, she decided to follow God's call rather than yielding to her parents' and others' wishes.

In analyzing BarBara's Stepp Cemetery performance, I have concentrated upon her oral formulaic utterances. These can be roughly divided into three categories: dialogue with the spirits, asides to the audiences, and prayer. In the course of the performance a definite rhythm emerges, alternating between moments of tension and relaxation, humor and extreme seriousness.

First, the question of audience involvement should be considered. All seven members of the audience, myself included, were members of the academic community in Bloomington, and most of us were folklorists. Except for Dr. Dégh, who asked occasional questions and replied to BarBara's remarks, we were relatively quiet and participated only by following BarBara from grave to grave. At one point, we were slightly unsettled by BarBara's question, "Has anyone here smoked dope?" It soon became clear, however, that she was referring to teen-aged visitors to the cemetery rather than members of the audience.

Upon entering the cemetery, BarBara asked us, "Are any of you scared?" This question, which elicited an affirmative response from Dr. Dégh and a denial from her husband, involved the audience in the first phase of the performance. After a moment of apparent nervousness and confusion, BarBara went to the first gravesite and immediately began to talk with the spirit she found there. In a low, almost sepulchral tone of voice, she asked, "What's the matter? What's the matter? I don't know where—What's the matter, darling? Tell me what's wrong!" Then she asked the audience, with similar repetition: "Is this a family tombstone? Is this a family tombstone?" Throughout the performance, transitions from dialogue with the spirits to dialogue with the audience happened rapidly and with apparent ease; unlike trance mediums, BarBara does not require an altered state of consciousness for her work.

Resuming her dialogue with the spirit, BarBara asked, "Do you have a baby?" Her question about the baby precipitated a moment of dramatic tension: the spirit ran away, and BarBara had some trouble getting her to return. Afterwards, she settled down into an affectionate dialogue with this spirit, who appeared to be the mother of a child.

Interrupting the dialogue to tell the audience what she was doing, BarBara explained, "I do not remember—*I do not remember* what they've said. When the sentence goes through me, it's not of me, it's not part of me, it—goes through me." She then repeated what the spirit had said and done: "And, uh, all I remember is that it was a family tombstone. She said she's lonely, she's lonely. I said, where's your baby, and she ran that way." Since BarBara seemed to have no difficulty recalling details of her conversations with the spirits, it can be assumed that her emphatic "I *do not remember*" was intended to enhance the dramatic effect of her performance.

The next sequence included several rapid transitions: praying, briefly reassuring the frightened spirit, and then introducing a note of tension by saying to the audience: "Somebody's hiding behind a big tombstone, but I thought it was closer than that." Then she suggested that multiple spirits might be present: "There are more than—there are more than one. There are more than one." Alternating between a brisk, almost impatient tone of voice and a slow, comforting rhythm, she urged the spirits to leave their gravesites: "No, it *isn't* your home." This exhortation was consistent with the goal that she frequently mentioned: sending troubled spirits to heaven.

BarBara's tone of voice in addressing the spirits was often that of a mother speaking to her child: ". . . you know what, God loves you now. And there are a lot of real, real good people, honey. And they can't believe in God. But as long as they're good, they have a right to go to heaven." In an earlier conversation with Linda Dégh, she had explained her feelings for the spirits: ". . . you know, I love them. I mean, I know it sounds crazy, but I love the starved spirits. You know what I feel like? I feel like I'm their mother." Having given birth to four children, now grown, and having suffered five miscarriages, BarBara had strong maternal feelings. When I visited her home later that month, she showed me a portrait of her five lost children, whom she regarded as her angels and guides. She told me that these children had gotten a good education in heaven and had gotten good jobs in science, teaching, and other fields.

Throughout the exorcism, BarBara introduced prayers in different ways. Some came abruptly, in the middle of a sentence: "So—uh—what we probably should do—uh—(prays) Dear angels of love, I ask you please to bring them all right here, and let's get them all to heaven." Other prayers, preceded by a pause, were slower and less perfunctory; for example, "Oh Father God, I ask you please. C'mon, c'mon (sighs). Dear angels, I ask you please to take this spirit into our heavenly school so that she may progress, and let them all be together." This type of prayer, with its slow, measured rhythm and almost ecstatic sigh, is set off more markedly from the rest of the performance, seeming to be more deeply significant.

Most of BarBara's prayers, particularly in the earlier part of the performance, are prayers of supplication that include the phrase "I ask you please." Her encounter with the most colorful character she found in Stepp Cemetery, "Isaac Newton," began after her prayer "If there is any need for my services, please let me serve." "Isaac Newton" was not the spirit's real name; resenting being disturbed, he told BarBara, "You're a funny girl!" His remarks injected some humor into the performance, culminating in BarBara's aside to the audience: "Well, he's, he's selling, 'Could I sell you some fish,' and he says, 'I gotta support a family!'"

Following the humorous interlude, BarBara had a long, serious talk with 'Isaac'; she insisted that his gravesite was not important and that he should join his family in heaven. At one point, she became almost tearful: "The important thing is that he's earthbound, because of material things. Like tombstones! And cemeteries! And families that are gone!" Then the tension broke again, and Indians entered the scene: "Come on, come on, all of you come. I know these woods are full of Indians, I know Indiana's full of Indians." In the course of this conversation, a number of Anglo-American clichés about Indians emerged: "happy hunting ground," "warground," and "great white spirit."

Speaking to another spirit not identified by name, BarBara tried to explain the limitations of being earthbound: "You see, we can't get up and just say, 'Well I want to be in California,' but you can. You can say, 'I want to be in Texas,' and you could be in Texas. You can say, 'I want to be *any place*,' and you can be there! You can go to the Riviera, of course! You can go any place you want to be." A similar oral formulaic tendency appeared when BarBara discussed one of her clients after the Stepp Cemetery exorcism: "He just picked up—and went! He's gone to California, he's gone to Texas, he's gone to Hawaii, he's gone any place he wanted to go, and all the time he's going he's been thinking to himself, 'Why am I going? I don't want to leave my wife. Why am I going? I don't want to leave my wife.'" This pattern of rhythmic repetition, integral to BarBara's style, adds fluidity to her anecdotes, exhortations, and prayers.

Toward the end of BarBara's performance, she encountered another female spirit: "This one—well, now this one I don't see in black. This one I see in gray." Although the most prominent character in Clements's and Lightfoot's Stepp Cemetery article is the "woman in black," there is also a mention that "If a person dies with his soul unprepared, a dark gray ghost will appear in the cemetery to indicate a soul in distress" (Clements and Lightfoot 1972, 95). BarBara explained, "This one I see in gray. But this one is barefooted and she *does* have a baby, and she goes like this! You know, she doesn't want anyone to touch that baby." As with the other spirits, she encouraged this one to leave the cemetery and go to heaven: "But dear, don't you know that you'll have a beautiful cradle, a bed for your baby in the heavenly realms? Don't you know that that baby can be sleeping, honey, and resting, and waking up and playing at all beautiful things with you? And you can sing it lullabies? Don't you know?" As before, rhythmic repetition gave her exhortation fluidity and eloquence.

Near the end, BarBara said, "I want to know if any of you know, could it be possible that somebody is using this graveyard for a witches' coven? A Satanist cult?" After Linda Dégh replied, "Kids come out on Halloween, but nothing like that," BarBara explained, "Because I know in Cleveland, there are an awful lot. All the big cities have these kind of things now, you know. And they gather in the cemeteries. And they've even dug up graves." Showing her familiarity with rumors and legends about Satanic cults, she expressed a concern that others in the Midwest shared.

Finally, BarBara blessed all of the audience members and paused to bless the "Warlock's Seat," where she briefly sat down; members of the audience took picture[s] of her there. Her blessing shifted to a semi-humorous encounter with the Warlock himself, who, BarBara said, refused to say whether or not he was a spirit. She determined that he was indeed a spirit and prayed for him to accompany her guardian angels to heaven. In this way, the performance ended on a positive note.

Exorcism of cemeteries is a relatively new occupation for BarBara; usually she is asked to perform the type of exorcism that others call "healing." In an interview for the Bloomington *Herald-Telephone* she explained how she usually conducts this kind of exorcism healing: "I always make passes around their shoulders, and around the front of them . . . If the spirit is very evil, or very stubborn, then the person has to stand up, and I make passes over their whole body. But that's very seldom; it doesn't happen very often."

When I spent a day with BarBara on May 28, 1975, I had a severe headache and asked her if she could help. She kindly agreed to try to heal me and asked me to sit down in a chair. First, she moved her hands around my head several times, saying "Whatever is not of God must *leave*," then she told me to repeat those same words three times. When she asked me how long I had suffered from headaches, I explained that I had had headaches

Early Studies

Figure 1.7. Creepy corridor in Indiana University's Eigenmann Hall, which used to be a graduate student residence. Photo by Elizabeth Tucker.

since the age of seven, when I was taking piano lessons. She told me that the spirit of a little girl who had once played the piano had entered my body through my fingertips, and her presence had given me headaches ever since. After BarBara had finished her exorcism, I was surprised to discover that my headache was actually getting better; it went away completely, and I had no further headaches for several weeks afterwards (Tucker 1975, 1–20).

EIGENMANN HALL, INDIANA UNIVERSITY

On May 28, 1975, I took BarBara Lee to Eigenmann Hall, the Indiana University residence hall where I lived and worked as a resident assistant. BarBara had heard students talk about the top floor of Eigenmann being a notorious location for students' suicide attempts. I had heard variants of this legend and had gone up to the top floor's stairwell a number of times with campus police and firemen during RA duty hours. I had even gone up to the top floor once with a narcotics agent who thought marijuana plants might be there. After visiting this liminal place so often, I felt comfortable inviting BarBara to come up to the top of the fourteenth floor on a legend trip of sorts. I did not, however, have any idea what would happen when BarBara summoned a ghost. Here is a summary of what happened:

> Halfway down the hallway of the fourteenth floor, BarBara stopped and pointed to one of the doors. "I smell funeral flowers here," she told me. "It's a funeral wreath." This wreath, BarBara said, marked the room of a student who had committed suicide by jumping out of a window. She led me to a window in the stairwell, then flattened herself against a wall as she struggled with the student's ghost. "He's trying to make me jump out too," she explained. After pushing the ghost away, she followed me out of the stairwell. Never having seen anyone fight off a ghost before, I felt shocked and surprised, but BarBara quickly recovered from the attack; finding ghosts and persuading them to go to heaven was her life's work (Tucker 2007, 67).

Although this was a rather unusual legend trip, involving a middle-aged Spiritualist exorcist and an eager young folklore graduate student, it fits the well-established pattern of adult Spiritualists' visits to haunted places, sometimes with others accompanying them. Back in the 1970s, folklore researchers were much more interested in adolescents' legend trips than in legend trips by adults. Even now, that is commonly the case.

All of these studies in the 1960s and 1970s set the stage for further scholarship. Documentation of participants' behavior during legend trips showed that this was a phenomenon well worth analyzing. By the early 1980s, scholars could begin asking new questions about legend trips and applying relevant theories.

NOTES

The following notes come from the original sources but have been renumbered to fit their sequence in this chapter.

1. Lack of sufficient data on the actual performance situation hampers [Thigpen] here, but there is indication of this three-part structure of ritual performance in the texts of the legends themselves. Also, additional data obtained from informants support this concept.

2. Dégh (1969a) suggests that a "scary" experience immediately preceding the legend-site creates the "general scary condition." I [Hall] would note that although the immediate area of the legend-site is certainly important in creating this legend "atmosphere," it does so only when it "sets" or brings to consciousness an atmosphere of fear already developed through legend telling.

3. Comment by D.M.: Female, 22, of Bedford, 1972. Indiana University Folklore Archives (Hall 1973: 150).

2

Legend Tripping in Ohio
A Behavioral Survey

Bill Ellis

As chapter 1 explains, some of the earliest studies of legend trips document teenagers' behavior. In particular, Clements and Lightfoot's "The Legend of Stepp Cemetery" offers a vivid description of young people "dancing around, throwing beer cans at, and shining automobile lights on the stump, mutilating dogs near the site, and overturning gravestones in the cemetery" (Clements and Lightfoot 1972, 130). This kind of rowdy, disrespectful behavior tends to shock adults. Thanks to the work of Bill Ellis, however, it does not shock legend scholars.

In this insightful, thought-provoking essay, Ellis defines adolescents' legend trip behavior as a ritual of rebellion. "Legend-Tripping in Ohio: A Behavioral Survey" (Ellis 1982–1983) places Ohio legends and legend trips in a maturational context. Based upon 218 legends told by 303 informants, it closely examines legend trippers' rebellious behavior. In addition, it categorizes Ohio legends by subject and location, covering 175 legend-trip locations.

Several points in this essay seem especially important. First, the strong statement "The trip, not the legend, is the thing" makes it very clear that scholars should closely examine legend trips. Second, the interpretation of legend trips as "ritual acts of rebellion" brings activities such as drinking, cursing, and tomb desecration into sharp focus.

Ellis suggests that legend trips offer "a way of playing chicken with adolescent anxieties." This intriguing statement highlights the significance of risk taking for teenagers. Some teens have played chicken by jumping in and out of their cars; others have played the game by dangling from railroad bridges while trains pass above them. All of us who have made it through adolescence to adulthood can reflect upon the kind of anxiety that generates risk taking.

Other questions raised in this essay encourage reflection. Why do teenagers give such vague directions to legend-trip locations? What is the meaning of the cars they drive to these places? And why are liminal figures so significant in the legends that inspire trips? Ellis suggests some answers but leaves plenty of room for further speculation.

Everywhere across Ohio, teenagers gather together, tell spooky stories about a local site, then travel by car to see the place for themselves. This ritual activity, recently christened "the legend-trip," has been studied by Linda Dégh, Kenneth Thigpen, Gary Hall, Sue Samuelson, and William Clements and William Lightfoot, among others.[1] Their analyses, however, have focused on single locations or on single legend motifs, and aside from Dégh's work, little effort has been made to characterize legend-trips in general. This paper does not attempt a deep study of any single Ohio tradition; rather, it draws some preliminary conclusions from a broad range of legend-trips reported in the Ohio State University Folklore Archives (OSUFA), especially about the behavioral patterns that remain constant over a variety of locations. This survey is based on 117 collections, supplemented by some original interviews, which relate 218 narratives attached to 175 locations, attested to by 303 informants.[2] A few generalizations about the tradition-bearers: all but one were white, and all came from middle- to upper-middle-class neighborhoods. No bias, other than European origin, was found in ethnic background, and none was seen in religious preference. Informants were about equally balanced male and female; some came from rural areas or towns of fewer than 5,000 residents, but the majority lived in towns of more than 10,000, with significant clusters around the major industrial areas of Cleveland, Youngstown, and Cincinnati. Most informants were interviewed while attending college, but they agreed that the peak age for participation was "cruising age"—sixteen to eighteen. The legend-trip thus is linked to the coming-of-age crisis among white small-town or suburban adolescents.

The destinations of these legend-trips were inevitably rural, however, and most were located along sparsely populated roads. Those in or near major cities appeared in undeveloped parks or along rural-seeming streets. The stories attached to these sites fell into three general categories. By far the most popular one involved persons who died violent or accidental deaths and, unable to rest in their graves, haunted the place of their deaths (motif E411.10). In all, eighty locations are said to be the setting of some gruesome accident, murder, hanging, or tragic natural death. Babies proved an especially popular subject, often associated with a "Cry-Baby

Bridge" where their mothers murdered them or where they were flung out the window of a crashing car, onto the path of an oncoming locomotive.[3] Decapitated revenants, usually looking for their lost heads (E422.1.1), also showed up frequently. The headless horseman still rides near Cincinnati, but near Sandusky he has become a headless motorcycle man, his head cut off by piano wire stretched across the road,[4] and near Cleveland the ghost is a headless little old lady in a yellow Volkswagen. Surprisingly, headless women are more popular than headless men,[5] and again are attached to bridges where they were murdered or died in car wrecks, the most popular being "Screaming Mimi's" outside Tiffin.

A second popular subject was the haunted graveyard (fifty-nine sites), with the common motif being the return of the dead to punish those who disturb graves (E235). Several such stories warned of mysterious deaths resulting from the desecration of an alleged witch's or warlock's burial site. Another, near Wheeling on the Ohio side of the river, simply promises death to whoever sits in a chair-like grave marker. Other tombstones are not cursed, but develop strange markings, sprout eyes at night, glow, or move around. One popular location near Carey is the grave of a murdered wife, whose portrait mysteriously appears on her tombstone, with the murderer's hands clutched around her neck.

Finally, many sites featured uncanny persons or creatures (seventy locations), some supernatural, some merely bizarre or eccentric. Witches, werewolves, zombies, and ghosts lurk around some places; but the more popular threats are maniacs and escaped mental patients who prowl around "parking" roads, looking for unwary carloads of teenagers to liquidate. "The Hook" in his various manifestations is perhaps the farthest traveled, having killed boyfriends in twenty Ohio locations and left his prosthetic murder weapon in car door latches in seven more. Less murderous is the "Green Man" near Youngstown; disfigured in an electrical accident, he simply seeks company. And some subjects of legend-trips are merely eccentric old ladies, like the "Stick Lady" of Waterville, who can be depended on to come out and scream at carloads of teenagers who disturb her.

The multiplicity of legends attached to such sites has been the downfall of most text-oriented collecting. Not only do many migratory legends circulate within a single community, but a single site will provoke as many versions of what happened there as there are informants to interview.[6] All graduates of Columbus high schools will agree that someone died near the Mooney Mansion on Walhalla Drive. But who? Did a father kill his promiscuous daughter, or did a jealous husband kill his cheating wife, or did a butler kill the maid, or did a maniac kill a young girl? Some say it was the husband, not the wife, who was killed, and others say no murder happened at all—a truck accidentally ran a girl down. The point is, *something* must have happened there, otherwise no legend-trip would be necessary. Or in other words, *some* legend, it doesn't matter which, is necessary to justify the traditional ritual. When we turn from the multiplicity of legends to the accounts of the trips themselves, we find remarkable unanimity.

Some of this agreement is at first puzzling. However hard a legend-trip site was to find, once it was reached it proved easy to recognize. The area was deeply rutted with tire tracks, which often led away from the haunted site into deep woods, while the place itself was littered with beer cans and remains of campfires or was marked by vivid graffiti. On rare occasions the inscriptions alluded to the legend, but more often they named "who loved whom," celebrated alcohol and drug use, or simply shouted obscenities. These markings may record the participants' successful passage of an initiation into manhood, which would explain why initials and class symbols are often found too (Dégh 1971, 65). But why the stress on drugs and male-female bonds? Similarly, although legends often warned against disturbing gravesites, I found all such cemeteries named were heavily vandalized. To say that desecrating a witch's tombstone fulfills the terms of an initiation ritual evades the issue: why should the ritual require vandalism? The answer seems to be that the legend-trip is more than an initiation into the supernatural; it functions in the same way as other adolescent automotive activities—that is, as a "ritual of rebellion" (see Licht 1974). The trip is the significant thing to the adolescent, and the legend serves mainly as an excuse to escape adult supervision, commit antisocial acts, and experiment illicitly with drugs and sex. Both legend and trip are ways of saying "screw you" to adult law and order; hence the obscene graffiti.

The locations of especially popular legend-trips are often described by participants, not as threatening, mysterious places, but as "party spots," where large numbers of teenagers gather to drink, smoke pot, and raise hell. An Athens informant described a local cemetery this way: "It doesn't look that scary right now, but at night it's pretty decent. On Halloween there's always parties here. Hank came down last Friday. He said there must have been about a thousand people there. They had a big fire going and beer cans were thrown all over the place" (OSUFA n.d.: Morosco 1976). Another informant from Union City described how a certain bridge was haunted by a werewolf that only appeared to groups of six or seven guys in a car and only if they had been drinking or smoking; to others it was invisible (OSUFA n.d.: Chew 1974). In fact, many haunted locations seem to exist only in the minds of the participants: instructions on how to find them are unusually, perhaps deliberately, vague. At night, after a few beers and joints, doubtless any old house, bridge, or graveyard can be the "right" one.

Witches, werewolves, and the like at first seem incongruous with the desire to get high, but in fact both are means of escaping from the symbolically sterile world governed by school, parents, and police. "Cruising" itself breeds on the excitement of breaking the law, and my students have confirmed that the last day one can cruise in good form is the last day before one's eighteenth birthday: the day one could (until recently) legally buy beer in Ohio. Drinking and pot-smoking, equally illegal for teens, are thus like visiting haunted sites in that both are "trips"—deliberate escapes into altered states of being where conventional laws do not operate. To this extent, actually participating in the supernatural is not a terror but a sought-after thrill. A Shelby informant, after recounting an experience of being chased by one graveyard haunt, commented, "All those stories added flavor to what would have been a dull high school year. Besides, being one of the few people to see Peter Ghoul, and one of the first, I felt rather privileged" (OSUFA n.d.: Daniel 1974). Just as the adolescent who gets drunkest and commits the most outrageous prank gains status among his peers, so too the participant who trips the farthest and sees the most tangible evidence of the supernatural is "privileged." The use of drugs or alcohol as a prerequisite to the visit makes it more likely that something out of the ordinary will be experienced; it also allows participants a rationalization for experiences that in retrospect seem *too* real.

Still more incongruously, many legend-trip sites are used for both scares and sex. Some frequently visited locations, in fact, appear first to have been lovers' lanes, yet when frightening legends became current, visits for sexual experimentation did not diminish. Strangely, the presence of ghosts and murderous maniacs seemed instead to encourage intimacy. While legends like "The Hook" can express female fears of sex, such an interpretation is based on female-to-female storytelling contexts (Dundes 1971). When told instead by an eager boyfriend to a timid girlfriend—alone together at the alleged site of the legend—the effect is aphrodisiac. One Dayton participant commented on "The Boyfriend's Death," localized at nearby Carpenter Road, "We used to use that one when we would go parkin' out there. You know—to scare chicks and make them want to slide a little closer. (Q: Did it work?) Fuck yea—you'd have to beat 'em off with a stick" (OSUFA n.d.: Coogan 1978). Why should a story describing a gruesome murder on a parking road serve as a sexual turn-on? Apparently, the couples continue to make out in spite of the threats. The illicit nature of the sexual adventure is the key: authority figures such as parents, teachers, and other chaperones are united in trying to keep the sexes apart, thus essentially castrating them until the age of socially recognized maturity. It is thus significant that the maniac or other threat is often identified with older, parental figures.[7] Sally Ann, one of the Mansfield-area witch-revenants, is characterized in life as a "dried-up [i.e., sterile] bitch" and in death as a puritanical ghost who "gets" couples who make out near her grave (OSUFA n.d.: Williams 1976). Likewise, one of the Columbus Walhalla Drive legends presents a ghost who behaves remarkably like a middle-class mother. She is said to "climb down the embankment and peer or pass the couple. Then she throws an emotional fit, stares at them again, and returns to the base of the grave. The results of the haunting are that the male becomes impotent or the girl just can't get it on anymore" (OSUFA n.d.: Stuts 1974).[8] It is not hard to see that these legends project social warnings about sex onto marginal figures like ghosts and lunatics whom the participants can defy in good conscience.

Finally, a little-examined but essential feature of a legend-trip is the automobile. The sites visited are not just spooky, they are also remote, sometimes twenty miles or more from the informants' neighborhoods. In part, then, the legend-trip is an extension of the car's normal function for adolescents—the creation of a personal, mobile territory where they are free to make their own rules.[9] But this territory is also a sanctuary from which conventional authorities can be safely challenged. Surely the least studied kind of legend-trip is that in which an eccentric person, usually an old lady, is harassed. A Toledo source describes a typical visit to the Stick Lady of nearby Waterville: ". . . you'd honk your horn once or twice and yell 'Hey, Stick Lady' at 'er and every now and again, if you had a good night, the Stick Lady would come out and chase you down the street and hopefully you would get away, as we always did" (OSUFA n.d.: Carroll 1975). The usual method of challenging the supernatural, interestingly, is the same: honking horns, blinking lights, shouting a name or, in one case, conducting a Chinese fire drill. In the same way the auto itself is a refuge from outside threats, since one could drive away from Stick Lady and haunts do not open car doors and get in. Even "The Hook" gets no closer than the door latch and kills only those stupid enough to get out. Nevertheless, the legends often express anxieties about the safety of this mobile territory. Many sites possess magical powers over cars, causing them to stall, refuse to start, develop mysterious electrical failures, or even roll toward cliffs. At Rogues' Hollow near Akron, ghosts are said to appear and run alongside cars as they approach a dangerous curve, hoping to startle drivers into speeding up and plunging over the ravine (OSUFA n.d.: Stripe 1975). "The Vanishing Hitchhiker" often is found in a sinister mood: if you don't stop to pick her up, you will wreck your car or she will race into the road in front of you, hoping to make you swerve into a tree or abutment.[10] If you see a little girl on the Randolph Hill Bridge outside of Steubenville, one informant advises (OSUFA n.d.: DeSeyn 1975), run over her! Such a spirit of defiance motivates trips to "Screaming Bridge" outside of Cincinnati as well. This site is supposed to be the scene of a car wreck that wiped out an entire family, yet the highlight of the trip is the successful negotiation of "Lose-It Curve" and "Lights-Out Straightaway," the last being a strip that participants covered at speeds of up to fifty-five miles per hour without the aid of headlights (OSUFA n.d.: Halverson 1977). In such cases, the legends not only express anxieties about this moving sanctuary, they also challenge adolescents to play chicken with these very anxieties. What better place than the scene of a horrible wreck to display one's fearless driving skills?

Extending this point, we could say that the legend-trip in general is a way of playing chicken with adolescent anxieties. At the same time that it dares participants to rebel against adult authority, it provides a psychologically safe way to defy the taboo against confronting fears of death itself. Violent death is at the heart of nearly all legend-trips, and if we strip away the melodrama, they are similar to today's news items. Bodies do turn up in isolated fields and roads. High schoolers are tragically killed in car wrecks. Husbands do go berserk and kill wives and family. Lunatics do haunt "parking" roads, killing whomever they find. In short, the same violence that confronts teenagers in raw form during the day is given structure during the night in these rituals. Mary Jane's Grave, for example, seems not to have been a popular spot to visit until two popular Mansfield teenagers were killed in a car wreck. The story that they had visited her grave and died on the way back seems to have been a post hoc imposition of logic on an otherwise senseless accident. Likewise, the cursed cement chair near Wheeling seems invented to embody the threat of mortality. If you sit in it, you die within the year, or, some say, within eight years, or, others say, either you or a close friend will die within eight years. Given such latitude the odds are good that the curse will take effect; thus, any tragic event, either within the high school or within an individual's family, can be given some sense of order through this legend. One informant recalled a tombstone in the same cemetery: "It's a big long story and you read it and come to the last line, it says if you read this story you will die" (OSUFA n.d.: Macri 1976). Actually, the stone reads, "Reader, remember all must die, as you are now, so once was I, as I am now thou soon must be, prepare for death and follow me."[11]

In a sense, then, the informant's paraphrase of the inscription is accurate: anyone who reads the stone will die, just as anyone who reads this

Figure 2.1. Visitors stand at the entrance to Moonville Tunnel, which legends say is haunted by the ghost of a decapitated brakeman. Photo by Lauren Pond.

essay will die. Mortality fears, first becoming intense during adolescence, need to be relieved, and adult white middle-class society is notorious for making such fears taboo in "polite" discussion, thus evading the psychological burdens of such feelings.[12] One function, then, of the legend trip is to create a means by which such fears can be localized, circumscribed, and defied without risk. Without actually putting oneself in physical danger (as in the literal car game of "chicken"), such activities allow adolescents to experience the emotions of being in death's presence and the exhilaration of having conquered their fears without adult assistance.

To conclude, the trip, not the legend, is the thing. To quote one former participant from Dover, "I am convinced that there is a basic need in people to be placed in terrifying positions where your life is in jeopardy. Very little in Dover serves as a threat, yet up on Ridge Road you can always find a full moon and a warlock. You get your adrenalin flowing on a boring evening, rush back home after a close brush with death, and somehow Dover doesn't seem so stagnant" (OSUFA n.d.: Rulon 1975). The legend provides the incentive to rebel against this "stagnant," adult-governed establishment and to confront a fictive death threat, but it is not the reflection of a passive acceptance of belief in warlocks, ghosts, maniacs, and the like. Rather, such legends are what adolescents *desire* to believe in, in spite of community norms. The trip, complete with illegal drinking and drug use, illicit sexual experimentation, and explicitly antisocial behavior such as vandalism, is from start to finish a way of "giving the finger" to adult rationality. If it is true that ritual acts of rebellion provide and inform many legend texts, much of what we have accepted as "supernatural legends" needs to be reconsidered, not as expression of belief in the extranormal, but as an excuse for what we adults would prefer to call juvenile delinquency.

NOTES

1. Linda Dégh's influential account of legend trips and their function is included in Dégh 1969a, 1971. As editor of *Indiana Folklore*, Dégh has printed several of her students' studies of legend trips, of which the following are the most comprehensive: Thigpen 1971; Hall 1973; and Clements and Lightfoot 1972. Sue Samuelson 1979 gives a rare view of the activity outside Indiana; she discusses a legend trip near San Francisco.

2. A more detailed breakdown of these figures by legend type is given in the appendix. My thanks to Patrick Mullen for assisting my search of the archives for material. All direct references to archival material are given in the body of the text by year and collector's last name.

3. Cognate material from Indiana is given in Dégh 1960a, esp. 73–75, 83–84.

4. A full set of texts for the headless motorcycle man is given in Rudinger 1976.

5. Discussion of the headless woman motif is given in Ellis 1982.

6. This conclusion is reached by Clements and Lightfoot 1972, 127–128, and by Dégh 1980a, 194.

7. Also observed by Samuelson 1979, 20–21, 24–25.

8. Cf. the consequences of the "White Witch's" appearance to parking couples: Samuelson 1979, 27.

9. Licht 1974 discusses this aspect of adolescent behavior in more detail (45–46, 51).

10. Also reported from Indiana by Janet Langlois (1980, 199), and from Louisiana by Patricia Alphonso (1981, 31–32).

11. Interestingly, Jacqueline Simpson records a "not very serious" belief of the same kind. According to legend, if you run around the tomb of a local eccentric seven times, he "will jump out and chase you; it is even asserted that the verses on the tomb (now very worn) say that this will happen. In fact, of course, they say nothing of the sort, but are simply the ordinary type of pious verse popular at that period [1793]" (1973, 45). The history of the legend trip before modern times, especially in England and Scotland, remains to be traced.

12. A treatment of this taboo in Western cultures is Aries 1974, 87ff.

APPENDIX
LEGEND-TRIPS IN OHIO: A CLASSIFICATION

A. Sites of Tragic Death Haunted by Ghosts

1. Baby or young child killed: 16 sites.
    Major sites
        Cry-Baby Bridge/Rogues' Hollow (southeast of Doylestown, Wayne County): Mother killed unwanted baby; ghost cries under bridge.

Gore Orphanage (south of Vermilion, Lorain County): Building burned with children inside; their ghosts scream at night.
2. Adult(s) killed in accident: 27 sites.
    Major sites
        Hills and Dales Park (Dayton, Montgomery County): Couple struck by lightning in tower; their ghosts scream.
        Moonville Tunnel (northeast of Zaleski, Vinton County): Brakeman decapitated in train wreck; light appears looking for head.
        Screaming Mimi's Bridge (north of Tiffin, Seneca County): Woman killed in car wreck; if lights blink, her ghost screams.
        Spook Light (ca. Sandusky, various sites in Erie and Ottawa Counties): Motorcyclist killed in wreck; ghostly light appears at site of death.
3. Adult(s) murdered: 22 sites.
    Major sites
        Dr. Crow's House (north of Kirtland Hills, Lake County): Doctor killed wife, self; ghostly lights appear in house.
        Walhalla Drive (Columbus, Franklin County): Woman killed by husband, father, or etc.; memorial statue moans or becomes animate.
4. Adult(s) committed suicide. 12 sites.
    Major site
        Walhalla Drive: Remorseful murderer hanged self from bridge; ghost of hanging body appears.
5. Adult(s) died natural death: 4 sites, none major.

B. *Graveyards Location of Uncanny Activity*

1. Spirit of witch cannot rest in grave: 11 sites.
    Major sites
        Mary Jane's Grave (north of Butler, Richmond County): Witch executed, buried in wilderness; if grave desecrated, death follows.
        Mary Stuckum's Grave (southeast of Coshocton, Coshocton County): Spirit of witch appears by grave, causes cars to malfunction.
2. Covens of witches hold meetings in graveyard: 7 sites.
    Major site
        Peach Ridge Cemetery/Mt. Nebo (north of Athens, Athens County): Witches' cemetery used for devil worship; animals dismembered; trespassers chased and killed.

3. Taboo: standing on grave; followed by death: 14 sites.
    Major site
        Scotch Ridge Cemetery (north of Martin's Ferry, Jefferson County): Those who sit on chair-like grave marker soon die.
4. Tombstones glow, move, display odd markings, etc.: 17 sites.
    Major sites
        Carey Tombstone (around Carey, various locations, Wyandot County): Woman murdered by husband; her face appears on stone.
        Horseshoe Grave (west of Somerset, Perry County): Man kicked to death by horse; red horseshoe appears on stone.
5. Ghostly figures, lights, sounds in graveyard: 10 sites, none major.

C. *Uncanny Persons or Creatures*
1. Eccentric humans: 12 sites, none major.
2. Freaks and retarded humans: 5 sites.
    Major sites
        The Green Man (east of Youngstown, in Pennsylvania): Linesman disfigured by electrical accident walks side roads.
        The Albino Farm (south of Chesterfield, Geauga County): Albinos keep commune secluded, chase away intruders.
3. Maniacs and murderers: 31 sites.
    Major sites
        Hills and Dales Park: After husband killed, woman went crazy; she attacks parkers with hatchet.
        Carpenter Road (east of Kettering, Greene County): Hook Man leaves prosthesis in car door, mutilates boyfriend when he leaves car. (Note: the migratory "Hook in the Door" is localized in six other places, the "Boyfriend's Death" in nineteen places).
4. Humanoid creatures: 16 sites, none major.
5. Other strange animals: 4 sites, none major.
        Fourteen other sites, none major, exhibited miscellaneous other unexplained lights, forces, or apparitions, mostly without explanatory legends.

3

Adolescent Legend Trips as Teenage Cultural Response
A Study of Lore in Context

Patricia M. Meley

Researched and written in the late 1980s and early 1990s, Patricia Meley's work with two specific adolescent legend trips offers an excellent in-depth case study of one small town's legendary traditions. Meley opens her essay with an explanation of ideas that will be familiar by now: the ritual nature of legend trips and their typical three-part structure. What distinguishes her research is that she worked with a single peer group (mixed gender and multiethnic) over an extended period of time, which allows her to "place [her] informants' experiences against the larger backdrop of legend-trip scholarship."

There are many "right" ways to study legends and legend trips. Lots of folklorists have used archival records or published legend texts in order to incorporate a large number of examples for comparative purposes. The texts found in archives and in published articles are useful and important to scholarship—they provide researchers with a sense of both the apparent limits of a given tradition and the range of dynamic variations that it encompasses. Meley's style of research, however, gives her a different level of understanding. She worked with her informants closely for over half a year. She became friends with them, coming to be seen as a "big sister" figure, as she puts it. This type of hands-on fieldwork, while generating texts much like those used by archival scholars, also generates a better sense of the "subtleties and complexities" of the legend trips.

Meley's chapter looks at two main legend trips that take place in Columbia, Pennsylvania. One is to a small nearby cemetery where the low wall that encircles the plots, known locally simply as "the Wall," becomes a site for supernatural events and daring stunts. "Haug's Road," the other site Meley focuses on, is a dirt road with an abandoned house at the end. Legend tells that a murder took place in the house, and visitors report seeing lights inside and hearing creepy noises. The teenagers in the essay describe a wide range of activities there, from intentional pranking to genuine confusion and fright (sometimes both in the same night!).

Among Meley's findings are some surprising elements: despite the common expectation (supported by prior research) that adolescent legend trips often feature alcohol or drug use, the young people of Colombia are adamant that such activities aren't a part of their traditions (and while we may suspect that young informants may not be honest about such a subject, Meley has her genuine connection with these teenagers working to her benefit—they admit to other types of inappropriate or illegal behavior in other contexts, so it's likely they wouldn't be lying about this). Legend tripping is often seen as a form of delinquency, accompanied by other delinquent behavior. But as Meley describes, while it may "superficially" incorporate "the face of antisocial activity," it is not actually delinquent. "It is not an overt challenge to society but is rendered a private ritual in which teenagers assert their independence from adult control innocuously."

The internal states being dramatized in the folk practice of legend tripping are not simple and straightforward. Teenagers in Columbia are ambivalent about their small hometown, defending it against outsiders and yet criticizing it to each other. Their practice of legend tripping encompasses this ambivalence, giving them a change to get away—albeit temporarily and mostly safely—from the norms of their community and test their maturity and bravery.

ONE WARM EVENING IN JUNE 1989, Jason, a fifteen-year-old boy who lived next door, called through my open window, "Can I come in and smoke a cigarette?" I welcomed him in, and as he sprawled his six-foot frame across the couch, he began to earnestly relate an account of a "trip" he had taken. To hear him tell it, it was a journey that took him far in emotion if not in distance:

> We went, you know, because Duane told us about it. There's this trailer where this guy shot his wife—shot her dead, y' know—she's gone—dead. And we stopped at this trailer and sat there and stared at it and we were all scared shitless. 'Cause it's just this narrow dirt road; trees surround it. And we sat there and this blue light goes on in this abandoned trailer where this man killed his wife. And if we didn't get out of there like nothing—I mean, we were gone. And then this car, it's a one-way road, there's no way to get out on it, this car just turned out of nowhere. There's a cliff—you fall off, you die—turned out of nowhere, just nowhere. I will never go back. I was so scared, I didn't sleep.

About two weeks later, while he was sitting outside waiting for a friend, Jason's seventeen-year-old brother, Paul, told me a brief but equally strange tale: There's a crazy man back there. He catches you—he hangs you upside down and cuts your balls off. There's a light that comes on and if you stare at it, you will be blind. Yeah, we go back there. We walked it—me and a bunch of my friends.

The teenagers who related these accounts to me are not juvenile delinquents; they are not drug addicts or mentally disturbed. They are healthy adolescents, and the activity that they describe, the legend trip, takes place near their hometown of Columbia, Pennsylvania. It also happens in sites all over America.

Legend trip research is a relatively new field of inquiry in folklore. The attention of earlier collectors centered on the textual analysis of adolescent legends. Recent trends in contextual analysis have refocused the research on the performance of the legend. Legend trip research has focused rather exclusively on the trip's function in the coming-of-age process of white, suburban, middle-class adolescents. Yet there are indications that the legend trip is an urban phenomenon as well, and as my own study shows, the trip is a multiracial experience.[1]

Kenneth A. Thigpen Jr.'s "Adolescent Legends in Brown County: A Survey," published in 1971, is an early study of adolescent legends that comments on the link between the narrative legend and its performance—the legend trip. Central to the ritual performance, in Thigpen's opinion, is the trip's three-part structure: the introduction, the enactment at the scene of the phenomenon, and the retrospective memorate. The introduction takes place before arrival at the legend trip site and "includes relating the past event and describing the current phenomenon" (204). The story is told by an experienced legend-tripper "in a manner that will heighten the anticipation of uninitiated and initiated alike, thus enhancing the receptive psychological state of all involved" (205).

The second part, the ritual enactment at the scene, is considered by Thigpen the "crucial" aspect of the trip. During this phase, teenagers "attempt to merge the supernatural realm described in the first part with reality" (Thigpen 1971, 205). The third and final aspect involves the telling and retelling of the event that the participants have experienced. These stories may in turn "be added to the basic legend complex to be told as the first part of the performance" (205). Thigpen concludes that the legend trip's primary function is the introduction of the "uninitiated to the realm of the supernatural" (204).

Gary Hall coined the term *legend trip* in his study "The Big Tunnel" (Hall 1973). Hall concentrates his discussion on the legend-telling aspect of the trip. The telling sets the scene for the trip. Hall concludes that the legend trip's function is "primarily recreational" and sees the "willing suspension of disbelief" as a crucial element of the trip's success (256). Similarly, William M. Clements's investigation of another Indiana legend trip in "The Chain on the Tombstone" concludes that the trips "provide a supernatural thrill as an escape from boredom" (Clements 1980, 264).

An extensive survey is Bill Ellis's "Legend-Tripping in Ohio: A Behavioral Study" (Ellis 1982–1983). Ellis proposes that adolescent legend trips are in part a "ritual of rebellion" in which the participants escape the reality-based, moralistic, and authoritarian world of parents, school, and police (64). Legend-trip sites are often physically remote, and the trips Ellis surveyed are opportunities for illegal activities like underage drinking, taking drugs, vandalism, and illicit sexual behavior. The presence of these activities reinforces his thesis that the trips function as "deliberate escapes into altered states where conventional rules do not operate" (65). In addition, Ellis examines the trips as a way for teens to confront adolescent anxieties of mortality in psychologically safe ways. He concludes that the "trip . . . is from start to finish a way of 'giving the finger' to adult rationality" (69).

My study contributes to adolescent legend-trip research because I worked with a single peer group over a six-month period; as a result, my fieldwork is an in-depth study of a normally closed folk group. I attempt to place my informants' experiences against the larger backdrop of legend-trip scholarship in order to draw comparisons and identify characteristics of a ritualized adolescent activity. By concentrating on the context of this ritual and by focusing on the folk group and its use of culture, I have been able to interpret the trips with a sense of the subtleties and complexities the study of adolescence demands.

I conducted my fieldwork in my hometown of Columbia, a small, working-class town located in south central Pennsylvania. Columbia's position on the Susquehanna River made it a natural gateway to the West, and early in the eighteenth century, a trio of English Quakers established a ferry there. Known as "Wright's Ferry," the settlement grew in prominence and was formally founded as the borough of Columbia in 1788. Reaching its zenith in the late nineteenth and early twentieth centuries, Columbia was a bustling center of river and railroad transportation, and home to many industries, including foundries, rolling mills, and lace mills.[2]

Colombia has, throughout its history, stood in marked contrast to its neighboring towns. In a region best known for its German Mennonite and Amish groups, Columbia's 10,000 residents are largely of German Catholic and Scots-Irish ancestry. A Democratic bastion in conservative

Republican Lancaster County, the industrial town lies among many agricultural communities.

Today, like many other small towns in America, Columbia must combat the stagnation brought on by unemployment, population decline, and lack of morale. Although Columbia has been in slow decline over the past few decades, many older residents show a fierce pride and are quick to point out the town's advantages. Colombians still sit "out front" on stoops and porches where they greet their neighbors by name, and the borough remains a relatively safe and appealing town in which to raise children. Children still gather to play in neighborhood groups, and the town is virtually surrounded by the natural playgrounds provided by wooded lots, and the banks of streams and the Susquehanna River. For adolescents, however, the community offers little entertainment and with many familiar, watchful eyes upon them, the town can seem repressive.

Teenagers in Columbia complain of the lack of places to congregate and of the absence of youth-oriented activities. Those that do exist are predictable or typically adult-run. During the winter months, social events tend to revolve around the school calendar and are most often limited to weekends. High school sporting events are well attended, and occasional school dances help break the monotony. Teens go to one another's homes (especially if parents are away or working) to watch MTV, play video games, and party—drink beer and occasionally smoke marijuana. Columbia has two video arcades where teenagers gather, "but you have to spend money or they throw you out." "Going to the mall" (Park City Mall in Lancaster) is a favorite cold-weather pastime, but one that requires cash, typically in short supply among Columbia's teens.

In warm weather, Columbia adolescents are out of doors as much as possible, away from adult eyes and interference. A local pizza parlor serves as a meeting-place, and the town's centrally located park is a favorite hang-out. Up and down Columbia's "main drag," Locust Street, teenagers gather in small groups, though the local police's efforts to crack down on loitering and cruising has put a damper on the crowds. In the summer, the town boasts a drive-in theater which specializes in horror and adventure movies and is popular as a party spot rather than a "passion pit." "Car parties," when teenagers drive to isolated country roads to drink, remain popular, as does cruising. It is during the summer months that legend trip activity is at a peak.

It has been this way since at least 1965, the earliest date that I have been able to trace legend trip activity. Although older Columbians related stories of cruising and other automotive activities, it appears that the legend trip is, in Columbia, a post-1950s teenage pastime.

I interviewed forty-one teenagers from July 1989 to January 1990. My informants composed a loosely affiliated peer group, racially and sexually mixed. The teens ranged in age from thirteen to nineteen; all were raised in Columbia and attended Columbia High School. Some were honor students, active in school activities such as sports and band; others were in trouble with parents, teachers, and the law. Most of the teenagers were of German ancestry, but I also talked with Black and Hispanic teens. The majority of the teenagers were from lower-income families, though at least two had professional parents. I was at first surprised at the diversity within the group; but in a school with a class size average of under eighty, everyone knows everyone else, and though cliques do exist, their boundaries are often blurred.

My first interview occurred at Marisa's sweet sixteen birthday party, held in her backyard in July 1989. Subsequent interviews took place in my home under a variety of circumstances: sometimes a lone teen, sometimes a group of twenty or more. Often these interviews were spontaneous, for in the course of my research, my informants came to look upon me as a "big sister." That, coupled with the fact that winter arrived and my apartment was warm and dry, gave me a unique opportunity to get to know the teenagers well. Although my original encounters with the teenagers were focused on legend trips, the interviews were characteristically informal, and we quickly expanded the relationship to include discussions about school, teachers they hated, relationships with parents, and their current love interests. When a large group showed up, the quality of my research suffered, and the meeting would quickly deteriorate from an impromptu "bull session" to a loud, unmanageable gathering.

I interviewed informants on many occasions under more advantageous conditions. They included Jason, a fifteen-year-old boy who was ambivalent about school and had a strained relationship with his parents. Jason's ultimate goal was to "get the hell out of this town." Paul, Jason's seventeen-year-old half-brother, was a more dedicated student and was involved in high school activities, like the football team. Paul was shyer than his exuberant younger brother, blushed easily, and often drove during the legend trips that the teens told me about. I had known both boys since they were toddlers, and for the last three years, they had been my neighbors. It was through Jason and Paul that I gained access to the peer group. The brothers served as a bridge between the various elements in the large peer group; Jason's friends were the wild bunch, while Paul's were more likely to maintain the status quo. La was a sixteen-year-old Black girl, soft-spoken and mature. La was always matter-of-fact in tone, even when she told me outrageous stories.

She recently began vocational training in horticulture and was pleased that she only had to attend Columbia High for half-days.

I chose to concentrate on two of the five legend trips sites my informants described. Known as "The Wall" and "Haug's Road," the two spots were cited by virtually all informants as the most popular and will be discussed in detail. The minor sites surveyed included "Toad Road" in York County, Pennsylvania. The site was identified by only three seventeen-year-old males who told me that they had gone there with "a bunch of older guys one night." According to several young men from Columbia, the site was an especially popular one in the early 1980s, but has apparently passed out of vogue. The "Gates of Hell" are located on the road; teenagers foolish enough to enter the gates are never seen or heard from again.

The other two legend trips identified by my informants are complex and deserve separate discussion. They are both "harassment trips," a type that Ellis describes as a trip where the object is to torment or abuse an elderly, eccentric, or handicapped individual. The "Midget House" was such a site. Only about fifteen of the teenagers told me that they had been there; four of the girls who went insisted that they only accompanied their boyfriends and did not "get out of the car and knock on the windows." One sixteen-year-old male told me that his friend had "run over one [a midget] in a cornfield one night," but most of the teenagers told me they thought this type of trip was "stupid." Jason asked, "Why would I want to bother them? They never did anything to me." Another harassment trip site was at the house of "The Troll," described as a "nut who will shoot you if you beep and holler." The site was known to virtually all of my informants because of the notoriety of an incident that occurred there in December of 1988 when Ralph Longenecker, "The Troll," shot at a carload of teens and injured one boy. Longenecker's story of years of harassment made the national press, and he was later acquitted of any wrongdoing.

"The Wall" is an early nineteenth-century graveyard on a lonely road on the outskirts of Marietta, Pennsylvania, another small town in Lancaster County, located about twenty minutes away from downtown Columbia. The cemetery is small, measuring about fifty feet by thirty feet, and is enclosed completely by a three-foot-high wall. A stone plaque on the wall reads, "Within this God's acre rest the descendants of Hans Graft."[3] Columbia teenagers contend that the cemetery is guarded by Indian ghosts who reside in the surrounding woods and cornfields. On nights with a full moon, or on any night at midnight (depending on the version), teenagers describe a ritual said to be performed at the site: "You walk around the wall seven times and spit, and you will die." Other versions vary the ritual: some say you must walk the wall thirteen times, some eliminate the spitting, and some say that death is not immediate but comes in the future without warning.

The ritual of circumambulation, though important to the site, does not have to be performed in order to make the trip successfully scary. In fact, not one informant admitted to completing the trek; most vehemently stated that they never even tried. Phil, fifteen, told me that he had heard of "a guy and some girl who walked it, and they disappeared; nobody ever found out what happened to them." Some of the more adventurous teenagers reported acts of vandalism; tombstones were overturned and tossed around. Most of the adolescents, however, are content to simply drive to the site, and they report strange sights and sounds.

The wind is held responsible for many scary experiences; on an otherwise calm night, the legend trip site is described as being unnaturally windy. For instance, one teenager reported that "a gust of wind nearly pushed the car off the road." Others claim to have had unexplainable car trouble and report that the car stalled repeatedly though "nothing was wrong with the engine, 'cause we checked." A group of teenagers referred to "the night we saw the gas cans," but when pressed for details, they could not tell me why the gas cans frightened them.

La's account of a legend trip to The Wall describes her first experience with legend-tripping:

> I went about two years ago, me, R.J., and Mike. We weren't scared or nothing. You know, we just wanted to go over there and see what was goin' on—see if it was scary or whatever. So we went over and as soon as we got to the road that it was on this big gush of wind pushed the car back—it was scary. We were really scared. We weren't even there yet. We didn't know where it was so . . . we seen it and, um, we just like looked at it for a while and this wind was pushin' the car and stuff. "I don't know if you want to get out of the car" [they said], and this one guy got out of the car—R.J. got out. And he, you know, looked over it and stuff, you know, and, you know, he was scared. And they're like, "Walk around it seven times." He never did. We just—the car stalled right in front of it—it was wild.

La's trip to The Wall was typical in many ways. Like many teens, she describes the unnatural wind and unexplainable car trouble, which, she told me later, continued to plague them until they were back in Columbia. None of the participants attempted to walk on the wall, although all three were aware of the existence of the ritual. The trip was typical, too, in that it included both male and female teenagers, though the group of three was relatively small.

Larger trips to The Wall were more common, like the one related to me by Paul, seventeen, and his eighteen-year-old friend:

B: Yeah, we go over there all the time. The last time was great. It was Paul and Phil and Helen . . . we had a whole carload of people.

P: Was that the time we thought we saw the gas can people? I was driving, yeah. And we pulled in real close to the Wall. And, uh—

B: Tara was there, too, 'cause she got out.

P: Oh, we were in the "Big Boat," weren't we? We had about ten people in there. Everybody was carrying on and shit. Did I get out that time? They paid me money to go 'cause I needed the gas money. It was after a football game. I was driving my dad's car.

B: The car was slidin'. And you kept puttin' that back thing down.

P: Yeah, the back window, and I got real close. And the girls were all screaming. I picked a tombstone up. We were driving away, and I like, I don't know, but you—

B: We saw those gas cans.

P: I don't know why we got scared, but the girls were sure screamin'. It was cool.

Like most of the trips related to me by older teens, Paul and his buddy stressed the social aspects of the trip. The gang had piled into his father's station wagon after the Friday night football game, and Paul described it for me as a celebratory occasion, with "everybody carrying on." Larger trips taken by older teenagers are related in an upbeat, joking tone. The teenagers are less serious in tone about the supernatural phenomenon and less emphatic about the details of the trip—who was there, what was seen, and how they were scared.

"Haug's Road" is the second trip surveyed, and it has a more complex legend cycle, with significant discrepancies among stories collected. The winding, partially paved road in York County, Pennsylvania, was for years the site of a harassment trip. Haug's Road was home to "an albino hermit who lived in a shack"; the site was popular among Columbia teens at least as far back as 1971.[4] As a teenager, I vividly remember trips to Haug's Road. My first legend trip was in the summer of 1977, when I was fifteen years old. Four friends and I rode in the back of my brother's pickup truck. After our initiation to the site, we returned many times, and though we never laid eyes on the hermit, our greatest fear (and the reason we went) was that he would shoot at us. The hermit died soon after I graduated from high school in 1979, and I assumed the lure of the site was buried with him. Yet teenagers report a variety of uncanny activity on the road: mysterious blue lights; houses that move and disappear; half-cat, half-fox animals with glowing eyes that run in front of moving cars and disappear over the road's steep sides. They also offer differing reasons for the road's haunted nature. Some teens claim that a "crazy man" lives on the road; some allude to the hermit, or his ghost; some maintain that the road was the site of a murder and attribute the haunted happenings to the victim's ghost or to the murderer (usually identified as a husband).

A fifteen-year-old female informant related to me the following account of a trip to Haug's Road:

> A friend and a couple of other friends went—Stan, Michelle, Tara, Courtney, me, and Mike. Stan drove. They were all there before. It was a Friday night last summer. We were just driving around town and Stan said, "Let's go over to Haug's Road." I said, "Where's that at?" He said, "Just come on. We'll all go there." I said, "All right," and all these people were in the car. And we're just on this dirt road. And it's all bumpy and we were driving on this bumpy road—real bumpy—and then we came upon this house. And there were no lights on and he [Stan] stopped the car and turned out his lights. And all of a sudden this light came on in this house and we tried to start the car and his car wouldn't start up. And we were all screamin' and shakin' the car. And then, um, and then . . . Stan said, "Look, what's that comin' out from the trees, walkin' down?" I said, "What is it?" We were all screamin'—we were so scared. And then we finally got the car started and we moved on. Then we came upon this like, little shack. And then he [Stan] said, "Get out and go see what's in there." And we said, "No, we ain't getting out." And I think that they already knew what was goin' on but I didn't. He said, "Go ahead, go ahead," and I said, "No, someone go with me," 'cause they were all pushin' me to go. I said, "I don't want to go." And so I got out of the car and like there was this door and I heard this creepin' noise. I run back in the—I tried to get back in the car and they had the doors locked. I was sittin' there banging on the doors and it was so scary. And then we made a U-turn and we came back. And we kept hearin' these noises outside the car and then he [Stan] got out. Someone musta been pretendin' like there was a flat tire and he got out and there was no flat tire. And he said, "Come on out here and look at this. Come on out here and look at this." We went out and he took off—left us standin' there for like ten minutes—me, Michelle, Courtney, and Tara. And we were by that house. So we start walking down the road and, uh, we saw this light flashin', but it was him in the car and he kept scaring us and we started runnin' down the road. And, uh, he was waiting like at the

beginning where we were at. We were cursing him out and screamin' at him. On the way home we were talking about it and they were laughin' at us. I haven't been back since.

In this narrative, the informant tells her story in a standard form, with a clear beginning, middle, and end. It is a story that she has told before, and one that she will repeat. Typical among my female informants, this teenager paid particular attention to detail, especially in noting who was there and the reactions of all participants.

The informant makes note of her status as an initiate: ". . . they already knew what was goin' on but I didn't." Because she was new to the trip, she was tricked by the group into performing a special task. Similarly, the boys, who were much older, "pranked" the girls by stranding them there.

Once initiated, teenagers take subsequent trips, and though they now know what to expect, the fun—and the scare—are in no way diminished. Describing what he later told me was "about my twentieth" trip, a sixteen-year-old boy included an account of what happened once the group returned to town:

Oh yeah, sure, we go over there all the time. We went about a month ago—right after school started. It was me and R.J. and Marisa and Julie. I drove Marisa's car. It was a Friday night and there was nothing going on so he says, somebody says, "Hey, let's go over to Haug's Road." And we went and everybody kept saying that whoever was in that trailer shot his wife and killed her. And this, this really freaked me out. We drove back there, you know, to Haug's Road, and all the windows fogged up. This is a dirt road in the middle of—like, it hadn't rained for a week. We came out with mud all over the car and the windows steamed up. There was no mud on that road 'cause it hadn't rained for a week The car was muddy—it was full of mud. Right up the road there's a barn and this blue light came on. Well, we got out of there quick. So we got back to town and go to the pizza place and saw this, uh, this group of people we know. And like we start telling them about what happened, you know, with the mud and all. And they could see it. So they said that they were gonna go and check it out.

Despite the divergent tales that surround the sites, teenagers are in agreement when describing the performance of the trips. Indeed, legend trips to both sites share many of the same features. That the physical trips are consistent and exhibit a pattern of behavior is significant, for the trip itself appears to have functions independent of the legends and may well be the more important aspect in uncovering adolescent motives and behavior.

The trips are described as either spontaneous or planned. A spontaneous legend trip usually occurs on a weekend night when "nothing else is happening." A group of teenagers, bored with cruising around town, suddenly decides to drive in the countryside, and someone suggests a trip. More commonly, however, legend trips are planned. Teenagers who have been to the sites will often plan to take an initiate to the site: "They heard I never was there," one informant told me, "so they took me." Occasionally a group will go to the site without an initiated teen: "We heard about it in school, so we went to look for it."

According to my informants, the mood inside the car as the trip begins is often rowdy and excited. The kids laugh and joke and talk about general topics: school, families, and members of the opposite sex. Once outside the town limits, however, the mood grows more serious. The topic of conversation switches to the approaching site, what happened there, what they saw the last time, what they heard happened to someone else. "If I was taking someone who's never been there," Jason explained, "I'd bullshit it up. You know, I'd tell them what had happened, but I'd drag it out and shit." By the time the car has reached the site, the teenagers are engrossed with the situation. They are quiet, tense, apprehensive.

Both legend trip sites have a central focus. The cemetery itself is the obvious place to stop in the first trip, and the old blue trailer on Haug's Road is reported as the focus in the second. The event itself may vary, depending on the audacity of the driver and the passengers. Some teens report getting out of the car, blowing the horn, even performing a Chinese Fire Drill to taunt the Fates. Some teens are more timid, and sit passively in the car.

When asked if he got out of the car at the Wall, a fifteen-year old boy told me, "No way! I wouldn't even look out the window. I was buried deep in someone." The central focus of the legend trip, the event at the site, is also the basis of most of the teenagers' narratives. They include many details of what happened at this central point, and they appear to vividly remember events, even if they occurred two to three years ago.

Leave-taking is usually abrupt and is markedly uncontrolled. Something happens, someone sees or hears something, and kids jump into the car, bury their faces, scream, and speed away. The frenzy inside the car generally lasts until the teenagers are back on the main highway; everyone talks at once, in bits and pieces of "Oh my god" and "Did you see?" As the teenagers calm, they begin to reconstruct the trip among themselves. They talk about what happened, and who saw what. Sometimes a teenager will attempt to rationalize a scary event, but most of the teenagers remain shaken. On the way back from Haug's Road one night, Jason maintains that they were so scared that he was "prayin' the rosary. La had this 'angel on her shoulder' and she kept sayin, 'I'm prayin' to my angel.'[5] And I said, 'The hell with your angel, I'm prayin' to God.' I kept asking for a sign, and we passed this guy on a motorcycle and he gave me a thumbs-up sign. After that we all felt better."

By the time they approach Columbia again, the mood is subdued, and the teenagers begin to talk of other topics. If it is earlier in the evening, however, the story is repeated several times; by the end of the night, it has taken a standard narrative form, to be repeated for the benefit of others and among themselves, and especially for the next trip.

The return to the hometown marks the end of the trip to the teenagers. One boy told me, "You know, you get home and go, 'Phew!'—like, 'I made it!' It feels good—it's fun." Another teenage boy offered: "At the time it's not fun, but when you get out of it, then it's like, you know, 'Ain't that cool?'"

The teenagers typically go on legend trips in the summertime; autumn, especially around Halloween, is also a popular time. During the winter, legend trip activity usually subsides. Weather conditions are sometimes a factor in deciding to go on a trip; foggy nights are ideal, and "on a night with a full moon," Jason tells me, "you almost have to go." Some teenagers had been at the sites as early as age thirteen; fifteen was more commonly named as the age for the first legend trip. The trips continue throughout adolescence, though older adolescents report less frequent visits. The seventeen-, eighteen-, and nineteen-year-old male informants interviewed offered different reasons for going as well: they were often enlisted as drivers for the younger crowd, or accompanied their younger girlfriends. Teenagers also report that the group can be as small as three or as large as ten; no one ever goes alone or as a couple; the group is usually mixed, male and female, though some boys sometimes go with a "gang of guys." No all female groups were ever reported.

In my interviews with the teenagers, I was continually impressed by the similarities in the information on legend trips they were sharing with me. I heard account after account that was virtually identical in content, form, and tone. The teenagers themselves were aware of this and grew impatient, insisting, "We already told you everything that happens." When asked to characterize the trips, the teens made sweeping generalizations: "You always go at night"; "You never go alone"; "Everyone knows what happens there." There appeared to be rules to follow and roles to play, and a list of necessary ingredients for a successful trip. Trips were taken at night, usually on the weekend; dark, gloomy nights, nights with full moons, and around midnight all enhanced the atmosphere. Trips were taken by groups, and "the more people you can cram in the car, the better." Boys act cool, girls scream a lot. Tricks are played on either newcomers or on the females. A sixteen-year-old boy, weary of my interminable questioning, succinctly summed up adolescent legend trips in Columbia: You know, you all get into the car and go over there. And you do something—something happens, like—and everybody gets all scared and stuff and you get the hell out of there and come home. That's all. It's just fun. Okay?

The ritual structure of legend trips parallels the model of rites of passage suggested by Arnold Van Gennep. Viewing traditional rites as cultural responses to "life crises" among tribal groups, Van Gennep's *The Rites of Passage* (1960) focused on the transitions in social identity that individuals and groups face: the passage from childhood to adulthood or from single to married status. Van Gennep distinguishes three phases within ceremonial rites of passage: separation, when initiates are figuratively or literally removed from the society, representing a break with the past status; transition, a liminal state when initiates must meet with tasks or challenges that symbolically prepare them for their new life; and incorporation, the ritual "welcoming" of the newly initiated into the membership of the community.

This three-part framework is still valid in modern industrialized societies, as Ray Raphael (1988) explicates in *The Men from the Boys: Rites of Passage in Male America*, because the functions of ritual initiations remains the same. Raphael writes, "The primary role of an initiation is to dramatize . . . change, and thereby to facilitate it. A rite of passage places a difficult problem of personal growth into a social context; it gives a public dimension to private problems; it calls upon the combined forces of a culture and all its traditions to help the individual get through this time of crisis" (12).

In our modern individualistic society, rites of passage may not be immediately recognizable. Ceremonies like Confirmations, Bar Mitzvahs, and high school graduations may appear to be rites of passage for adolescents in America, but are often rendered impotent. Solon Kimball, in his introduction to Van Gennep's *The Rites of Passage*, states that "perfunctory ritual may be pleasant but meaningless" (1960, xvii). Yet there is still a need for transition, particularly from extended adolescence into adulthood, as Raphael points out. This transition, according to Raphael, Bronner, and others, is not met by public, uniform ritual in America. It is therefore privatized, differentiated, and spontaneous.

A comparison of trips from various sources with the trips of Columbia teens establishes the legend trip tradition as a ritualized activity of modern American adolescents. The physical location of documented legend trip sites is consistently rural or isolated, thus requiring a passage from home and community to a liminal area or state. Legend trip sites, in addition to having a rural setting, are usually an extended distance from the teenagers' homes. To reach their destination, teenagers must make a twenty- to thirty-minute drive away from the sanctuary of their hometown (Ellis 1982–1983, 66; Hall 1973, 233). The trips that Bill Ellis surveyed were "invariably rural . . . located along sparsely populated roads" (61). Gary Hall describes a "winding road . . . shrouded invariably in dense fog" (233). Another legend trip site in Abington, Indiana, stands "on the edge of a dense woods" (Knox 1971, 1). And Stewart Blankenhorn's description of a popular legend trip site near suburban Philadelphia, Pennsylvania, is virtually identical to Columbia teenagers' accounts of Haug's Road: ". . . the paved road stops . . . At this point, there are no more street lights . . . The roads, which are only a carwidth, are dirt roads that seem to wind without any particular destination" (Blankenhorn 1983, 2).

Another consistent feature of a legend trip is that it is a communal activity shared by adolescents. A "typical" trip almost always includes a mixed-sex group of adolescents. Stewart Blankenhorn relates, "The typical carload is at least three people, not necessarily all of the same sex. However a carload of boys is common and a carload consisting of only girls has not been recorded. I recall one situation when I went [to a legend-trip destination] in a station wagon packed with twelve boys" (Blankenhorn 1983, 2). Gary Hall reports that the trips are usually practiced by "a carload or two of young people . . . Usually boys and girls ride in the same car, but seldom as couples" (Hall 1973, 232–233).

Informants in recorded trips generally mention drugs and alcohol as an ingredient of a successful trip. In *The Rites of Passage*, Van Gennep (1960) also reports mood-altering substances as a frequent feature of the symbolic, vivid nature of rituals. An informant related the circumstances leading to a legend trip to collector Mark Knox: "We had been drinking one night during our junior year and he took me to the bridge where he said the Moss Man lived" (1971, 1). Similarly, Stewart Blankenhorn reported, "People who visit Pitcarin usually are drinking or have been drinking" (1983, 1).

Unlike many of the sites collected by Bill Ellis, the Wall and Haug's Road were not used by teenagers as party or parking spots. Ellis notes that the sites were marked by the great number of beer cans strewn around, and many sites were identified as lovers' lanes (1982–1983, 64–65). Yet my informants were adamant about this point: no one ever went to the legend trip sites to drink or to neck. One informant asked, "Are you crazy? We go parking where it's safe." He offered the local high school parking lot as a prudent site. Among my informants, moreover, the consumption of alcohol on a legend trip was seen as unimportant; many teens claimed to have gone on trips "stone cold sober."

The three-part structure that Kenneth Thigpen discusses was found to be a valid pattern in my research. The same structure—introduction, ritual enactment, and retrospective memorate—parallels the structure of the rites of passage and is apparent in other legend trip accounts. Stewart Blankenhorn relates, "[On] the journey . . . legends about the Pitcarin family and area are exchanged adding suspense to the ride" (Blankenhorn 1983, 2). Gary Hall's "The Big Tunnel" (1973) contains a transcript of a taped ride to a legend trip site that clearly demonstrates the role of legend-telling as an introduction to the site. Further, Linda Dégh discusses the cyclical aspect of how each successive performance evolves into a narrative which is then added to the extant legends of the site (Dégh 1969a, 77–78).

The legend trip functions as a response to the stresses generated by the transitions inherent in adolescence, transitions that must be managed without adult guidance. The age segregation of American teens, coupled with the lack of socially approved means of ritual transition, results in adolescents finding their own standards of behavior and their own rites of initiation.[6] The legend trip is an initiation into the family of the peer group, a sign of acceptance by other members and a sign of acceptance by the initiate of the rules and customs that govern that group. It is an initiation into adulthood, a ritual "trying on" of adult roles, and a means of internalizing the demands of adulthood. Finally, it is an initiation of identity, a rite of passage into a self-awakening in adolescence.

The role of ritual in the development of adolescent identity is related to the role of the crisis during the adolescent years (Erikson 1968, 17). A crisis—a conflict or choice—is a necessary impetus to identity definition. The legend trip is a self-induced crisis, deliberately sought by teenagers, for it compels the peer group to contemplate behavior and to emerge transformed. Invoking rituals such as a legend trip, teenagers make the crisis more manageable (Bronner 1990, 101–115). It becomes a safe way to experiment with various ideologies and feelings, to deal with issues of sexuality, mortality, and autonomy, and a viable means of asserting independence and maturity.

Legend trips serve to strengthen and bind the society of a peer group; teens are adamant about "who went which night." Being invited to go on a legend trip can be a sign of acceptance into a group; my youngest informant. Bill, thirteen years old, was proud of his inclusion on several trips and, among his younger peers, enjoyed a certain notoriety and elevated status by virtue of his acceptance by the older teens. Another teenager who was not well liked asserted her status as a member of the group by the fact that she had been included on a certain legend trip. She silenced the cries of derision and dismissals of "You weren't there" and "No, you weren't with us" by describing a specific incident from the night in question. As a result, her precarious fringe status was improved, at least for the moment.

In addition, the trips facilitate the preservation of the group's collective identity. As a group, teen boys and girls think of the legend trip sites as private domain, belonging exclusively to them. All of my informants were surprised to learn that Haug's Road was a popular legend trip site throughout the 1970s. By naming and renaming sites, teenagers indicate their sense of ownership of a site. Similar to the impulse of pioneers setting out away from the "old" community, teenagers, by virtue of naming a spot, claim it as their own. Moreover, they exert control over their environment and reserve the site for themselves. Grown-ups may know of the Hans Graft Cemetery, but they do not recognize the appellation "The Wall." Even Haug's Road shares a subtle element of this. "Haug" is a common name in the area and is pronounced "howg"; teenagers go legend-tripping on "Hog's Road."

When I ask teenagers, "Why do you go?" the younger teens invariably answer, "It's the thing to do" or "*Everybody* goes." Again, this indicates the need for approval from outside of oneself. Older adolescents are better able to internalize their approval, and do not need the peer group's permission to act or make choices. Older teenagers commented on the "fun" aspects of the trip more, and talked about the trips as big, crazy social gatherings, similar in tone to parties.

Participants in legend trips around Columbia have expectations for socially appropriate behavior according to gender. Teenagers insisted that girls never, under any circumstances, went on legend trips "alone," in an all-female group. In addition, I did not encounter a single episode where a girl drove a mixed-sex group, though many of the girls I interviewed had access to a car. Rather, boys drove the girls to the spots, and at the sites, the girls often exhibited different reactions. They screamed more, and as one boy explained, "They grab you and stuff. It's kind of neat."

When boys go on legend trips by themselves, it is a different kind of experience. In all-male groups, the object of the trip is to contain the fear, to dismiss the anxiety, and to belittle the frightening aspects of the trip. Paul bragged about walking the length of Haug's Road with his buddies, and one teenage boy told me, "When just the guys go, it's a macho thing."

When describing trips in general, the older male adolescents tend to describe their exploits in a confident tone. The boys perform more daring acts, such as getting out of the car, walking on The Wall, and throwing tombstones. One sixteen-year-old boy told me, "Me and Webby got on top of the car and rode on the roof" at Haug's Road. Girls of all ages and the younger boys focus on the supernatural elements of the trips. The youngest informant interviewed told me that just talking about the trips gave him the "creeps," and after about twenty minutes he refused to go on.

As a rite of passage that serves to socialize an individual, the legend trip's rigid gender roles suggest that boys and girls must learn different lessons in their process of becoming men and women. The girls stressed cooperation and interdependence in the performance and narrative of the legend trips; they elaborate on the details of the trip—who went along and what kind of interaction took place during the trip. While the teenage boys brag about their bravado in the face of danger, the girls discuss the trips in terms of "we": "we were scared," "we all screamed," and "we all saw it." The girls also exhibit a passivity and dependence on the males of the group; they never go alone and seem to rely on the boys for both protection and to tease them about their fright.

The boys, on the other hand, display a competitive denial of fear. Many times in my interviews, boys would point out that while others were losing composure, they themselves remained calm: "You know, they were all screaming and shit, I told them to chill out." When describing trips, they tended to use words like "neat," "wild," "crazy," and "great" compared to the females' "scary" and "awful." Male teenagers use the trips to test and prove their masculinity; only the boys talked about attempting daring feats at legend trip sites.

The legend trip also helps to alleviate the sexual anxiety of both the boys and the girls. Despite the apparent sexual sophistication of my informants, the fear of rejection remains intense. The nature of the trips—mixed-sex groups crammed into close quarters—gives teenagers an opportunity to be physically close without having to express the desire to touch. In the frenzy that takes place inside the car, both boys and girls have a chance to satisfy needs for physical contact without excess, commitment, or fear of rejection.

Newly acquired skills in reasoning enable teenagers to contemplate death in a new way. Adolescents can become almost obsessed with death, drawn to the morbid and supernatural, or indulge in fantasies about their own deaths. Paradoxically, to the outside world, teenagers may appear completely unconcerned with death, and may actually tempt fate with reckless, death-defying behavior. "The way I figure it," one informant told me in an offhand manner, "is we all have to die sometime."

This nonchalant attitude belies the sometimes profound fear that adolescents have of their own mortality associated with independence. In a world like ours, death and destruction are daily fodder for the media. At the same time, adult society does not condone open discussion of death and dying. This point was especially apparent in the course of my research. A sixteen-year-old informant with leukemia died in March after a long struggle with the disease. The other teenagers were visibly shaken and several gathered in my apartment after the viewing. One boy related that in school that day there were counselors to assist the students. "I went to talk with one," the boy told me. "She told me to go and eat lunch and that was supposed to make me feel better." He was openly disgusted with adult guidance.

In lieu of a support system and an acceptable method of dealing with death and dying, teenagers are once again left to their own means. The ritual of the legend trip is an aid in helping teenagers confront issues of death and mortality in a psychologically safe way. Without risking their lives, teenagers can simulate the experience of looking death in the face, and this helps them to "exorcise" their fears about dying.

My informants expressed an ambivalence about their hometown. Well aware of Columbia's "black sheep" status among neighboring communities, the teenagers are distrustful of outsiders and are easily and often provoked into fighting to defend their town's honor. At the same time, among themselves, they complain bitterly about Columbia. "This town sucks," one boy casually summed it up. Most teens express a desire to "get out" as quickly as possible. For many of my informants, the chance will not come. For these teenagers, the legend trip may be a symbolic escape out of town.

Ellis interprets the legend trip as a ritual of rebellion. The trips include features of acts against social norms and expectations, demonstrated by the underage drinking and acts of vandalism, but the rebelliousness is more an outcome than a purpose of the ritual. Because the rebellion is ritualized, it is transformed; through the ritualization of the challenge to adult authority, teenagers make their challenge both manageable and comprehensible. The activity takes place deliberately away from the locus of adult power and control, and is guarded against the possibility of adult interference or even knowledge. The legend trip, though superficially incorporating the face of antisocial activity, is not a delinquent behavior. It is not an overt challenge to society but is rendered a private ritual in which teenagers assert their independence from adult control innocuously.

The search for independence is a primary motivation for legend trips. This is reinforced by the physical structure of the trips. Legend trip sites are removed through time and space from the adolescents' hometown. Unlike party or parking spots, which are chosen for their convenience as well as their seclusion from prying adults, the legend trip site requires a journey of considerable distance from the town. Although a number of cemeteries and sites could be characterized as "spooky" within the town's limits, teenagers deliberately travel away from what they consider to be the locus of parental and societal control in order to have a chance to try on adult roles for themselves.

The legend trip provides teenagers with a setting in which to test their newfound adult courage. It gives teenagers an opportunity to prove their ability to take care of themselves in a crisis. Finally, the legend trip also offers teenagers the chance to return to the sanctuary of home when they have had enough of the adult world of risk and responsibility. Without a chance to test the limits, to question authority, to live and learn, teenagers cannot incorporate the values, the lessons, the judgment and, essentially, the integrated identity they will need to cross the threshold to maturity, able and willing to meet the stresses and challenges of adulthood in modern American society.

In the absence of meaningful, adult-sanctioned rites of passage, teenagers must create their own. The legend trip serves this function in modern society, for unlike tribal cultures, which celebrate initiation rites rarely in an individual's lifetime, modern American teenagers must repeat the ritual over and over again. Because their incorporation into adult society is not acknowledged by that society, teenagers must, on an individual basis, make a judgment about their own level of maturity. The repetition of the legend trip throughout the adolescent years reinforces and validates the teenagers' growth as individuals and as young adults.

The vitality of the teenage tradition of the legend trip is thus strengthened, and the continuity of trips is assured. A sixteen-year-old girl shared the story of her first legend trip with me and revealed how the trips will continue in Columbia. Having never been on a legend trip, she was ambivalent about going, but yielded to peer pressure: "They said they couldn't believe that I wasn't ever there before. They kept telling me all this weird stuff about it, you know, and man, I didn't want to go. But they were all saying, 'Oh, you gotta go' and all." Once at the site, she reports that the boys "showed off" by getting out of the car, and they teased the girls for their timidity, saying, "'C'mon, get out and walk the wall.'" The girls, true to their legend trip role, "wouldn't, you know. We were just sitting in the car saying, 'You're crazy.'" The event climaxed when "this dog, it sounded like a wolf, it started barking and somebody said that it was twelve o'clock midnight, and we started screaming and flipping out. So the guys get back in the car and we got out of there real fast." But that was not the end of the trip for my informant. She now had a story to tell, and, importantly, an experience to share: "When we got home I was still shaking, but it was cool, you know, because the next day, I told my girlfriend about it, and I told her that she had to go. So we're gonna take her, maybe this weekend."

The context she provides for her adolescent folklore helps to uncover the base compelling reasons why teenagers "have to go" on legend trips. Ultimately she, like others, speaks of transition from adolescence to adulthood, a transition made all the more stressful in a fragmented, individualistic society. The legend trip provides teenagers with a culturally appropriate and comprehensible response.

NOTES

1. Though published literature on the urban legend trip is scant, brief interviews reveal that the tradition is found within the city limits. A thirty-five-year-old Harrisburg man told me that, as a teenager, he and his friends walked to a city graveyard to see "Fidget Widgets," creatures that he described as "outer spacemen." Teenagers at the Harrisburg Middle School report going to the same cemetery to see the Fidget Widgets, but they claim the scary creatures are video game characters.

2. A thorough recent history of Columbia, Pennsylvania, remains to be written. One available source is *History of Lancaster County* by Franklin Ellis and Samuel Evans, published in Philadelphia by Everts and Peck in 1883. An invaluable glimpse of Columbia at the height of the town's prosperity is provided by James D. Slade's *A Complete Business Directory of Columbia, Lancaster County, Pennsylvania, Together with a Few of the Most Important Events of the Borough's Past and a Correct Pen Picture of Columbia in 1887*, published in Columbia by the Evening Star Job Office in 1887. I also relied on the information I acquired at Wright's Ferry Mansion, a private museum in Columbia where I worked as a tour guide in 1988.

3. I have been unsuccessful in my attempt to identify Hans Graft.

4. My brother, Nick Meley, born in 1955, told me that his first legend trip to Haug's Road was as a high school sophomore in 1970.

5. "Angel on my shoulder" refers to a tiny angel pin worn on the shoulder for a blessing or as a good-luck charm. The pins are popular in Columbia among both children and adults.

6. Bronner 1988 discusses how children in modern America similarly use folklore in lieu of adult guidance. Raphael 1988 argues similarly for young males in American society.

APPENDIX

INFORMANTS: ORAL SOURCES

1. Jason, 15, German, Catholic
2. Paul, 17, German, Protestant
3. La, 16, Black, African Methodist
4. Julie, 15, German, Catholic
5. Charlie, 16, German, Catholic
6. Rob, 16, German, Episcopalian

Adolescent Legend Trips as Teenage Cultural Response

7. Jen, 16, German, Episcopalian
8. Hosee, 16, Filipino, Catholic
9. Kathy, 15, German, Lutheran
10. Danielle, 16, Italian, Catholic
11. Brandi, 16, German, Catholic
12. Marisa, 16, German, Lutheran
13. Amita, 17, Indian, Hindu
14. Angie, 16, German, Catholic
15. Bill, 17, German, Catholic
16. Wolfgang, 16, German, Lutheran
17. Randy, 16, German, Methodist
18. Faith, 16, Black/German, Baptist
19. Duane, 19, Black/Hispanic, African Methodist
20. Bill, 13, German, Catholic
21. Bucket, 17, Black 24
22. Tara, 18, Black
23. Helen, 14, Irish/Italian/Black
24. Nestor, 15, Black/Hispanic, Baptist
25. Amy, 16, Mexican, Pentecostal
26. Evie, 17, German, Atheist
27. Chris, 14, German, Protestant
28. Latrease, 18, Black, Baptist
29. R.J., 18, German
30. Phil, 15, German, Lutheran
31. Michelle, 19, Black/German
32. Scott, 17, Black/German, African Methodist
33. Heidi, 15, German, Catholic
34. Bo, 18, Black
35. Carol, 17, German, Mormon
36. Tiekey, 17, Black, Baptist
37. Emily, 14, German, Catholic
38. Jeff, 15, Black/Hispanic, African Methodist
39. Mike, 18, Black, Baptist
40. Phil, 17, Black, Baptist
41. Kurt, 17, Black, Baptist

4

Legend Trips and Satanism
Adolescents' Ostensive Traditions as "Cult" Activity

Bill Ellis

Linda Dégh's and Andrew Vázsonyi's "Does the Word 'Dog' Bite? Ostensive Action: A Means of Legend-Telling" (Dégh and Vázsonyi 1983) argues that "presentation as contrasted to representation" constitutes an extremely important form of the legend (6). Dégh and Vázsonyi propose three kinds of ostension: pseudo-ostension, a hoax; proto-ostension, appropriation of a legend's content as personal experience; and quasi-ostension, misunderstanding of a legend (18–20).

Bill Ellis's "Legend-Trips and Satanism: Adolescents' Ostensive Traditions as 'Cult' Activity" (Ellis 1991) applies Dégh's and Vázsonyi's terms to legend-trip behavior during the Satanism scare of the 1980s, which frightened many people and fascinated folklore scholars. During this time period, it was not unusual for police officers to ask folklorists to explain whether or not devilish-looking artifacts found in public parks had been placed there by Satanists. Tucker was one of the folklorists of the 1980s who accepted police officers' invitations to scrutinize sodden piles of ashes, candles, and other objects in a local park. What, asked the police, did these odd objects mean? Were Satanists really infiltrating parks where innocent children played? And if so, how could the police find and stop these evildoers?

Like Ellis, Tucker concluded that teenagers, not Satanists, had put together a pile of objects that looked like they might have been used in devil worship, but she did not apply legend theory to this phenomenon. Ellis made an important contribution to legend-trip scholarship by explaining that approximations of Satanic rituals can be part of teenagers' ostension during legend trips. His insightful, detailed analysis of adolescent behavior in relation to the mysterious "Toledo Dig" helps readers understand the genesis of "Satanic panic" in the American Midwest and northeastern Pennsylvania from the late 1960s to the 1980s. Jeffrey S. Victor's (1993) Satanic Panic: The Creation of a Contemporary Legend further documents this extremely interesting phenomenon.

ONE OF THE MOST INTRIGUING FOLK TRADITIONS active in the United States today is the adolescent legend-trip, or ritual visit to an allegedly haunted or marginal site. It normally involves the ostension, or literal acting out, of local supernatural legends. Frequently, the trip encourages teens to enter abandoned churches and leave graffiti or to vandalize tombstones to prove their courage.

Rumor-panics about alleged Satanic cults frequently stem from the traces of legend-trip activity. Such trips are intended to be illegal and to shock adults; still, they are forms of entertainment, not religious rites, and the groups who commit them cannot be termed "cults." This essay will examine a variety of legend-trips reported from rural areas in the Midwest and in northeastern Pennsylvania, areas hard hit by Satanic rumor-panics. We will see how from the 1960s on folklorists have documented as normal adolescent activities what Satan-hunters present as evidence for "cult" activity. In particular, we will see how a knowledge of such folklore would help us understand the background of dramatic events like the 1984 "Toledo Dig."

THE DYNAMICS OF LEGEND-TRIPPING

Claims about Satanic cults have been supported by evidence such as "Satanic" graffiti, desecration of churches and cemeteries, animal mutilations, stone circles in fields or decorated rooms in abandoned houses that apparently served as "altars" for occult rites, sightings of robed figures in graveyards or remote spots, and rumors about blood-drinking or cannibalism (Lanning 1989; Ellis 1989a; Victor 1990). Such finds may seem to be hard evidence for devil-worship practices; in fact these phenomena are more likely to be reflections of adolescents' legend tripping.

FOLKLORISTIC STUDY OF LEGEND-TRIPS

Documentation of the legend-trip as a U.S folk tradition began with a 1969 article by folklorist Linda Dégh, who paraphrased an undergraduate term paper on a haunted bridge near Avon, Indiana. Dégh supplemented this account with materials documenting similar visits in Indiana, Tennessee, South Carolina, and Michigan. In traditional legends, supernatural experiences simply happen unexpectedly to a witness, but in the legend-trip, Dégh noted, "the bridge-visitors condition themselves mentally for a vision they desire to have [and] perform a series of designated acts known to be effective to prompt the ghosts to appear." She suggested that belief or disbelief in supernatural phenomena was less important than the visit's role as an "initiation ritual" through which young males prove their adulthood (1969a, 77–81).

Other early surveys described legend-tripping at other Indiana sites (Mitchell 1969; Baker 1969, 1970, 1972; Gutowski 1970; Clements and Lightfoot 1972), and studied the dynamics of the participating adolescent groups in more detail (Thigpen 1971; Hall 1973). Kenneth A. Thigpen, in particular, recognized that teens' legend complexes reflected a three-part ritual consisting of (1) initiation into the story, (2) performing the acts that "cause the fulfillment of the legend," and (3) retrospective discussion of what participants believed happened, which then fed back into the core story into which newcomers were initiated (Thigpen 1971, 204–205). Scattered documentation of legend-tripping in other areas has confirmed this basic description (Harling 1971; Fisher 1975; Rudinger 1976; Samuelson 1979; Moss 1979; Alphonso 1981; Baker 1982; Ellis 1982–1983; Johnson 1984; Glazer 1989; Orso 1989).

CULTS AND FOLK GROUPS

The total number of teens participating in this tradition is unknown, but it must be large. Thigpen, surveying all grades of a rural high school, found 14 percent familiar with legend-tripping (Thigpen 1971,144); Johnson (1984), surveying college students at the University of Iowa, found that 28 percent had visited the "Black Angel," a local legend-trip site. Further, some legend-trippers become "experts" in the tradition, visiting the same or similar sites dozens, perhaps hundreds of times. Thigpen identified six teens who had formed a coherent group focused on "The Watcher," a malign spirit invoked by secret covens of witches in the Indiana countryside. Johnson found that "five [students] had made multiple trips, ranging from several to one hundred" (Johnson 1984, 6). Such small clusters of teens may specialize in "ghost-hunting," but they hardly constitute a "cult."

The popular image of a "Satanic cult" assumes that the adolescent mind is somehow helpless in the face of adult "recruiters."[1] Yet teens' firsthand descriptions of legend-trips make it clear that adults are not involved or welcome. "Trippers" who are eighteen or older are largely shunned as outsiders. Likewise, since the philosophy of the legend-trip involves defiance of "adult" norms, it would be highly unlikely that such a visit would be organized and enforced by an older cult "recruiter." Some popular teens strongly interested in the occult may indeed gain control of some groups that engage in legend-tripping. Still, most visits are spontaneous and frequently involve skeptics. In any case, it would be hard to see anything in the normal dynamics of the tradition that would require belief in the supernatural phenomena invoked; in fact, as Thigpen notes, participation in legend-trips seems not to have any "profound or stable influence on one's belief system" (Thigpen 1971, 207).

It seems more accurate to say that such a cluster of adolescents is a folk group, a collection of individuals that share informal, face-to-face contacts and so generate and share specialized information and attitudes (Ben-Amos 1972; Toelken 1979). A cluster that specializes in visits to "haunted" spots may thus be termed an "occult-oriented folk group," since members often gather and share knowledge about other aspects of the supernatural and anomalous: UFOs, Bigfoot, Ouija boards, and the like. We can infer that such folk groups—not "cults"—are responsible for most of what police "experts" claim is evidence of "Satanism." Further, we may infer that, as adults become hypersensitive to certain activities as "Satanic," many such adolescent groups will adopt (or pretend to adopt) these acts out of protest.

LEGEND-TRIPS AS OSTENSION

Traditional folklore analysis, based on performed texts, is ill equipped to deal with legend-tripping. However, recent research has given us fresh ways of looking at the phenomenon. Dégh and Vázsonyi (1971) have argued that legends were not primarily "kinds of stories" that express "belief" but rather traditional ways of testing the credibility of certain beliefs. Thus they have redefined legend-telling as a "repeated group rite" (Dégh and Vázsonyi 1978, 269). To deal with legends as behavior, Dégh and Vázsonyi borrow from semiotics the term *ostension*: an action that gains its primary meaning by being part of a recognized story. A person who uses a legend as a guideline for a criminal act, for instance, is performing that legend through an act of ostension; hence, "copycat" crimes based on urban legends are themselves types of legend performance.

Two common variations, they propose, are "quasi-ostension," or mistaken judgment, and "pseudo-ostension," or hoaxing (1983, 18–20). Legend-trips, then, can best be understood as a ritual activity driven by varying forms of ostension that interpenetrate and rely on each other for meaning:

- Ostension: as part of the legend-trip's characteristic invocation of the supernatural, teens will commit ritual acts that may suggest Satanism.
- Pseudo-ostension: adolescents seeking to frighten peers or parents will briefly impersonate "Satanists" or fabricate evidence of "cult" rituals.

- Quasi-ostension: normal adolescent acts having nothing to do with occult practices are nevertheless seen by authorities as being part of "Satanic" rites.

Some of this complex interplay between "cults" and legend-trip activities can be documented from archival and published sources.

FORMS OF OSTENSION IN LEGEND-TRIPPING

Quasi-Ostension: Mistaken Perception

GRAFFITI

Although few participants' descriptions of legend-trips allude to writing graffiti, nearly all locations that I have visited have been covered with inscriptions of all kinds. In only a few cases, moreover, do these graffiti allude to the legend that motivates the trip. More often, bridges were simply covered with names of loved ones, high school names and mottos, and favored rock bands or albums. When graffiti are mentioned in legend-trip descriptions, they are generally put in terms of high school rivalries or courtship customs: at a haunted house near Portsmouth, Ohio, for instance, there is a room with a huge heart painted on it. If you put your initials and those of your girlfriend inside the heart, then add a number, you will marry and have that many children (OSUFA n.d.: Jones). Even at alleged "devil-worship" sites, occult graffiti have made up a tiny minority of inscriptions. Typical is a derelict hunting lodge just north of Hazleton that was identified as a "cult" meeting place by a student of mine, who showed me several snapshots of graffiti incorporating pentangles and the number 666. When I visited the site (which had been used for teenage parties), I had difficulty finding those particular items among a welter of doodles, linked initials, and other public notices.

It is important, therefore, not to give "Satanic" inscriptions and symbols a disproportionate weight. A few places may sport deliberately "Satanic" inscriptions, but less to invite occult practices than to heighten a site's atmosphere. Seen from the teens' point of view, these graffiti seem neither particularly unusual nor threatening.

"ALTARS"

In some cases, these may be the result of ostension proper: members of occult-oriented folk groups may set aside spots for some kind of home-grown "worship." More often, rock circles are simply indications of legend-trip sites' status as party spots. Peach Ridge, near Athens, Ohio, has been connected with evil witchcraft cults at least since the 1940s (Ellis 1989a, 206–208), but this has not stopped teens and college students from congregating there in great numbers. Although some circles may be deliberately set up for improvised rites, most probably have a beer keg, not an altar, as their focus.

This suggests an explanation for the many rumors about mysterious groups of devil-worshippers whom some groups of legend-trippers try to spy on. Generally, the legend has it, if you can catch the "witches" or cult members at the right time, you will find them standing around a fire, dressed in black (or white) robes, chanting and preparing to sacrifice an animal. This is dangerous, as you may be spotted and chased by the "witches" or have a mysterious car accident on the way home. A Cleveland-area account is typical:

> And it's supposively [sic] where a group of people that worship there every full moon and they're like in these monk outfits and they have a fire burning and they sacrifice things like animals . . .
>
> I've heard things like seeing rings of witches and balls of fire and crowds of people around the fire . . . umm, the cops won't even bother them, the cops know better. People said they seen them standing—it's kinda like the Klu Klux Klan [sic] that it, it's like something to do with Satan. (OSUFA n.d.: Cannata)

In 1985, police investigating a peaceful public gathering of 140 neopagans near Bloomington, Indiana, showed a similar reluctance to intervene. A deputy sheriff, primed with information obtained through a network of police specialists on Satanic cults, told news reporters that he had directly witnessed "people drinking blood, eating raw meat, dancing around the flames naked . . . wearing devil-like costumes, and having a ceremony with burning candles in the graveyard" (Guinee 1987, 3). The deputy said only that he could not stop the Satanic rites because of "freedom of religion," but police reported that one of the "Satanists," arrested for possession of marijuana, had told them "something bad was going to happen." Shortly afterwards, the arresting officers' police car was rear-ended by another motorist (not a Satanist); two officers and one "disoriented" police dog had to be taken to area clinics (21). Local police obviously believed that confronting Satanists directly would put them into supernatural or physical danger.

Ironically, in most cases, nothing more complex than a loud party is going on. A colleague of the deputy cited above who lacked special training in cult detection saw only "a large group of people holding hands, dancing, and yelling around a large fire" (Guinee 1987, 3). And other accounts collected from adolescents describe the same cautious police behavior, only from the perspective of the party. One Hazleton-area teen related several stories about an abandoned mental institute in the White Haven area that was said to have been taken over by Satanists. She continued:

> John said the one time they were like—it was the middle of the summer or something and they said they were all looking for a place to party, right, and they didn't want to get busted . . . So he went up to—he went up there with like a bunch of his friends; they had carloads. And he said they walked up there at night.
>
> They had like barrels [kegs of beer], you know. They started a big fire. He said you could see the fire from like everywhere. They said you could see it from anywhere.
>
> And they were walking back down and they could see like cops going by their cars, but they wouldn't even frigging stop; the cops wouldn't even go up there. So they didn't even care. They just let it go. Cops won't even go up there and that's really weird, the fact that they—[Interviewer: Then they know something.] Everybody knows for a fact that there's devil worshippers up there, and they won't even go up there. The cops won't even go up there and stop them or stop you from partying.
>
> They don't even care if you trespass. They just let you go; they won't touch you. It's really weird . . . I can't wait to go up there, personally. (PSUHFA n.d.: Watkins)

For some teens, then, the reluctance of police to confront Satanists holding their rites must come as a godsend. In fact, one of the reasons for circulating rumors that certain popular party spots are "devil-worship" sites might well be to keep unwelcome freshmen and interfering adults away, so that they can drink and party in peace. Legend-trippers must find it richly comic that the tradition lets them party in plain sight of patrolling police.

Pseudo-Ostension: Hoaxing and Role-Playing
ANIMAL MUTILATIONS

A common allegation is that cults kill small animals as part of their ceremonies, frequently draining their blood out and hanging the corpse from a tree. Some instances can be blamed on quasi-ostension: in fact the animals have been killed by cars or mutilated by predators. In New Hampshire, apparent animal sacrifices were road kills waiting to be picked up by highway crews (Hicks 1989, A22–23). But it is also true that many legend-trips locate dead or mutilated animals specifically at the "haunted" sites. Teens in the Hazleton area claim to know several places where Satanists leave dead animals. One informant told a student of mine: We walked for about a quarter mile beyond the cemetery and John [a "Satanist" friend] showed me a huge stone altar covered with blood and huge stone candle urns. I turned my flashlight upward to the trees and I saw thirteen dead puppies hanging from them. (PSUHFA n.d.: Pipech)

Some of these may be adolescent boasts or creations of imagination, but some are acts of pseudo-ostension. During the spring of 1987, in the midst of persistent rumors about Satanic cults in the Hazleton area, a group of teens stole a lamb from the Hazle Park Packing Company, slaughtered it, and left it inside a stone ring not far from "Markle's Grave," a statue that is said to grow devil's horns under a full moon. Although State Police investigated and identified the group responsible, the sensation caused by the "mutilation" was partially responsible for a rumor-panic that broke out later that spring in area high schools (Ellis 1990). In such cases, animals were killed (perhaps intentionally) by teens and left in conspicuous places, but closer study showed that no occult ceremony was ever performed.

"CARETAKERS"

A somewhat more complex situation of pseudo-ostension takes place when humans confront humans. One of the common elements in most legend-trips is the danger presented by some adult who chases and tries to punish intruders into the legend-trip site. In some cases, the "caretaker" is a supernatural being like "The Watcher," but in many traditions, he or she is a human, though perhaps with crazed, superhuman powers. At some sites, it may be a parent who, driven mad by the death of a child, attacks any teen who resembles his/her murderer. In others, the caretaker may simply he a local eccentric or farmer who tries to scare kids away. And, indeed, some locals have accepted their legendary status and set up sound systems to broadcast bloodcurdling screams or pop out of bushes to frighten carloads of teens. More often the teens themselves play at becoming "The Caretaker" temporarily. Many legend-trip accounts include descriptions of simple or elaborate hoaxes played on peers. Some are no more than reaching a hand out the back window and then into the front to tap a girl on the shoulder; others involve hiding underneath a haunted bridge to make weird noises when the next carload drives up. Some teens succeed with even more elaborate forms of impersonation. Some students have confessed to putting on a Halloween costume and prowling around "Weatherly Cemetery," a typical neglected graveyard outside of Hazleton, jumping out of bushes and chasing carloads of their peers.

This kind of pseudo-ostension seems integral to the legend-trip tradition, since it not only gives skeptics a chance to prove their adulthood by tricking more credulous peers, but it also, ironically, provides those who are hoaxed with a more complex, entertaining experience to discuss and share with others. The possibility that one might have been tricked, in many teens' accounts, does not seem to matter much, so long as the trick was carried out well. The twin benefits of pseudo-ostension, then, are that it allows the hoaxer to embody the threat invoked by the legend, while also giving the witness a chance to act as if he or she were genuinely in the presence of a witch, angel of death, or ghoul. An uneventful visit to the haunted site is, for committed legend-trippers, the worst outcome.

Ostension: Vandalism and Supernatural Rites
SMASHED GRAVESTONES AND EXHUMED CORPSES

One complex of legend-trip beliefs, derived from older English superstitions, attributes living qualities to stones. Many such beliefs are jocular, like college stories about statues that move when virgins graduate, since they refer to events that can never happen (Williamson and Bellamy 1983, 122). But more serious beliefs are fully paralleled in adolescents' legend-trips, where tombstones often move, glow, become hot, and return mysteriously if stolen. Mary Jane's gravestone, near Mansfield, Ohio, is one of many that punishes vandals. One story relates how two youths tried to steal her tombstone but were killed in a car wreck on their way home. The next day Mary Jane's marker was back in place (OSUFA n.d.: Willett).

Often these rituals are accompanied by complex graveyard "ceremonies," said to bring sinister results: those who carry them out summon devils or evil ghosts or bring untimely deaths upon themselves. Yet all the sites named in these traditions have in fact been heavily patronized and vandalized over a long period of time. Mary Jane's gravestone is conspicuous for being perhaps the most completely damaged marker in the churchyard. The legend, therefore, cannot be artificially distinguished from the trip that it motivates, which tests adolescents' bravery by creating an imaginative supernatural threat, then defying it. Still, there is no evidence that such rites actually do raise evil spirits or lead to sudden deaths. Graphic as the "friend-of-a-friend" stories are, firsthand stories of defying the curse tend to be no more dramatic than cars that won't start, near or minor fender-benders, and sudden gusts of wind. Although such acts are ostensive, directly acting out the events that the legend says will lead to supernatural dangers, on some level they are collective fantasies that the adolescents can and do distinguish from genuine religious rites.

One of the most dramatic "signs" of cults is grave robbing: in a number of cases, mausoleums have been broken into and burial vaults dug up. "Experts" suggest that Satanists are after skulls or other bones to use as amulets or ritual objects. Although firsthand accounts of grave robbing are absent from folklore archives, cases in which teens have been apprehended with skulls or body parts have pointed more toward a legend-tripping context than toward cult activities. In February 1990, for instance, two youths were arrested for entering a Lancaster, Pennsylvania, mausoleum to smash a skeleton with a hammer. Although the cemetery association's president blamed Satanic cults, police discounted this theory. An accompanying photograph shows typical adolescent graffiti on the opened tomb and others nearby (AP release, February 20, 1990).

"Dabbling" and Ostension

The prevalence and consistency of legend-trip stories and associated vandalism do not provide evidence for cults directing such actions. Children's folklore has been found to be surprisingly consistent in even small details across state and national boundaries, and it can spread surprisingly quickly through letters, telephone calls, friendships made during vacations, and the electronic media. So too adolescents' folklore tends to be "silent" yet remarkably uniform, with names and motifs cropping up in widely divergent places. Because legend-trips appeal to universal adolescent anxieties, it is no surprise that we find similar actions throughout the country.

An adult uninitiated into the tradition of ostension might well accept the presence of mutilated dogs, black-robed figures, and smashed gravestones as evidence that adolescents are "dabbling with Satanism." Such teens, they might think, are playing a dangerous game with rituals that might seem to give them real-life powers. Perhaps because Satan gives them extra powers, perhaps because they become confused and want to act out their fantasies, they may be enticed into performing more elaborate rituals that involve killing animals or humans.

The fallacy in such an argument is that there is no direct evidence that adolescents participating in legend-trips confuse reality and imagination. Gary A. Hall, examining a complex of beliefs and rituals attached to "The Big Tunnel" in southeastern Indiana, observed that adolescents consider legend-tripping primarily as a recreational event. Its effect, like that of a popular horror movie, relies on a "willing suspension of disbelief" in supernatural phenomena. Just as the movie may be enjoyed both by those who believe in the horrors portrayed and also by those who are skeptical, so too participants in legend-trips may or may not believe that their rituals are producing real effects. "Questions of actual belief or non-belief are largely irrelevant during the drama and excitement of the trip," Hall concluded; rather, the essence of legend-trips is "collectively shared emotions of apprehension and fear" (Hall 1973, 170–171).

The dynamics resemble those observed in professional "haunted houses" set up by charities near Halloween, during which local teens and adults impersonate cultural scare figures like Dracula. Some psychologists have suggested that such attractions are dysfunctional, giving visitors the message "that it is fun to pretend to kill people and chop them up" (quoted in Ellis 1989a, 201). But Sabina Magliocco (1985) observed that adolescents who go through such attractions adopt well-known "roles," females reacting with exaggerated fright, males with overdone macho displays. In short, both performer and audience collaborate in a dramatic event, heightening the aesthetic effect of the "scare." Similarly, no discussion of legend-trips has ever suggested that participants "embodied" the characters of legend plots in anything more sinister than hoaxes. Real-life murders committed by teenage "Satanists" likewise have shown no direct connection to legend-trips, role-playing games, or haunted houses.

Allowing oneself to become "engrossed" in the reality of self-generated plots is quite different from actively believing in them (Fine 1983; Ellis 1982). Engrossment involves creating a fantasy self that is appropriate to a given play situation. It may draw on real-life roles and generate powerful emotions, but ultimately it is set off from common-sense definitions of reality. The ability to become engrossed in such situations is mastered around the age of twelve and remains a fascinating challenge throughout adolescence. The ostensive traditions reflected in legend-trips are best understood as part of this complex recreational activity, not as attempts to control entities or forces that affect common-sense reality. When adults deny teens' ability to suspend disbelief and enjoy self-generated fantasy plots, they inappropriately class their activities—and their minds—with those of children. Simultaneously, they miss the real value of their folk culture.

LEGEND-TRIPPING AND THE TOLEDO DIG

When adults fail to understand adolescents' folk traditions, or try to interpret them in a simplistic fashion, the results can be bizarre and politically dangerous. One event that illustrates this confusion is the excavation of a wooded lot in Lucas County, Ohio, by deputy sheriffs seeking the graves of sixty human sacrifices. The so-called Toledo Dig was to some observers a total fiasco, turning up piles of rubbish and no confirmable evidence for cult activities. To others, it was a qualified success: while no bodies were located, "experts" said they found "a headless doll with nails driven through its feet and a pentagram attached to its arm," identified as part of a "death ritual," along with "a nine-foot wooden cross with ligatures attached, sacks of folded children's clothing, sixty male children's left shoes, assorted hatchets and knives, and an anatomy dissection book" (Lyons 1989, 3).

The truth is rather less sensational. Sorting out the site's history and the "clues" followed by authorities, we can see that the deputies probably excavated a legend-trip site frequented by local teens for partying and imaginative scares. Nevertheless, Lucas County police were tied up for several days during the excavation, and two innocent families were publicly harassed as "child killers" after their homes were described in local papers as "cult houses" (*Cleveland Plain Dealer*, July 7, 1985). And as recently as March 1989, results from the dig were used uncritically as proof for human-sacrifice cults in the Ohio/Michigan area (Victor 1990).

Area Adolescents' Legends

The Toledo area is an especially rich one for legend-trippers. A short drive can take a teen south along U.S. 24 to Waterville to visit "Stick Lady," then a bit farther to harass "Shotgun Lady," then farther south into a rural area known to teens as "Zombieland." Here you can watch zombies with glowing red eyes run through fields carrying parts of dead bodies, or sitting comatose in barns with folded arms (OSUFA n.d.: Carroll). About eleven miles south of Toledo lies the rural village of Tontogany, where for two generations suburban teens have driven to see the face of the devil appear on the side of a barn in the light of the full moon. By the 1980s, this legend-trip had expanded to include ritual visits to the tombstone of a cult sacrifice victim who had allegedly been found "all mutilated and his body organs . . . missing," with the word "revenge" written in blood beside his body. The "revenge" was taken to be the penalty the victim's spirit would exact on anyone who dared to touch his tombstone. Local teens described trips in which a member would be encouraged to hug the tombstone; the others would shout, "The guy's coming!" and the visit would end with a frenzied dash back to the car (OSUFA n.d.: Weekley).

Farther south, in Napoleon, an abandoned house is said to be the haunt of the first white woman in the Northwest Territory. Trippers report that, as early as 1975, the walls of the building had been covered with inscriptions relating to Satan and witchcraft (OSUFA n.d.: Evans). A short drive east brings you to the Headless Motorcycle Man's several roads. To the west of Toledo one might visit Salisbury Graveyard, near Swanton. This site features a flattened gravestone that stands up straight at midnight and a caretaker who might fire a shotgun at you, not to mention witches who hold occult rituals nearby (OSUFA n.d.: Kosonovich).

North of Toledo, along the Michigan border, the "Candlemen" hold strange rituals, standing in a circle, holding candles. Adolescents believed that these strange people held a human sacrifice once a year, and if they realized that they were being observed, they would grab you, strip you naked, stab you, and leave you hanging from a nearby tree. This particular legend-trip tradition is similar to several others found elsewhere in Ohio (Ellis 1989a). Well before police found rumors of teenage cults credible, then, legend-trips were a widespread and popular activity in the Toledo area.

Police Folklore and "Experts"

The Toledo area had been affected by persistent rumors about cults since a sensational case in which Leroy Freeman had fled from the area in 1982 with his granddaughter Charity. The child was later found unharmed in California (*Costa Mesa* [CA] *Daily Pilot*, October 24, 1988), but in the meantime, police officials repeatedly aired their fears that Charity had been the victim of a cult sacrifice. These rumors became more intense in the spring of 1985, when Lucas County sheriff James A. Telb was told by an informant that a cult was planning to meet on April 30 near Holland, just west of Toledo. The informant led deputies to within 500 feet of an abandoned farmhouse, where they watched and tape-recorded about 100 "worshippers" chanting for about two hours. Later, in June, a nearby Methodist church was desecrated: Satanic symbols were soaped on the stained glass windows and altar and a Bible was burned.

At this point, Sheriff Telb requested assistance from Ohio cult "experts," who claimed that animal mutilations were "routine" and that as many as five covens of thirteen people each were operating in a typical rural Ohio county (*Cleveland Plain Dealer*, June 21, 1985). Prominent among these was Dale Griffis, a police captain in nearby Tiffin, who had been interpreting cult-like evidence in Ohio and Indiana communities since the early 1980s (Guinee 1987, 6–10). His public pronouncements make it clear that he saw cults as a deadly danger for both adolescents and law officers. Fully a third of kids in Satanic cults are willing to kill, he claimed, and he illustrated this point with a "story that circulated among police agencies" about two officers who were killed by devil worshippers when they "crossed the boundaries of a five-pointed star used for a ritual" (Dorfman 1985, 47). Griffis admitted that he could not document this incident. But the *Necronomicon*, one of the occult books he had collected to learn about cultists, warned: If thou happenest upon such a Cult in the midst of their Rituals, do but hide well so that they do not see thee, else they will surely kill thee and make of thee a sacrifice to their Gods. (*Columbus Dispatch* [*Capitol Magazine*], July 15, 1984).

Griffis also had special information linking northern Ohio to human sacrifices. Through hypnosis, Griffis had allowed "Jane," an Ohio cult "survivor," to recall that eleven years previously she had been taken to "a mass meeting of about 100 practitioners at a huge open field in a remote area of northern Ohio." There she had watched in horror as the ritual's leader ordered an initiate to give him her baby, then cut the child's throat. Griffis admitted that "Jane's" story was impossible to confirm, but concluded, "There are indications throughout the United States that there have been babies used for sacrifice" (*Columbus Dispatch* [*Capitol Magazine*], July 15, 1984). Her testimony appeared to be corroborated by another anonymous "survivor" from Monroe County, Michigan, who told police that she had seen Satanists bury a child near the site of the Toledo Dig (Dr. Michael Pratt, personal communication).

Griffis likewise allowed traditional narratives to shape his perception of what he was helping uncover. His involvement was another form of ostension; the difference was that Griffis, unlike most teenagers, fully believed that he was confronting evil, diabolical forces. As he told a Toledo reporter shortly after the dig, "I like going to an area where I can do my thing and leave and ride out on a white horse and never be seen again" (Dorfman 1985, 47).

The Site of the Dig: Artifacts and History

Fitting together local folklore and information from such experts, Sheriff Telb announced that a 200-member devil-worship cult was active in the Toledo area and that since 1969 they had sacrificed five persons a year, mostly children, carving them to death "in homage to Satan" in cult rituals that included sex and drug use. Little Charity Freeman, he announced, had probably been one of the children sacrificed (*Cleveland Plain Dealer*, June 21, 1985). On June 20, 1985, he raided two "cult houses," seizing cult paraphernalia like a *Raiders of the Lost Ark* poster, and began excavating a vacant lot rumored to be the site of the sacrifices. Meantime, deputies probed through two abandoned houses and several apparent garbage dumps in the area.

Perceptions of what they found varied: a "cross" with "ligatures" looked to one reporter rather more like "half of a clothes line post" (*Akron Beacon Journal*, June 21, 1985). One reporter said a headless doll was found nailed to a board and holding a "pentagram"; another said it had simply been stapled to a base to make it stand alone and had been tangled up in pink yarn with other trash: an amusement-park medallion decorated with a five-pointed star, a rag, and a telephone receiver (*Cleveland Plain Dealer*, June 21, 1985; Dr. Michael Pratt, personal communication). A more telling sign were the "cryptic symbols" found around the site, including large numbers of papers with backward writing on them and "a symbol depicting horns, eyes and a goat's head painted in red on the interior of a ramshackle cabin" (*Cleveland Plain Dealer*, June 22, 1985).

Follow-up work determined that an Afro-American drifter named Lewis Williams had settled in the building a few years previously. A local deputy sheriff recalled him as a harmless eccentric who would go "off his rocker" occasionally. The site was isolated, yet easily reached from the main road, so it was often used by adolescents as a lovers' lane, and Williams apparently enjoyed scaring them away. For a while he raised hogs (hundreds of animal bones were found by police nearby) and when one would die, he would bleach out the skull and set it on a stake beside the road. He would also take road-killed dogs and hang them alongside the house. As an additional touch, he would post the property with "Keep out" signs decorated with skulls and backward writing. When couples ignored these warnings, he would wait until cars were parked, then put on a large Santa Claus beard painted black and pop out of the woods. Other times, he might wave a small "voodoo bag" or homemade cross in his hand and threaten intruders with a curse. "Kids would leave," the township sheriff recalled: "Sometimes they'd even leave their cars there" (*Cleveland Plain Dealer*, July 7, 1985; James Meredith, personal communication).

Obviously the drifter's shack was a legend-trip site, with Williams and the "lovers" engaging in a mutual pseudo-ostensive relationship. The eccentric's actions were in line with those of other legendary figures who haunted isolated shacks in the area, and the skulls, hanging dogs, and cryptic signs clearly spawned a cycle of adolescent rumors about Williams as a local "lunatic" or "witch." After Williams moved on, the drifter's shack, like others in northern Ohio, remained the focus of visits, and more cryptic inscriptions began to accumulate. Teenagers, doubtless, were willing to let police believe that their illegal beer blasts were ceremonies of "chanting" devil-worshippers.

Meanwhile, adults were engaged in their own rituals of ostension. "Expert" Satan-hunters collated "survivor" tales, urban legends, and muddled legend-trip traditions to produce the temporarily convincing claim that real "Candlemen" were responsible for an unsolved "abduction" and a troublesome vandalism case. The outcome was an act of "therapeutic magic": a public act intended to focus and bring to closure a variety of diffuse and "unnamed" anxieties (Ellis 1990). By digging up a likely area on the date of the solar equinox (supposedly the date of the next human sacrifice), Lucas County Police forestalled further "Satanic" acts by a show of force. They also convinced fellow believers that they were doing something concrete to fight cults and all they represented.

As often with such public acts, witnesses interpreted the "evidence" to suit their worldviews: out of several houses and piles of junk came a few items that for the faithful confirmed their beliefs in cults. For others, the dramatic nature of the dig, contrasted with the triviality of the finds, showed that fears were unnecessary. In either case, the dig cleared the air. By acting out a scenario drawn from police folklore, officials reduced anxieties fueled by inability to resolve the Charity Freeman "abduction" and teenage acts of vandalism and partying.

In truth, Sheriff Telb probably did uncover evidence of clandestine ceremonies. An Ohio teenager familiar with the Tontogany "cult victim" legend-trip freely linked the police search with adolescent rituals: The legend in fact is so popular that it made officers in the area start up a search for satanic cults supposedly in the area. In fact the city officials a couple of years back dug up around a house that was supposed to have dead bodies buried in their yard because a satanic ritual was [supposed] to have taken place there. Nothing was ever found but the legend lives on in the minds of the locals and also the city officials because the search for the satanic cult is still at large in Tontogany (OSUFA n.d.: Weekley).

The scenario officials constructed had little to do with the silent adolescent rituals being enacted around this county. The same teen called the dig an "enormous snowball that has gotten out of hand," commenting that the legend-trip was no more than a "means of escape from the everyday doldrum" for youths, "and the thrill of getting away with something they aren't supposed to just encourages them on." For adults, by contrast, the legend is "a threat to their world," and so they "are out to get rid of the harm and the problem the legend provides" (OSUFA n.d.: Weekley). For youths, the legend is an opportunity to play with daylight problems, but the adult response, far from eliminating harm, resulted in real daylight penalties for the people falsely accused of "cult" involvement.

CONCLUSIONS: HOW SHOULD WE STUDY LEGEND-TRIPS?

Legend ostension may include genuinely violent acts by teens that incorporate "Satanic" elements. But these are rare, and the media attention they receive is misleading. To understand adolescents' use of legends, we must study the many less sensational ostensive acts that represent the norm of the legend-trip tradition. I have called this tradition "silent"—but not because it is secretive. Materials used in this essay were freely volunteered by adolescents whenever academics were willing to ask them about their lore. We understand little about legend-trips simply because we rarely talk with teens or pay attention to their culture.

Additional study of adolescents' supernatural legends and legend-trips is badly needed. Many misconceptions could have been clarified more quickly, had legend-trip materials been widely available to researchers. We know that the legend-trip is popular from New Jersey westward to California, but we do not know its exact national distribution. We know little about occult-oriented folk groups except that they are responsible for much of the tradition's vitality. What is the peak age for participation? Do males' patterns of participation differ from females'? What religious backgrounds stand out among trippers? Psychological questions also need to be asked about activities that might be linked with legend-tripping. Are frequent participants also interested in other common activities based on engrossment, such as storytelling, role-playing games, or school dramas?

Adolescents who freely identify themselves as practicing Satanists also deserve more objective attention. Bourget, Gagnon, and Bradford (1988) suggest that individuals identified as "Satanists" by parents and authorities are likely to be prone to substance abuse and express self-destructive or violent ideas. Is the same true for frequent legend-trippers? To what extent does the population of teens who participate in "Satanic" group activities overlap that of occult-oriented folk groups? A case study of a self-identified "coven" in Georgia described rituals drawn from Anton LaVey's *Satanic Bible* conducted at the community's legend-trip site, a haunted bridge. But Kathleen S. Lowney (1995) found that the coven's membership was distinct from other adolescent groups that also indulged in legend-tripping. Can teen Satanists and legend-trippers be distinguished in other parts of the country, or do "normal" and "Satanic" legend-tripping frequently overlap?

We can arm ourselves against official misinformation about fictitious "cults" by studying the folk groups that do exist and educating others about the functions that legend-trips perform. Occult-oriented folk groups are not "cults." Ostension of supernatural legends is not the same as "dabbling" in "witchcraft." Folklorists and sociologists should cooperate to collect data that would combat these dangerous misperceptions.

Considerable time and money have been invested by local and state police to pay for "expert" information made up of garbled adolescent legends and police folklore. Religious figures like Cardinal John O'Connor of

New York City have given warrant to such claims, assuring parents that Satan is ready and waiting to hypnotize teens into conducting gruesome black masses in graveyards. When the academy ignores legend-trips as a "trivial" subject, these three estates cooperate to perpetuate ignorance of our own folk culture.

Through the Satanic scare, Americans are paying for their lack of cultural self-knowledge. Unless we cooperate to understand the rituals quietly played out in nearly every rural or suburban community in this country, we will continue to pay the price of this ignorance through painful and unnecessary misperceptions.

NOTES

Research on which this essay is based was partially funded by a Research Development Grant from Pennsylvania State University. Thanks are especially due to Patrick Mullen for allowing me access to the Ohio State Folklore Archives, and to Jeffrey S. Victor and Rita Swan for making newspaper releases about Satanism available to me.

1. See, for example, *Jay's Journal*, a book that purports to be the journal of a sixteen-year-old who committed suicide, preserved by the boy's mother and "edited by" Beatrice Sparks. Introduced to transcendental meditation by an adult occult "missionary," the alleged author dabbles with PK (psychokinesis), voodoo, angel dust, sadistic sex, Presbyterianism, strangling kittens, drinking blood, and cattle mutilation before falling completely under the occultists' control; they force him to bathe in blood and devote his soul to Satan. The Library of Congress catalogues the book as "juvenile fiction." Over and over, Jay claims to have no control over what he does, commenting, "The occult movement is kind of a Pied Piper sort of thing: we want to go but we don't want to go . . . in the end we have no choice . . . we've just got to see what's in the mountain" (Sparks 1979, 112; ellipses in original). Many religious leaders assume that rock and roll music exerts a similar "hypnotic" control over teens, especially through the effect of subliminal "Satanic" messages recorded backwards on some pieces (McIver 1988).

5

Playing with Fear
Interpreting the Adolescent Legend Trip

S. Elizabeth Bird

As S. Elizabeth Bird explains in her essay about the legendary Black Angel statue in Iowa City's Oakland Cemetery, the "truth" of a legend lies as much (if not more) in the doing of the legend as in the telling of it. The central legend explored in this essay, and the physical monument associated with it, is a major source of legend-tripping activity for people, especially college students. Most scholars suggest that legend tripping is largely an adolescent activity, but Bird's work shows that people of many different ages are familiar with the legend and the ritual, and that they may have quite different motivations for sharing the story and participating in the legend trip. Bird's case study of the Black Angel highlights, as she puts it, that "different people tell different stories"—children playing in the cemetery during the afternoon don't tell the same story as college students visiting at midnight.

Cemetery statuary is a common focal point for legends and legend trips and quests. Folklorists often seek underlying meanings in legends and ostensive activities, trying to uncover through textual and performative analysis the cultural messages that are encapsulated in the traditions. Sometimes the explanation for why folklore surrounds certain places or objects is simple, at least initially. Monuments that stand out visually on the landscape always draw attention; as Bird suggests, the Black Angel demands explanation "simply by being there." The statue is unlike any other grave marker in the cemetery; it makes sense that people would seek an explanation for its presence.

Folklorist Jeannie B. Thomas has studied legends about cemetery statuary, and her work touches on some of the same themes that Bird's work addresses: gender and sexuality. As Thomas explains, "The legends mirror what is most noticeable in a cemetery: statues of women. Not only are they fairly common but they are also, significantly, often more visible and dramatic than the markers around them" (2003, 21). Thomas points out that female figures in cemeteries typically aren't depicting the women buried there. They instead serve as "surrogate mourners"; if they don't depict a beautiful young woman, they typically show an idealized maternal figure. These limitations on the expected roles of women are evident in the legends that are told about the Black Angel. The stories reveal that the emphasis in the narrative is almost always on the "sin" the woman commits; even when the man is said to have committed the same infidelity, his behavior is dismissed.

This gender inequality is reflected in the legends trips as well. Bird shows us that males and females behave differently on legend trips, and this different behavior is expected of them. Males are expected to act tough: testing, or even mocking, the frightening figure of the Black Angel. While some females behave similarly, there is a greater expectation that they'll be scared (or at least that they'll act scared), and that they'll provide an audience for the male bravado. The potential for physical interaction—perhaps cuddling in response to fear—makes the potential danger of the encounter worth it. Scholars of horror films have dubbed this concept the "snuggle theory of horror," the idea that "horror films can provide a setting for amorous adolescents to react in socially sanctioned, gender-specific ways and cuddle up in the semidarkness of the cinema" (Clasen 2012, 227). Like a darkened movie theater, the nighttime setting of a legend trip provides a setting for the enactment of specific gender roles.

Of course, not everyone enjoys or appreciates those stereotypical gender roles; some young adults find themselves pushing back against the expectations of the legend trip, making this traditional activity a significant backdrop for practicing and enacting one's own self-expression. The belief that a virgin's touch will make the statue turn white again reveals how manipulative a legend trip can be. As one of Bird's informants says of her experience touching the statue, only to be pranked by her boyfriend's friends, "I was so scared and really mad."

Bird's essay is a valuable example of just how much may be going on within a single legend complex. Different ages and different genders, explanatory functions and psychological functions, embracing and pushing back against expected norms—the Black Angel covers it all.

I<small>N</small> 1924, T<small>ERESA</small> F<small>ELDEVERT</small> <small>DIED IN</small> I<small>OWA</small> C<small>ITY</small>, Iowa. More than sixty years later, her grave is a site for beer bashes and Halloween pilgrimages, where adolescents meet to share stories, superstitions, and fears, and to act them out in games that try to tempt fate.

The "legend trip," as it has become known by folklorists (see Ellis 1983, 1988; Meley 1990), is a widespread phenomenon. Many communities have their haunted houses, spooky bridges, or other sites where adolescents drive on dark nights so that they can terrify themselves and live to tell about it (see Baker 1970; Clements 1980; Clements and Lightfoot 1972; Dégh 1969a; Hall 1980).

As its name suggests, the "legend trip" centers around stories or legends shared among people who travel to a particular place; the legends surrounding it are often disseminated actually at the site. Such is the legend of Iowa City's "Black Angel," the grave of the Feldevert family. From an analysis of the texts and context of the Black Angel legend, I aim to show how the site is used to play out the values, fears, and concerns of those who perpetuate the tradition. While this particular site is local, the legend trip as an adolescent communication activity is widespread.

Over the last few years, University of Iowa graduate student Don Johnson has collected accounts of Black Angel stories and legend trips from over 100 individuals, using questionnaires and unstructured interviews. Involvement with the legend-trip behavior varied among his informants. A few who knew angel stories had never visited the cemetery, although most had. While some had made only one visit, others had made multiple trips, ranging to over 100 visits. Johnson's collection, drawn from questionnaires and interviews with over 100 individuals, makes up the main body of lore from which my interpretation of the event is made; I use the words of the participants wherever possible in order to evoke the experiential context of the event.

Earlier scholarship on legend concentrated primarily on text, the stories themselves. More recently, an extensive and growing body of literature has been examining the legend in context, including the dynamics of performance (see, for example, Bennett 1988, 1989a, 1989b; Boyes 1984; Ellis 1988, 1989a). Most often these analyses concentrate on the performance and circulation of legends that, while localized, are variations of wider legend types. Less common is an analysis of the dynamic context of local legend telling. The local legend frequently circulates in a specific context, the "legend trip"; the trip itself is inextricably bound to a particular site, and it involves more activities than, say, a legend-telling session in a dorm room. It is in this context that the meaning of local legend becomes clearest. As Bruner writes, "We know that stories must be seen as rooted in society and as experienced and performed by individuals in cultural settings" (Bruner 1984, 5). To understand the impact of the Black Angel lore, it must be studied in its cultural setting, providing an appreciation of the complete experience that is the legend trip.

I view the legend trip as play involving not only storytelling but also *doing* particular things. The emotional power of the experience derives from a combination of setting, narratives, and actions, all of which are interdependent.

Playing with Fear   115

Figure 5.1. Black Angel monument in Oakland Cemetery, Iowa City.
Photo by S. Elizabeth Bird.

THE SETTING

Any interpretation of the event must start with the setting, the Black Angel itself. Why is it special, and why has it become the center of so much folklore?

The Black Angel monument, which stands on raised ground in Oakland Cemetery in Iowa City, comprises a flat slab surmounted by a granite base bearing the inscription Rodina Feldevertova—the Feldevert family. The angel itself, which is about nine feet tall, stands with arms and wings outstretched, looking down from the granite base. Beside the statue is another marker in the form of a stone tree stump bearing the name Eddie Dolezal.

The facts behind the erection of the monument are recorded in local histories. Teresa Feldevert went to Iowa City from what is now Czechoslovakia in the late nineteenth century, as did many others. By her first marriage, she had a son, Edward Dolezal, who died in Iowa City in 1891, his grave marked by the tree stump. Teresa had the bronze angel statue sculpted in Chicago, and it was erected in the cemetery in 1912. The ashes of her second husband, Nicholas Feldevert, were placed in a repository at its base. Teresa died in 1924, and her ashes were placed beside her husband's. The monument bears the birth and death date of Nicholas, but Teresa's birth date only—1836. The metal statue apparently oxidized when exposed to air and is now almost completely black.

It is well documented that local legends tend to develop around particular types of places—bridges, cemeteries, unusual graves, deserted houses, and so on. As Mullen (1972) points out, legend particularly thrives on ambiguity, where questions arise that cannot be answered by ordinary means. The Black Angel is extremely ambiguous. It is the only statue of its kind in the cemetery and stands in an elevated, prominent position. It contains several inscriptions, all in a language which, though common in Iowa City once, is no longer understood. One name mentioned is given a birth date, but no death date.

But most of all, the statue is a Black Angel, which in our culture is a contradiction in terms. Black, of course, is a potent symbol that in various contexts may connote darkness, evil, death, sin, sorrow. Angels, too, are potent, multifaceted symbols (Koske 1981), but they connote the opposite: light, goodness, eternal life, purity, bliss. Angels are white; the two together do not make sense.

Simply by being there, the Black Angel demands explanation, and much of the lore that has grown up around the statue is intended to explain its existence. The narratives do not explain the angel away; rather they validate it as an anomalous phenomenon that continues to exert power long after the supposed events in the stories are over. Once the stories have become firmly established, the site and the narratives become inseparable; "if a story becomes 'embedded' in features of the landscape, story and place are mutually supportive" (Leach 1984, 358).

THE LEGENDS

In the eighty years since the statue was erected, a large body of oral tradition has grown up around it, ranging from quite detailed explanatory legends to brief rumors and superstitions. Angel lore is widely known among high school and University of Iowa students, as well as among older residents. The lore varies among cultural groups, but it all attempts to explain the existence of the angel with reference to the symbols of "black" and "angel" and the various connotations these symbols have.

Different people tell different stories, and there seems to be some correspondence between age and themes in the stories, such that the possible meanings of the two dominant, dissonant symbols vary in prominence. As Bruner writes, "Cultural narratives become personal narratives. Further, the individuals who experience the story do so at a particular point in life career, at a given age and phase in the life cycle, so that tellings always involve an intersection of culture and autobiography" (Bruner 1984, 6).

Many middle-aged and older adults tell stories about the angel that emphasize the motif of a mother grieving for a child, with the angel turning black in sympathy (Bird 1983). Other stories, such as a version told by a forty-five-year-old woman, explain that an atheist chose a white angel monument for his grave and then challenged God to turn it black if he really existed. Naturally, God did just that once the man was buried under the statue (1984, questionnaire 24). For older people, the "legend trip" may entail a casual walk to the cemetery and perhaps the narration of a story about the statue's origins to a friend or out-of-town visitor. Often these stories pick up on the associations of blackness and angels with death and sorrow. Young children frequently exchange stories that see the angel as a "boogeyman" figure that will punish them if they stay out late or litter the cemetery.

However, when we look at the majority of the lore from adolescents and young adults, different patterns emerge. The central ambiguity of the Black Angel is still dominant, but the ambiguous message is decoded through reference to different facets of the dominant symbols. The opposition between life and death, light and dark, is still present, but another set of oppositions comes to the fore, namely, black as representing sin and corruption versus the angel as whiteness and purity. In these examples, the angel is black because of a sin, more specifically infidelity. The angel was always originally white, never bronze, thus emphasizing the opposition. It can become white again by contact with a virgin, at which moment we should see briefly how the angel appeared before sin corrupted it.

There are numerous individual variations of the tales that explain the Black Angel, but many share a common thread. The white, marble statue was brought by sea from Europe by a man and his new bride. During the voyage the woman died, and the grieving widower placed the statue on her grave. However, it turned out that she had been unfaithful to him, either on board ship or earlier, and the statue turned black to expose her sins. One variant is told by a twenty-year-old man who heard the story in high school:

> I heard she was being shipped over by this one guy in Europe somewhere. This one rich guy was mailing it over to his sweetheart in America. And she was unfaithful to him one night—on its shipment over here to America. And supposedly during that night she conceived a child or whatever. And on that night by some mysterious powers, it turned black in the middle of the ocean. And when it got to the United States, she thought it was a white angel, because that's what her lover had said. So she was expecting a white angel. But, when she saw the black angel, she said, "Oh, my God, what did I do," and all this other crap. And then nine months later she had the kid. The kid supposedly died right away. And that's about as much as I know. Then they say if you kiss the black angel at night, at midnight, you'll die within 24 hours. (1985, interview 2)

A twenty-three-year-old woman tells a briefer version stressing the wife's general wickedness: The black angel was purchased by the dead woman's husband. It had been ordered from somewhere in Europe. When the statue arrived here it turned black, because the deceased woman was very evil; she was a witch (1981, interview 91).

A less typical example is told by an eighteen-year-old woman. Here, the relationship is transformed to father and daughter, but the woman's sins, if a little updated, remain constant: Another one is that the father thought his daughter was a perfect angel who was good and pure so he decided to buy her an angel for her grave so everyone would know how perfect she was. But when the Angel was placed upon her grave it turned black because she was an evil person, she drank and did drugs and she was a known slut (1986, interview 3).

In this group of legends, sin is specifically assigned to women, not men, a pattern that, like other symbolic representations in the legends, goes beyond this particular message and into the symbolic representation of women in other aspects of culture. As well as the potent symbols of black and angel, the coding of the message of "woman" varies between contexts and between receivers. We are all familiar with the many images of "woman" embodied in our culture, such as woman as wife and mother versus mistress, virgin versus whore, or witch (Williams 1978).

In some older people's stories, the dominant image was woman as mother. In the young adults' versions, the dominant image is woman as sexual sinner. Angels are pure; a good woman is "a perfect angel." So the black angel must be a fallen angel, a witch, and stands as a symbol of what society holds for deviant women. Their sins will find them out and be shown up for all the world to see.

In the examples where the woman is the adulteress, which are the most common, she is labeled wicked, evil, cursed, a witch. There are a few tales, however, in which the man is the unfaithful partner. Nevertheless, invariably in these stories the man's infidelity is a technicality, as the wife is already dead. A seventeen-year-old girl tells this version:

> A man and his wife were traveling from America over to Europe on a ship and she was really sick and she was going to die, so the man bought her this huge tombstone in the shape of an angel and she said she was afraid he was going to be unfaithful to her and she said, if you are unfaithful to me I will be able to tell by the tombstone. And she died in Europe and they were bringing the tombstone back and her body and when they—oh, he did have a shipboard romance—when they brought the tombstone up out of the hull it had turned black. (1981, interview 3)

In this story and others like it, the language is hardly condemnatory—"a shipboard romance." The woman is still responsible for the Black Angel, since she invoked the curse. The pattern is maintained in some other examples where the husband dies and the wife is "unfaithful" after his death. She squanders her husband's money, abandons his grave, and disappears with a younger lover, as in this version learned from a college room-mate by a now twenty-seven-year-old man:

> Around the turn of the century, there was a married couple and the husband had a considerable amount of money. As I say, they were married, and he became ill. So, they decided that they were going to be buried together in Iowa City. So they went ahead and purchased a monument and it was a white, supposedly a white angel. So they purchased it and had it moved here, and soon after that the husband died and he was buried with the angel as his gravestone. And not too long after his death, the wife, the widow, ran off and left town with a younger man taking all of her ex-husband's money. Soon after this happened, then the white angel turned black and her head sort of fell, and the wings also. And to this day if you go to the cemetery, the black angel is still there, and there is no date of death on the woman's nameplate on the gravestone, so she is still not buried there. And part of the story is that if you go out and gaze into the black angel's eyes, it will put a curse on you and bad things will happen to you, or whatever. (1984, interview 11)

This representation of women is not unique to these legends, of course. In his surveys of modern legends, Brunvand (1981, 1984) discusses the ambivalent attitude in them toward women who control their own sexuality, and we find the same themes recurring in all genres of popular culture, such as the notorious "slasher" movies. Both the folklore and popular culture of adolescents and young adults are extremely concerned with sex, morality, and guilt, with different representations of male and female within these themes. It seems entirely consistent that this section of the population should also apply a similar framework of cultural references to the Black Angel enigma.

THE ADOLESCENT LEGEND TRIP

While the texts of the Black Angel stories are revealing in themselves, they become more so when we look at the context. Mullen (1972) suggests that legend should be studied not only for structure and content, but also for the role it plays in particular collective activities. Contemporary legends may indeed articulate "many of the hopes, fears, anxieties and submerged desires of our times" (Brunvand 1981, 2), but they can only do so if they are told and retold. A crucial element in the interpretation of the legend is an understanding of the dynamics of the legend-tellings, during which the texts come alive.

Black Angel stories often have two main elements: an explanation of the existence of such an anomalous object, and a warning of what happens to someone who touches, kisses, or otherwise bothers the angel. Typically, the offender will die within twenty-four hours, seven years, or at an unspecified time, and rumors circulate about specific instances of this happening: "If you make fun of it, you will die. Once, some guy did make fun of it, and he was struck by lightning" (1984, interview 41, female, age 14). Even informants who scoff at such ideas may seem just a little unconvincing in their skepticism: My sister went there when she was in high school to write an article for the school newspaper, she kissed the angel at midnight on Halloween (gasp!) and set out to prove that she wouldn't die within the year. (She didn't by the way; she was run over by a Good Humor wagon the week after, though) (1984, questionnaire 15, male, age 20).

Young people tell the legends as a mood setter before visiting the angel, during the visit itself, and sometimes afterwards as well. Much of the action during a legend trip involves challenging these prophecies of doom, touching, kissing, and defiling the angel, or staring into its eyes. A "typical" legend trip is made late at night in a group of young people. College students, particularly those from out of town, for whom the angel is new, do participate in legend trips, but the trips are more commonly a high school activity. Groups are usually all male or mixed sex, rarely if ever all female, a phenomenon also noted by Meley (1991). The group has often been drinking, driving around, watching a horror movie, or generally partying, and is looking for something to do to relieve boredom or heighten existing excitement. Someone, usually male, suggests visiting the Black Angel. Once there, the group may continue drinking, telling stories, and then "legend testing." Members of the group will work themselves up with frightening stories, games of hide and seek, and sometimes alcohol or drugs. They will then challenge the statue, kissing, defacing, or insulting it. Typically, males do the testing, while females sit protesting and warning, or even refuse to get out of the car. When everyone is thoroughly scared, the group leaves, and will either disperse or go on to more partying and post-trip discussion.

One of the questions that often arises around legends is whether those who tell them believe them, and folklorists traditionally discussed this question at length (see Dégh and Vazsonyi 1973). Our informants were in fact asked if they believed the stories about the Black Angel; they almost invariably said they did not. However, this in itself shows why the study of legend texts out of context can only tell part of the story (see Bennett 1988).

On sober reflection, the explanatory legends are far from convincing, and very few people, in the cold light of day, will believe that a statue in a cemetery can kill you. Put those same people in a dark cemetery, add a few beers, the discourse of friends whose conversation centers on death and evil, and you have a very different situation. In this context, people exhibit the well-known "willing suspension of disbelief" that is part of many games, rituals, or dramatic performances.

Several informants mentioned that the mood was set by watching a horror movie, one mentioning that whenever *Friday the 13th* or its sequels showed in town, high school students would visit the angel before or after the movie. Bennett (1988), in her analysis of a dorm-room legend-telling session, makes very clear the intertextuality between legends, the horror movies that draw on them, and the "media narraforms" that in turn feed oral tradition. Do viewers "believe" in the events that happen in horror movies? Probably not, but as long as the game of watching the movie continues, they are willing and eager to be terrified.

Comments from participants capture some sense of the ambivalence and special atmosphere of exhilaration and fear that characterizes the legend trip:

> I get a high feeling when I go over there . . . the adrenalin in me starts flowing. (1984, telephone interview 3, male, age 16)

One night we went to the Black Angel and the guys were climbing up to her and kissing her etc. Shelli and I got scared so we ran to the car. I remember looking up at the Black Angel's face and her eyes were white. That was so scary. It happened to me once before when my sister, my friend Jenny, and I went to the Black Angel. It wasn't completely dark and since we had heard a lot about her but never seen her before we wanted to scope her out. When I first looked at her she was just this black statue—even her eyes were black. I tried to read what was on the grave but I couldn't really make it out so I looked up at her face again and her eyes were white, and Brenda noticed it too. We grabbed Jenny and ran as fast as we could to the car. Later we laughed about it but the whole experience was *so* scary. (1986, questionnaire 3, female, age 18)

Well, I was scared when I was there in front of her because it was dark, and the clouds were moving in front of the moon. It was kind of an eerie feeling. I was scared, but I don't think I really believed in them (the legends) . . . First, when the boys were up there goofing around in front of it, one boy kind of tripped, and her wing hit his head. And it was kind of strange because nobody really knew how it happened. But he was kind of teasing us that she moved and hit him and that he didn't move. And he hit his head and got a big knot on his head. And then when the girls were standing in front of it, a guy took off and they started running around the cemetery. And so we were running and hiding, and one girl tripped over a grave marker and hurt her ankle . . . Everybody was just kind of spooked. And we were making jokes about it, that it was true, that people were going to die within a year . . . Everybody, kind of in the back of their heads thought it was quite a coincidence that people were getting hurt who were there. (1984, interview 8, female, age 22)

Well, I can't say that I'm generally a believer in rumors and stories like that, but I figure why push that sort of thing—don't have any good reason to. (1984, interview 3, male, age 28)

In 1972, a group of friends of mine, we decided to stake out the Black Angel on Halloween, because apparently strange things happen. And we went there on Halloween and about 10 minutes till (midnight), a fog developed and it was so thick you couldn't see your hand in front of your face. And at that time there was a dredging project, or some sort of fixing up of whatever, there was an open pit around, so no one wanted to walk around. And in the fog, we heard the flapping of wings, big wings, and about 10 minutes after midnight the fog lifted. And we couldn't explain the fog. (1984, interview 23, male, age 24)

I acted like I believed it . . . being there in the cemetery was spooky. (1984, questionnaire 10, female, age 19)

It was a lot easier to believe the stories when you're actually there. I really never believed the stories, but was never tempted to find out if they were true. (1984, questionnaire 19, male, age 19)

>   While standing in front of the BA after a midnight stroll through
>   the cemetery, the laughs were just a little bit forced. After all, who really
>   knows? (1984, questionnaire 25, male, age 28)
>
>   If I believed them, I wouldn't have kissed the statue. I mean, that's, I
>   guess, a test of . . . you know, like, I'm not out to kill myself. So I guess I'd
>   have to say no, I don't believe them. But under the influence of marijuana,
>   it was more believable. (1984, interview 14, female, age 26)

Ellis (1988, 1989b) suggests that the issue of belief is essentially beside the point. Indeed, rather than worrying about belief as such, we must try to capture the essence of the experience in its full affective context. As Honko writes, "The mere folklore text as such . . . is empty—whether it be stored in the memory or some archive. It only acquires meaning in context, in use, when charged by actual feelings, attitudes, values, its user's intentions and its listener's reactions" (1984, 99).

Young people actually use the legend trip as a form of play, deliberately suspending the normal laws of the real world and entering a world of heightened reality, or fantasy, much as dedicated players of fantasy games do (Fine 1983). With such play comes a loss of control; in fact the abandonment of ordinary controls over behavior is the object of the play. Through legend as play, "we can temporarily set aside normal definitions of reality without being considered deviant" (Ellis 1989b, 33).

During the legend trip, within a frame of playful fear, young people are able to explore and confront some of the concerns that face them in "real" life, through the potent interaction of texts, environment, and action. The legend texts have little power on their own. As one former University of Iowa student put it, "It wasn't something you just talk about" (1984, interview 14, female, age 26). "The truth of a legend lies in its telling" (Nicolaisen 1984, 173), but in the case of the legend trip, the truth also lies in the doing, the "playing" of the legend.

The legends about the origins of the statue and about the dire consequences of defiling her are intimately concerned with death, sex, and morality, and the texts provide a narrative frame for the event itself. The adolescents who legend trip are confronting the anxieties that accompany maturity and approaching adulthood. For, as Omvedt comments, while play is a form of fantasy, it is "defined by a double reference, on the one hand to our normal world (the real things that are to be transformed or bracketed) and on the other to the unreality given to them" (Omvedt 1966, 6). Through fantasy play, real concerns are transformed and explored.

However, while this is true for all adolescents, the game is different for males and females. For young men, it seems to act as some sort of initiation rite into adulthood, during which they test themselves and their fear of the unknown in a situation that is entirely peer-oriented, without adult supervision. In fact, the fear of discovery by police or other authority figures is often cited as adding "spice" to the event. The event serves to prove a young man's adulthood, as he discusses and then tempts death in the symbolic frame of the legend-telling, followed by legend-testing. The sense of the trip as a rite of passage is recognized by many participants: "You can't graduate from City (High) unless you know about the Black Angel" (1984, interview 33, female, age 18). The initiatory aspect is also dramatized in the legends and rumors about either Satanic rituals or fraternity hazings at the angel:

> I do remember back in the, probably late 60's, early 70's, I remember a wedding took place. This one in particular was between a witch and somebody else, dressed in black, and they had a black cat as a witness. (1984, interview 25, female, age 28)

> The strange things started to happen when a fraternity in Iowa City decided to do a sacrifice as an initiation stunt. And one of the initiates was supposed to go up and smear blood on the breasts and kiss the black angel. And from what I understand, according to legend, when he did this, out of a clear blue sky a bolt of lightning killed him. (1984, interview 23, male, age 24)

While groups visiting the angel are often mixed sex, they are also frequently made up only of young males, who dare each other to go further and further in testing the superstitions, and who even in the telling show echoes of the bravado of the event: They got drunk and climbed the damn thing! One guy kissed it on the lips. (He lives!!) (1984, questionnaire 3, male, age 23). The "rules" of the game are that no one should show undue fear, at least until everybody else does, and those who show weakness are taunted and tormented, as in this account: We had a good time when we went over there because we had one guy that was real scared. We pried this guy's door open on his car. So after he kissed it, he jumped into the car and he couldn't even close his door, so he was scared. We were in the back seat telling him it was going to get him and shit. He was panicking (1984, interview 9, male, age 21).

In these all-male affairs, the object is to show fearlessness and daring, confronting the promise of death that is so clear in the atmosphere created in the dark cemetery and the tales of doom told at the base of the angel. For males, the most important element in the angel lore tends to be the stories about the consequence of touching, kissing or defacing the angel, rather than the legends about its origins, although these are certainly told in order to establish the supernatural and eerie nature of the statue. Bennett (1989b) evokes the image of "playful chaos," an atmosphere developing as friends meet and tell stories, each building on the other. In the case of the dorm room she discusses, the playful chaos is one of "general silliness," as close friends assert their intimacy with each other through chaotic, interweaving narratives. For the angel legend trippers, the "playful chaos" seems to be a heady concoction of fear and hilarity, but it also serves to cement the group identity of the participants; "the focus has shifted from the content of the interaction to the interaction itself" (198–212).

Proving one's masculinity is not only about confronting death, but also about confronting sex, and the angel provides for this too. With the inclusion of females in the party, the bravado gains an added dimension for the young men. The tests of bravery and manhood are still there, but they are performed to an apparently admiring female audience, who are appropriately terrified:

> We went with a couple of girls. And when we said that we were going to get out and touch it or something, they'd just, you know, "No, don't," and they kept refusing, and locking the doors, and wouldn't let us out. We got out once and touched it and stuff, and when we came back to the car, they didn't want to talk to us or nothing. Well, they'd just, "Don't mess with me, because you've been messing," just a bunch of stuff like that. They'd say, "Have you heard that before, you know, what happens?" I'd go, "yeah." (1984, interview 27, male, age 16)

Females do sometimes participate in legend testing, such as the girl who set out to test the angel for her school newspaper. As a rule, college-age women are more likely to take part in the "dares" than their high school counterparts. In the setting of the high school legend trip, the more usual pattern is for them to remain in the car, hang back, egg the boys on, plead with them to stop, or all of the above (see Meley 1991). The female audience adds a different dimension to the experience from the male point of view, as boys have to prove their masculinity not only to each other but also to the girls, who essentially have the power to validate the boys' demonstrations of masculinity.

In addition, the goal of the males is often to scare the girls and assert their sexual power over them: These guys took some of the girls over there and some other guys were over there waiting for them. And they were going to spook them, they were like hiding behind trees, and they had sheets on and stuff, and they were going to come out and try to scare them (1984, interview 6, male, age 22).

Scaring the girls was seen as a potentially useful technique in breaking down their assumed resistance to various levels of sexual activity—the arousal produced by fear just might be translated into sexual arousal. Girls are taken to the cemetery "to scare the piss out of them, more cuddling. I used to take my girlfriend up there and get her scared." Generally, the young men gave little evidence that this actually worked, but the belief that it might is essentially one element in the complex folklore surrounding the angel. The plan may even backfire, as this young man went on to explain. In this case, the group managed to scare themselves too much: "We heard some noises, and we thought 'Oh no, all the dead people are coming to life,' so we took off. And this guy kept saying 'her wings are moving, her wings are moving'" (1985, interview 2, male, age 20). From this viewpoint, the legend trip can be seen also as a sexual challenge, equating fear with compliance on the part of the girls involved.

From the female point of view, both the legend trip experience and the legends themselves have a different meaning. For girls, the tales of the angel's origins seem often to be more important than for boys, specifically because they act as cautionary tales about sexual activity. Girls and young women report telling the tales at slumber parties, along with the many modern legends that equate sexual activity with death, such as the madman with the hook, the axe murderer in the dorm, and so on (Brunvand 1981). In these legends, as in the slasher movies often derived from them, sexually active women die; "good girls" survive.

In the legend trip itself, the dares and the male legend-testing are intimately connected with fear, and then with the possibility of being tricked or seduced into sexual activity. A female taking part in a legend trip is faced with something of a dilemma. She is "supposed" to act frightened while also being impressed with the courage of the males. But she also has to be prepared to act the role of "good girl," fending off male advances, or else run the risk of falling into the role of "bad girl," or black angel. The explanatory legend tells her that sexual activity is evil; the boys themselves are telling her this when they narrate them. She may hear another common motif—that when a virgin kisses the angel it will momentarily turn white—and she may be pushed into the impossible position of demonstrating her "purity" in this way. She is aware that the boys are judgmental about female sexual virtue while at the same time they are creating a situation in which they hope to take advantage of the girls' fear.

It is perhaps unsurprising, therefore, that several females reported feeling angry about the legend trip. One woman described her experience as a high school sophomore, when she was taken against her wishes to the cemetery by her boyfriend, who forced her to touch the angel. "At the moment that I touched the black angel, all of his buddies from the football team jumped out from behind the bushes and were screaming and yelling and flashing their flashlights; it just scared the shit out of me. I was so scared and really mad" (interview, female, age 25, May 8, 1984).

She believed that the event had been "set up" to "soften her up" for the boyfriend, as, perhaps, did the girls who refused to be touched by their male companions. This is not to say that all females felt this way; many reported feelings of excitement similar to the males'. But the potential for aggressive use of the trip by males is certainly there. And it seems that for girls the fantasy dangers confronted in the cemetery may be closer to the "real world" than the abstract challenge to death that the experience is for males.

CONCLUSION

In almost any discussion of popular culture, there is the danger that the power and exhilaration of play is diffused by the analysis. As Leach comments, "if we are too serious about what is palpably foolish, we shall only make fools of ourselves" (Leach 1984, 364). An event like the Black Angel legend trip is, after all, done for fun and excitement, not to make statements about sex, fear, and death. But if we believe that the mesh of symbols that is culture is constantly being shaped and reshaped through communicative acts, we must examine any and all such acts. James W. Carey discusses the process of cultural interpretation through which meaning is teased out: This is a process of making large claims for small matters: studying particular rituals, poems, plays, conversations, songs, dances, theories, and myths and gingerly reaching out to the full relations within a culture or a total way of life (Carey 1977, 424).

The Black Angel is an object that historical accident and layer upon layer of narrative and activity have turned into a powerful symbol of ambiguity. Its meaning has become so foreboding that some people reported avoiding it even in daylight, or contemplating it and trying to understand their fear. For once it has "acquired this story-based existence, the landscape itself acquires the power of 'telling the story'" (Leach 1984, 358). The angel provides a setting for young people to play, exploring their fears in a make-believe world that, at least while the game continues, may seem very real. The stories alone are only curiosities; even the cemetery is for most people just a pleasant place to walk on a sunny afternoon. Only in the context of the midnight pilgrimage does the Black Angel become fully powerful, when place, time, stories, and actions intersect: "The message, if there is one, is somehow embedded in the collective jumble rather than in any linear sequence . . . we see, hear, touch, taste, and smell. Although we can experience the result, we cannot describe it in words" (Leach 1984, 362).

But although the legend trip is indeed often a jumble of narratives, actions, and emotions, these are not arbitrary, but are specific and relevant to the players. The legend trip is part only of adolescent subculture, although the Black Angel is known by all age groups. The trip is one of the few events that belong to adolescents, without adult supervision and even awareness. During the trip, they explore the rules of the fast-approaching, real, adult world through the rules of their game, a game of which adults may be but dimly aware (see Meley 1991). The experience is an act of resistance to adult rules; the young people in effect write the script for the play.

Nevertheless, the participants are subject to the cultural prescriptions that define the direction that script will take. For within the adolescent subculture, there are different subcultures for boys and girls. Girls learn that the world of sexual maturity is a dangerous place in which they need protection from men, who are themselves the predators. They learn also that fear is allowable, and even expected from girls. Boys, on the other hand, learn that they must confront danger and avoid showing fear, they must bond with other males but also compete with them, and they must learn to be the predator while distinguishing between "good" and "bad" women. The game's central figures may be the mythical adulteress and the ever-present statue herself, but the real protagonists are the teenagers playing at the feet of the angel.

6

"Shame Old Roads Can't Talk"
Narrative, Experience, and Belief in the Framing of Legend Trips as Performance

Tim Prizer

At the start of Tim Prizer's essay he briefly explains one of the major disciplinary shifts in the field of folklore studies: the move from a focus only on texts to a focus on context (the social and cultural settings in which texts are performed) as well. This move highlights the blending of folklore's two main disciplines of origin; folklore studies grew out of both anthropology and literature scholarship, and retains perspectives and methods from both. A more literary approach to folklore may use textual or narrative analysis to approach stories, rituals, and customs, while a more anthropological approach may emphasize the norms and expectations of the folk group in which those forms circulate. Ideally, folkloristic scholarship blends both these approaches.

Prizer explains that he's using Erving Goffman's concept of "framing" to consider the legends and legend trips of the Ghost Road in Brooklet, Georgia. Goffman was a very influential sociologist in the twentieth century; he pioneered a perspective called dramaturgy that uses theater as a metaphor for human social interaction. His concept of "frame analysis" is a way to understand how people organize and make sense of social situations and activities. As he explains, "From an individual's particular point of view, while one thing may momentarily appear to be what is really going on, in fact what is actually happening is plainly a joke, or a dream, or an accident, or a mistake, or a misunderstanding, or a deception, or a theatrical performance, and so forth" (Goffman 1974, 10). In other words, the way an interaction is framed determines how the people taking part in it will understand what is going on.

The case study of the Ghost Road highlights that different people have different frames, and that we can't assume that the frames of belief and disbelief are mutually exclusive. Even within a folk group where the generally assumed worldview (way of perceiving the world) may be one of supernatural belief over scientific evidence, individual people who encounter a legend may have an attitude of disbelief. Prizer explains how different legend tellers can manipulate frames in order to bridge these gaps, reframing a legend within a listener's worldview in order to create a deeper connection despite potential disagreement about the reality of the supernatural. Prizer also reminds us that disbelief can be just as traditional as belief; always trusting to a scientific perspective is just as much a matter of personal faith as always trusting to a supernatural one. As folklorist David Hufford explains, scientific explanations for supernatural experiences usually only offer different, rather than better, logic than the legends themselves. As he says, "From this perspective, atheists are believers as much as the faithful are. The religionist is as much a skeptic of the materialist framework as is the materialist a skeptic of the supernatural" (Hufford 1982, 48).

> She kept asking me if the stories were true. I kept asking if it mattered. Finally we gave up. She was looking for a place to stand and I wanted a place to fly. (Brian Andreas 1993, 61)

> Fright, threads, and horror make strange bedfellows with fun. (Bill Ellis 2001, 44)

A FORMER UNIVERSITY OF IOWA CLASSMATE of the great Southern author Flannery O'Connor once recalled to an interviewer that O'Connor was fascinated by zoos. She would sit fixed, for hours, her unflinching gaze directed at the primitive life she saw before her. Only she was transfixed less by the wildlife confined to cages and tanks than she was by the wildness she saw in the humans peering anthropocentrically into these recreated habitats. O'Connor felt that zoos revealed much more about human nature than they did that of any ostensibly "lesser" species (Allen 1986, 256–266).[1] Her gaze, diverted from the form in zoos, provides the folklorist with a powerfully didactic metaphor. Folklorists, especially over the past quarter century, have redirected their own gaze from folk forms (which could be collected, analyzed, exhibited, and gawked at like caged matter) to the study of the ways in which the nature of these forms is only revealed—brought to life, if you will—through human interaction with them.[2]

This shift is perhaps most evident in folklorists' work within the genre of legends. Once collected as texts and placed side by side in edited volumes that made no serious attempts at contextualization, legends were placed on display as quaint and inherently irrational beliefs that somehow still managed to survive on the margins of society. The transformation of folklore's central paradigm from a text-centered approach to one that concentrates on performance amid context has shed light on the notion that legends occur in complex performative situations in the course of everyday discourse and in ongoing conversations in social interaction. Legends are now recognized not as folk literature, but rather as folk *behavior* (Ellis 2001, 10). They are not texts to be collected, transcribed, dissected, and archived; they are, in Bill Ellis's terms, "maps for action" (235). Bauman (1977) has demonstrated the ways in which any oral text transmitted to paper and analyzed as a static account misses the point and sets the folklorist up for egregious error. In *Verbal Art as Performance*, he observes that investigating the emergent and performative qualities of the oral literary text promises to reconceptualize the nature of the text, "freeing it from the apparent fixity it assumes when abstracted from performance and placed on the written page" (40). Bauman' s language encourages the use of the O'Connor metaphor: the unconscious specimens put on display as *beau ideals* for human enjoyment (like the animals at the zoo or the printed legends in an edited volume with no serious attempt at contextualization) must be "freed" from their cage of the written page by exploring how they come to 1ife through human interaction. We then become less interested in the stories themselves and much more so in how human beings use the stories in everyday performances.

A parallel development in legend scholarship, surfacing also in the late 1960s, has been the work of folklorists Linda Dégh and the aforementioned Bill Ellis on the concepts of *legend tripping* and *ostension*, which simply describe the processes by which legends may be *enacted* as well as told (Dégh 1969a; Ellis, chapter 4). Ellis defines ostensive behavior as "contrived events in which a group . . . venture[s] out to challenge supernatural beings, confront them in consciously dramatized form, then return to safety" (Ellis 2001, 165). Likewise, Dégh notes that in traditional legends, supernatural experiences occur unpredictably to witnesses, but in the ostensive behavior of the legend trip, visitors "condition themselves mentally for a vision they desire to have [and] perform a series of designated acts known to be effective to prompt ghosts to appear" (Dégh 1969a, 77–81). Ellis, in keeping with a dynamics-centered approach to the legend, notes that the sheer variability of the legends that inspire these trips demonstrates that it is the trip—and not the legend—that is most important in the tradition. Like O'Connor's focus on the people's interaction with the "forms," Ellis observes that "the stories alone cannot be understood without setting them into the context of this more complex folk tradition of deviant play" (Ellis 2004, 114). From this view, the primary function of the legend itself is merely to establish a mood of anticipation, perhaps even fear, necessary to the more significant *event* in which human interaction becomes essential (Ellis 2004, 114–115).

I ground this paper theoretically in Goffman's concept of framing. My exploration of this concept is twofold. First, I look at the means by which the stories people tell *about* the phenomenon and their experiences with it are presented to audiences for the purposes of achieving some latent social function. Second, I explore the host of ways legend-trippers involved in *experience* have of answering Goffman's fundamental question, "What is it that is going on here?" (Goffman 1974, 8). It is always the case that the framing devices employed in the performance of the legend *narrative* affect an audience's subsequent *experience* of the legend-trip, even if not in the way or to the degree the performer intended. Indeed, as I later explain in more detail, the narrative frame may influence an individual to experience and interpret the phenomenon in a way that is directly contrary to the performer's tacit intention. It is also true that one's framing of the *experience* in turn affects the way one will frame the *narrative* in later performances. I thus use framing as a springboard into an interwoven exploration of performance, performative competence, experience, and degrees of belief and disbelief (as constructed in the work of folklorists like David Hufford [1982], Dégh and Vázsonyi [1976], and Bill Ellis [2001, 2004, chapter 4]). I argue that legend trips are not merely an example of ostension where oral traditions become social events or actions; rather, they are a form of performance in their own right that rely on techniques of framing to attempt to convince or dissuade an "audience" of supernatural materialization. These attempts are complicated by the fact that they fall on the ears of individuals who hold a set of beliefs and skepticisms that fall anywhere along what I term a complex belief-disbelief continuum. I contend that the notion of a worldview shared by all in a given society or community must be seen as a reality only to the extent that the conflicting sub-beliefs of the individuals who comprise that society operate within a common framework. In addition, I argue contrary to Bill Ellis's claim that "the events narrated and experienced have a trivial impact on adolescents' belief systems" (1996, 440) and attempt to highlight the ways in which a legend framed effectively and told to individuals with an ability to suspend disbelief may indeed profoundly impact individuals' systems of belief after confronting on a legend trip what is thought to be a manifestation of the supernatural.

FIELDWORK AND "DISCOVERIES"

I first encountered the phenomenon of the legend-trip as a freshman at Georgia Southern University, long before I had even considered the concepts of performance, context, or even folklore as a discipline of academic study. I sat cramped in my room late one night in the freshman dormitory, overloaded with homework, half-empty pizza boxes, and Ramen noodles, when my friends rapped upon my door and insisted that I cram into even tighter confinement in the bed of a pickup truck for a wind-battering trip from Statesboro out to what they called "Ghost Road" in nearby Brooklet. I went, several times actually over the next couple of years, and my fascination with the stories, the beliefs, and indeed the eerie glow that undeniably exists there in some form, intensified. It would be misleading to suggest that I came to folklore *because* of this interest or even that it influenced my decision to move out of my then-current affiliation with the journalism department and align myself with the anthropologists. But when I did make this shift and enrolled in an introductory folklore course for the spring semester of 2003, I decided that my goal for the required fieldwork project and paper would be to explore the ins and outs of this local tradition so popular among students. I thus distributed broad surveys in freshman residence halls and in freshman classrooms, on which I asked if they would be willing to later discuss their experiences and knowledge of the phenomenon with me on a one-on-one basis. I received a moderate response, and began conducting interviews with students over coffee or in the library commons.[3] I also knew that I needed to speak with those who lived nearest to the "sites of experience," and I began looking for networks of individuals that would lead me into contact with Brooklet residents. Once established, I conducted interviews with three families in the area: Alvis and Joann Tyson, Truman and Vivinea Page (and their niece Samantha Blake, also a student at Georgia Southern), and the family of Jesse and Eleanor Wise. In this paper, I use my fieldwork experience as a foundation from which to explore the theoretical underpinnings of legendtripping, and I intend for my ethnographic research to provide an example of these theories at work that both upholds and challenges certain components of said theories.

My decision to interview both college students and Brooklet residents turned out to be essential to my attempt at a full representation of the tradition. Not only did this approach enable me to encounter a great degree of variation within story and experience, it also revealed to me several distinct explanations to describe phenomena at essentially two principal (and equally discrete) locations, each of which corresponds almost exclusively to two separate spheres of activity: that of Georgia Southern University students and that of Brooklet residents. Though the legend-trips of students and locals are made to the same plot of heavily wooded acreage, the specific sites of experience are self-contained in that they occur on two—and *only* two—of the many dirt roads that dissect the same plot of land. Students

Figure 6.1. Legend-tripping students from Georgia Southern University park their cars near this point on Robertson Road. An eerie light, in the form of a man digging, is said to appear on the left near the end of the road. Photo by Tim Prizer.

venture from Statesboro to Brooklet on Highway 80 and make a sharp left onto an unmarked strip of dirt and sand called Railroad Bed Road. They then hunt for Robertson Road, which is known to them as nothing other than "Ghost Road." Brooklet residents, even those who live on Railroad Bed Road, expressed no knowledge of the ghost on Robertson Road. Nor had they ever encountered the term "Ghost Road." Students are equally ignorant of the legends told among Brooklet residents, which hold that the ghostly light is in fact on Railroad Bed Road. Very few had ever heard of anything called "the railroad bed" or, for that matter, Railroad Bed Road. On the other hand, "Ghost Road" is as common and esoterically understood a reference among students as is the term "keg party."

Students visiting "Ghost Road" are usually instructed to drive about halfway down the road and then to stop, turn off the car, and kill the headlights. They then exit their vehicles, stand in the middle of the road, and pose a fixed, unflinching stare toward Highway 80, down the chute of trees along either side of the path. In addition to glowing balls of light, students most commonly report to have witnessed moving transparent figures and shadows of people otherwise undetectable. Their explanations for these sightings are almost comically diverse. Among their

"Shame Old Roads Can't Talk"

Figure 6.2. According to student accounts, the glow appears very near this point at the end of Robertson Road. Photo by Tim Prizer.

accounts are: a slave picking cotton and his master shooting him; a slave on his wagon; the ghosts of several slaves; a man standing with a lantern; a gang of farmers, workers, and women; a lady swaying in a swing; slave spirits beside a white plantation house; a slave who died working in the cotton fields; a man swinging a blade of some sort; a man with a shovel digging his own grave; a man with a shovel digging a grave for his wife; a slave with a shovel digging his master's grave; and merely a breeze blowing the limbs of a bush to and fro. Most student accounts maintain that, for whatever reason, the ghostly glow of a man repeatedly thrusts a shovel into the ground and heaves the dirt over his shoulder. Supposedly, the man also lays his shovel down on occasion and then drifts up the road toward observers.

The stories local Brooklet inhabitants relate, on the other hand, speak of an eerie "orange glow" that hovers over and drifts down Railroad Bed Road. Most stories among Brooklet residents resemble the story related by Jesse Wise, sixty-nine years old and residing in the home closest to the site where the ghost light is most commonly seen. Wise was born on Railroad Bed Road in 1934, and his father recounted as early as 1920 the same story that circulates in Brooklet today. "Dad used to sit around and tell us the story of the 'headless light,' as we called it," he says:

Figure 6.3. Inhabitants of Brooklet have long known the story of "the ghost down at the railroad bed." Interestingly, this ghost is said to appear only on Railroad Bed Road. Photo by Tim Prizer.

> There used to be, when the train used to run out here, they was having some problems on the track one night . . . The switchman on the back of the train, he had a lantern with him, and so they said that he had some trouble. So he went up kind of towards the engine of the train, and for some reason he fell down in between the tracks. And when the engineer saw the light move as if for him to move the train now, he fell and his head come across the tracks and the train wheels cut his head off. And they've never been able to find the head. And so what they say is that it's the switchman, or the man in the back caboose had the lantern still in his hand, and he was looking for his head.

Another of the most interesting "discoveries" I made through choosing to speak with both students and Brooklet residents came long after my fieldwork and final paper were written. I discovered much later that my ethnographic research challenges one of the definitional components of the legend-trip as defined by the subject's most prolific scholar, Bill Ellis. Ellis's writings insist time and again that legend-tripping is exclusively confined to adolescents, a contention that my fieldwork proves false. Ellis argues that "the philosophy of the legend-trip involves defiance of 'adult' norms and that teens' first-hand descriptions of legend-trips make it clear that adults are not involved or welcome. 'Trippers' who are 18 or older are largely shunned as outsiders" (1996a, 169). My simultaneous interviewing of three generations (ranging in age from twelve to sixty-nine) of Railroad Bed Road legend-trippers in the Wise family reveals that Ellis's assertion may describe a situation of typicality, but not one of invariability.

Even though Brooklet residents have grown up with the ghost and the stories told about it in their backyard—quite literally for some—it continues to excite their imaginations. Some in the Brooklet community do approach the story passively, but for others, the story serves much the same social-ritualistic purpose it does for college students residing outside of the community. Alvis Tyson, the postmaster of Brooklet from 1969 to 1992, is old enough to recall a day when the famed railroad traversing Railroad Bed Road was still very much in use. In the 1980s, over forty years after officials removed the railroad, Tyson remembers that "the ghost down at the railroad bed was the talk of the town." For Brooklet residents during this time, the story produced a large social event as cars turned out in droves to line Railroad Bed Road in search of the light. He recollects: "I believe the full moon had something to do with it. It was unreal the number of people who used to come out . . . It was just a gathering like it was going to be a show or something. They was there like to see the show. They would be strung, probably thirty or more of them . . . Sort of like a family reunion, they just didn't have nothing to eat . . . Parking places was gone, done sold out." Indeed, as the vast majority of Brooklet legend-trippers are college students from nearby Statesboro, only a very small fraction of participants are under the age of eighteen.

So this is a narrative tradition that doubles as social event; it seems many are in as determined a pursuit for the ghost as is the ghost for its head. Though participation is intergenerational, leading this mission are Georgia Southern University students who, perhaps since the school accepted Brooklet residents at its opening as the First District A&M School in 1906, have scoured the marsh lands and pines along Brooklet's Railroad Bed Road in search of paranormal fulfillment. The tradition continues to thrive on the Statesboro campus, especially in dormitories where the story circulates quickly among every batch of incoming freshmen each August. Students venture out of their residence halls and down Highway 80 to track the ghost under strikingly similar circumstances. Most students spend the evening drinking either at Statesboro's local establishments or in their dorms before heading out to Brooklet often after midnight, a factor that may or may not affect their vision and perception—and thus their memory—of the ghost lights they see at the railroad bed. These excursions are rarely planned and

Figure 6.4. Ralph Kearney, Eleanor Wise, Jesse Wise, Ryan Kearney, and Matt Kearney represent three generations of Wise family legend-trippers who love on the same property as Robertson Road and Railroad Bed Road. The story of "the ghost down at the railroad bed" is as powerful for them today as it was for Jesse Wise's father, who told the story as early as 1920. Photo by Tim Prizer.

usually occur under the whimsical insistence of one student or a group. Though many venture out on "boring weeknights just to scare girls," the ritual is especially common on nights ranging from full moons and meteor showers to Halloween and Friday the Thirteenth. Typically, large groups of students pile into pickup trucks or small cars for the trip east to Brooklet.

DEFINING THE LEGEND-TRIP

"A ritual; teenagers hear a legend about uncanny events said to occur at a particular spot, then visit the site to test the legend" (Ellis 1996b, 439). Bill Ellis begins his definition with this concise, elementary statement. Starting here and proceeding to its end, throughout its simplicity and its complexity, the definition speaks to virtually every detail of the trips made to the railroad bed in small-town southeast Georgia. Dating back to at least the fourth century (Ellis 2004, 118–119), the pilgrimages nearly always focus on "spooky" places such as a bridge, an abandoned house, a graveyard or, as in this case, an unlit and heavily forested road near an inactive railroad track. The potential for terror fails to deter the trips; to the contrary, they often function as dares that encourage repeated visits to invoke danger.[4] One of the stories collected in my fieldwork—the one found almost exclusively among Brooklet locals and confined to Railroad Bed Road—is widespread enough in legend tripping for Ellis to include as one of the many beliefs, "a person—a man or a woman—was decapitated in an accident and a ghostly light lingers at the site of the tragedy" (1996, 439). He goes on to cite perhaps the most famous of these specific types, which folklorists first collected in the town of Maco in eastern North Carolina in the latter half of the nineteenth century. His description of the Maco story is most directly adaptable to the phenomena said to occur on Railroad Bed Road in Brooklet: "Near Maco, North Carolina, generations of teens have come to witness a mysterious light along a railroad track, said to be a headless brakeman looking for his head" (439). As Ellis goes on, his definition continues to capture the essence of many of the trips to Brooklet. "The visit is usually made by automobile, and illegal drinking [and] recreational drug use . . . are integral parts of the 'trip'" (439). For some, the trips are nothing more than chances to "drink beer, smoke pot, make out, and talk about what's 'real'" (Ellis 2001, 191).[5]

The performative aspects of the legend-trip begin to surface in the recognition that the event could be said to "begin" before the trippers crank their car engines for the ride to the site and to "end" well after the trippers have returned to the safety of their homes or residence halls. Ellis notes that legend-trips have a tripartite structure which in elementary terms can be broken down to *before, during, and after* the pilgrimage. Literally by definition, Ellis suggests, the events begin with the oral transmission from one or several individuals to any number of others. The telling may occur at parties, in the classroom, in dormitories, or even as the group travels to the site. Regardless of when the process of text transmission begins, the group usually uses the time it takes to travel to the remote location to intensify anxiety and excitement by sharing "origin legends" about why the site is haunted and "proof legends" confirming supposed encounters with the occult on previous visits.

The second performative component of the legend-trip transpires upon arrival. It is then that the brave are expected to engage in the very acts said to put them in the most danger. This often involves turning off the car engine or leaving the security of the vehicle, and it may also require further ritual actions such as honking the car horn, flashing the headlights, hollering at the ghostly manifestation, or physically approaching what is thought to be the materialization of the supernatural—all of which are commonly thought essential to students' trips in the Brooklet situation. "The trip often climaxes," Ellis accurately notes, "when something unexpected happens—a noise, a sudden wind, even a prearranged hoax . . .—and the visit often ends with a panicked retreat to the car" (Ellis 1996, 440).

The final stage of the three-part structure of legend-trips occurs, like the first stage, in any number of locations—a dorm room, a bar, or on the ride home. It too involves a performative narrative event in which retrospective personal experience narratives, in the form of "proof legends" or negative accounts, are shared about what happened at the site. In the next section, I discuss the ways in which each of the three components of the legend-trip structure can be viewed from the angle of a performative event and how aspects of performance affect, and are affected by, experience and belief.

FRAMING, PERFORMANCE, AND COMPETENCE IN THE LEGEND-TRIP

Talk of structure and stages of performance should not suggest that the legend-trip is a self-contained linear sequence that moves from beginning (telling the initial narrative), to middle (making the trip), and finally to a clear and conclusive end (sharing experiences and interpretations among the trippers). Such a model would suggest that the legend-trip flashes and fades, that it is nascent at nearly the same moment that it begins to die, evaporating as quickly as it was born. But legend-trips involve a complex coincidence of these stages. Not only is it the case that individuals perpetuate a *circular* and unending sequence in which they hear (as audience), experience (as participant), and then tell (as performer), thus inciting others to set the process in motion anew, it is also so that the initial narrative may be told during the trip or that new narratives form at the site of experience as people encounter the phenomena at hand. The legend trip—narratives *and* experience forming its totality—should thus be seen as emergent and created through cooperative interaction among individuals.

It is in the third stage that we most clearly see the continuity and remolding of tradition, for here in this "final" stage, where individuals retreat to gather and discuss their experiences at the site, we simultaneously see the first stage begin anew. Any unusual event that took place at the site, Ellis writes, will be "interpreted as a brush with the supernatural and become the core of a personal experience story that will then be passed around among the teens' peers" (Ellis 2004, 115). Undoubtedly, these stories will be told to the uninitiated and thus incorporated into the basic legend complex. Thus, here we find the retrospective reports of personal experience circling back to encompass later trippers' first stage of the performance (115). So, all three stages can equally be viewed through the lens of performance, and in fact since none are isolable in the *process* of the legend-trip, we must consider them as overlapping components of an ongoing whole. Framing is intimately involved in this interminable process as well. Individuals experience and select a series of frames and framing devices (1) in their encounter with the story, (2) in their being presented with the possibility of partaking in the legend as event, (3) in their experience of the phenomenon, and (4) ultimately, in their interpretive narratives after experience.

The framing devices employed in the Ghost Road tradition are as many and as varied as the stories themselves. The stories often begin with a statement of their indisputable veracity: "I know for a fact that the story is true because it happened to *me*" or because "I *saw* it." As often, they are placed upon a credible witness through reported speech: "This happened to my friend, who is completely sane, I swear." It is the style, or the skillful stringing together of convincing utterances, that makes one's truth claim convincing. It may additionally have everything to do with the teller's demeanor and emotion. A powerful raconteur may shift between authoritative or rational tones of voice and "an intense quivering intonation" to demand authority from his audience (Ellis 2001, 93), all the while consciously excluding any "rational" explanations he may have heard to counter the story.

But before delving into all of the ways that legends are framed, whether as truth or as complete fabrication, it is important to note first of all that to view the legend in terms of performance requires a different lens than is used in nearly every other prose-narrative genre. Not only does a legend occur in the course of everyday speech like the sagacious parable, very rarely delimited clearly for the sake of its own performance as would be a self-contained joke or tale, it also features no clear break between performer and audience. The boundaries between performer and audience are unclear in legends, as Dégh and Vázsonyi note, because "the [legend] teller is not a self-conscious artist who is recognized and admired for his creative fantasy, like the storyteller. He is just one of the group, whose other members share the same knowledge and act as audience or often as associate contributors to his story" (Dégh and Vázsonyi 1976, 101). Also, the legend performer(s) rarely claims authorship; rather, reported speech is relied upon to establish authority in an outside source by claiming that the events being recounted have in no way been altered from the way they left the horse's mouth (102). In this sense, the events of the legend have already been interpreted before the teller reports on what was heard. Yet, as my fieldwork in Brooklet confirms, some tellers do declare authorship in the sense that they claim to have *experienced firsthand* the events they recount. It is they who interpreted the event through primary experiences and sensory impressions.[6]

Dégh and Vázsonyi's contention that the legend performer is not a "self-conscious artist" is correct only to a certain extent. Some legend-trippers do partake in the pilgrimages so frequently that they become "experts" in the tradition, visiting the same or similar sites dozens, perhaps hundreds of times (Ellis 1996a, 169). Thus, with this experience and familiarity may come a competence due to the fact that they possess knowledge the others have not yet encountered (Dégh and Vázsonyi 1976, 101). Their expertise is borne out in the telling of the legend and framing of the event that follows it. They may more effectively employ framing devices and achieve from their audience a greater respect for their ability to stir fear, excitement, or curiosity. These emotions, stimulated effectively, can lead to a competence for the performer that depends not at all upon his ability to convince his audience of the truth of the legend. It rather depends, to use Ellis's term, on the *suspension of disbelief*, or the audience member's ability to become engrossed in and get carried away by an idea that he or she may or may not fully perceive as reality. What is most important, in this case, is maintaining the *illusion* of reality. The legend is thus *presented* (or framed) as reality, but *understood* as fantasy (Ellis 2001, 29). In this way, by superimposing the make-believe upon real life, legend-trippers are able to interact with ideas of fear and terror without ever actually worrying for their personal safety (Ellis 2001, 173–174). But it is also highly possible, contrary to Ellis's argument that ostensive behavior has no serious impact on individuals' belief systems, that this illusion may grow so intense that it is transformed into an actual perception of reality. I can say personally that I was highly skeptical of ghosts before my experience at the railroad bed and, though I began the experience with simple entertainment and fantasy in mind, the nearly indisputable vision of someone digging has forced me to accept that the "correct" explanation *may* indeed be the appeal to the supernatural. This same sentiment was repeated in others' accounts throughout my fieldwork.

The so-called experts are active bearers of tradition who often designate as their primary objective the persuasion of others to the stories' veracity and to convince them that a trip to the site would be well worth their time. Rarely, however, is this persuasion conducted overtly. The real "experts" find more subtle ways to influence. It is thus they who, in likely the most artful use of framing, will ground their stories in the nonbeliever's world by either claiming not to know if the legend is true (but arguing that one should definitely find out for oneself), speaking of the ways in which their skepticism was shattered by experience, or through reported speech, referring solely to others' narratives of encounter. It is here that we find the convergence of the two spheres of legend framing activity: that of the legend itself and that of the experience with the legend on the legend-trip.

In the first sphere, as Glenn Hinson has observed, "the details *surrounding* encounter (rather than the experienced specifics *of* encounter) become centrally important, in that they establish an experiential common ground" (Hinson 2001, 18). If this is achieved and, the teller hopes, interest in the legend-trip is established, one may safely say, as Hinson does, that "by locating [supernatural] experience firmly in the nonbeliever's world, they affirm the commonality of hearer and teller, and thus invite belief" (18). Georgia Southern University students told me time and time again, "I didn't believe it either before I went out there. I didn't believe in ghosts at all. But *something's* there. God knows what, but it's not of this world." Here we see the legend-trip process come full circle, as this student's framing technique is likely identical to the way the story was originally presented to him. He has reestablished the frame based on his own and others' experiences, he has tempted one as he was to make the trip, and he has thus invited belief from even the most obdurate skeptic.

But it must also be noted that simply telling a legend text as true does not necessarily mean that the teller believes this is so. Though "the teller is trying to convince his audience and to make his listeners believe what he is telling," Dégh and Vázsonyi write, he "'might lie, he might make fun of the believers, he might pretend in order to attract public interest or to gain popularity, or he might simply be following tradition by making use of the available formulae common to oral genres of narration. The text alone cannot tell us whether the raconteur believes his story" (1976, 98).

It should be acknowledged then that those who instigate the trips to the railroad bed may be held accountable by the standards of performance to display a certain degree of competence depending upon the way in which they frame the phenomenon and the event. If framed as unarguable truth in *the narrative*, as is often the case, the performers' "audience" is especially likely to *experience* the phenomenon with an eye toward the believability of the performers' version of what they are supposedly witnessing. Yet the individuals who comprise the audience are bound to encompass a wide range of beliefs and disbeliefs, and thus may perceive the performers' interpretation of the phenomenon as false not on terms of the absurdity of supernatural belief, but rather on terms of an incorrect interpretation that stems from a logical foundation of tacit belief in ghosts and other forms of the supernatural. In other words, though the stories themselves may come under fire for embroidering what one feels is a natural phenomenon, the *premises* of belief upon which all similar convictions are founded—the likelihood of the existence of a supernatural realm on which humans may speculate but never fully know—are rarely called into question.

PERFORMANCE, BELIEF, VARIATION, AND "CONDUITS"

I refer above to the "wide range of beliefs and disbeliefs" of individuals in a single audience through which any legend must pass. Dégh and Vázsonyi (1976) call this web of transmission and belief the "legend conduit." They explain their coinage of the concept in these terms: "The fact that recipients acquire their information . . . through specific communicative channels is much more important than the question of objective truth. The way in which the intricate process of legend transmission . . . is conducted might be termed the *legend conduit* . . . By *legend conduit* we understand the sequence of individuals who qualify as legend receivers and transmitters" (1976, 96). They go on to explain that all participants in a legend performance—legend advocates, audience members, and performers—may be grouped into any of five categories—believers, indifferents, skeptics, nonbelievers, and opponents—and that these are fluid categories; that is, one individual may vacillate among any of the five designations (117). They are interested in "the procedure by which legends are . . . generated, formulated, transmuted, and crystallized by means of communication through the legend conduit" and the fact that "legend carriers—believers or non-believers—usually accept, pass on, and are fed back the verbal communication they themselves have launched" (96). It may thus be so that the mere echo of one's own statement "acts as substantial proof for the legend, rather than the real facts" (96).

The complexity of the web of transmission and belief among a group of individuals is complicated even more by the range of belief and wavering negotiation that may occur within a *single* individual regarding a belief in both the supernatural realm and the particular legend at hand. In the dynamics of the group, we see that "some people believe in one story, others believe in another" (Dégh and Vázsonyi 1976, 99). But on the level of the individual, we may discover that one person "might take one portion of a legend for granted but reject the rest" or that it is possible for one "both to believe unconditionally and to believe with some second thoughts, with a trace of doubt or with mixed feelings." The point is that, as Dégh and Vázsonyi correctly observe, "this fluctuation of attitudes toward belief cannot be discerned from the text of the legend alone." Thus, even the nonbeliever can fuel legend dispersion. Conversely, no matter how aporetic the raconteur may be of his legend, regardless of how thoroughly he insists that his story is untrue, some individuals in his audience may accept it as truth (99). "The germ wrapped in the shell of incredulity might fall into fertile soil" (118).

Despite this complexity on the level of the individual, there is still a common premise of cultural logic. If ethnography can be defined as trying to uncover the "scripts" by which humans make cultural sense of their world and of each other, we must determine what lies at the foundation for *all* members of a group and *then* try to determine how that foundation leads individuals in different directions. It is thus that I feel an extension is needed to the model of the legend conduit. If we can imagine the Dégh-Vázsonyi model (1976, 118) as branches of individual potentialities of belief, we may also construct a "trunk" to represent the common foundation from which stem the degrees of belief represented in any legend performance. This trunk signifies the shared understandings comprised in a common worldview that allow, for example, two or more individuals to even begin speaking about a ghost in the first place. My point is that irrespective of the discord that may divide any two individuals' beliefs in or interpretations of the supernatural, the *concept* of an order of existence beyond the observable universe is implicit and intermutual in the individuals' shared worldview. No group of people, however large or small, is capable of producing a legend, or any information for that matter, without a common foundation that supports it (Dégh and Vázsonyi 1976, 102). All members who share culture, as Barre Toelken notes, are "inclined to view . . . phenomena in those conceptual terms which seem 'logical' to [their] society." They are taught by society "*how* to see" (1975, 265). It is this worldview that forms the foundation of the supernatural legend in all its variation and that must serve also as the foundation for the folklorist's exploration of its dynamics.

Though Toelken recommends that we "pass over the idiosyncrasy of the particular individual in the culture" (1975, 269) and focus instead entirely upon this foundation, I argue that this leads us to misleading generalizations and only a superficial understanding of any group of people, irrespective of size. We must study the ways in which a coherent system of belief is constructed in the conflicting sub-beliefs of individuals, beliefs that seem to threaten the structure but which, because of how deeply ingrained worldview is in every one of us, operate comfortably within the boundaries of a shared logic. "The actual belief manifest at the time of the [legend] telling," Dégh and Vázsonyi note, "is always the result of the dichotomous relationship between the communal belief system, inherited in tradition and sanctioned by enculturation, and the personal belief[s] of the individual[s]" (1976, 102–103).

In terms of this complex conduit, then, it should be obvious that, with legends involving tripping, variation in the stories told may arise on several levels. In performance (in the sense of the social event) and in interaction with the light, variants form not only through the transmission of oral accounts (as with legends simply *told*), but also through varying interpretations of *experience* that are molded from the start by *individuals'* preconceived systems of belief and by the particular framing devices employed in the initial performance of the legend text. Goffman observes on the subject of the framing of experience and event that "when participant roles in an activity are differentiated—a common circumstance—the view that one person has of what is going on is likely to be quite different from that of another. There is a sense in which what is play for the golfer is work for the caddy" (Goffman 1974, 8). Thus, when beliefs diverge and lead experience to do the same, we see that the personal-experience narratives that form the ever-growing body of legend texts and which make up the third stage of performance as cited above are fated for incessant variation. Put another way, stories *about* the phenomenon flourish as experiences and interactions *with* the phenomenon take place, thus creating a never-ending process of emergence and creation. Variation arises in performance; no one story can encompass the whole of student/local belief due to the emergent and unique quality of each performance or interaction with the story or event. When legend-trippers retreat from the site—some for reasons of fear, others of boredom—to talk about the event, this process begins. I appeal here once again to Erving Goffman: "It is plain that retrospective characterization of the 'same' event or social occasion may differ very widely, that an individual's role in an undertaking can provide him with a distinctive evaluative assessment of what sort of an instance of the type the particular undertaking was. In that sense it has been argued, for example, that opposing rooters at a football game do not experience the 'same' game" (Goffman 1974, 9). The "texts" and the experiences, then, are inextricably linked components of the same process.

Ostension may be said to be performative in nature as well. Such ritual activities as shutting off the car's motor, flashing headlights, or walking up the darkened path toward the ghost are examples of performative ostension in two respects. First, these taunting mechanisms attempt to merge the supernatural realm referenced in the preparatory narrative with the reality of the live situation (Ellis 2004, 115). Second, and a natural extension of the first, is that this action connotes a performance in that, as characterized by Kenneth Thigpen, "whether the words of the legend are spoken or not, the awareness of all present centers on its message" (quoted in Ellis 2004, 115). The message, then, is only in small part constituted in the performance of the orally narrated legend. Here again we find that it is only through *experience* that the message is borne out in full.

The simple or elaborate hoaxes commonly carried out by legend trippers are also a type of performative ostension whereby individuals exploit the heightened tension and anxiety that come naturally with the trip in order to temporarily terrify other trippers. Contrary once again to Ellis's insistence on ostension as a sphere of strictly adolescent activity, this form of ostensive behavior in Brooklet is most commonly—at least most elaborately—executed in the playful yet potentially petrifying actions of adults. While college students certainly scare unsuspecting peers by way of a jolting scream or touch, Brooklet locals exploit the unexplainable phenomenon in remarkably innovative ways. Annually, the Wise family's local church hosts a hayride along Railroad Bed Road and the surrounding property for young children in the congregation. This long-standing tradition is a favorite pastime of local children and adults alike, and it is here that Jesse Wise feels he gets his chance to shine as a storyteller. "It's easier to lead the kids when you can look at their faces," he says. "Sitting around the campfire, you can look at their faces and know how deep you can go with them. You can *really* pull it out yourself." Before embarking on the hay-covered wagon behind Wise's tractor, the children settle in for the introduction of his liberally embroidered story of the headless flagman. And as if the mysterious balls of light were not enough to scare the children out of their wits, Wise continues his story as the tractor creeps through the pines. Furthermore, the adults make this a community effort, and thus an event much larger than the children ever imagined. Enacting both the (super?)natural phenomenon and the legends to explain it, one hoaxer often stands a good distance down the road from the approaching wagon with a flashlight and a piece of orange cellophane while another enthroned atop the fire tower lowers a dangling lantern from the end of a rope with in grabbing distance of the wagon. As Jesse Wise fondly recalls, "Those kids like to have had a heart attack."

In looking at these hoaxes as a form of performance in which performative competence relies on the success of the hoax, we see that the performers—well aware of the contrived nature of the event—deliberately withhold this information from the uninitiated (Ellis 1996a, 174). Following Erving Goffman (1974), these activities are designed to cause an audience "to have a false sense of what it is that is going on." Or, to use Bateson's theory of play, the goal is to walk the tightrope between the illusion of reality and the shared understanding that "these actions, in which we now engage, do not denote what would be denoted by those actions which these actions denote" (Bateson 1972, 180).[7] And the legend-trippers, though often terrified by it, usually welcome this manipulation. To this effect, Bill Ellis notes that "the possibility that one might have been tricked . . . does not seem to matter much, so long as the trick was carried out well . . . An uneventful visit to the haunted site is, for committed legend-trippers, the worst outcome" (1996a, 174). Thus, the "audience" in this case—perhaps unconsciously due to the performer's careful use of deception—holds the performer accountable for a display of performative competence; indeed, their "fun" relies on it.

Elaborate ostensive hoaxes are also performative in a number of other respects. For instance, Jesse Wise's introductory narrative event begins as usual before the trip, but continues throughout. In carrying the performance of the narrative from stage one to stage two of the legend-trip's tripartite structure, Wise reveals the common but often overlooked synchronicity of the phases of legendtripping process. Also, in speaking of "how deep you can go" in the performance of the narrative, Wise acknowledges that he assesses the audience's reactions in order to know how to present the story and how elaborate he can make it while still presenting at least the illusion of reality. He knows that he must employ framing devices that confer competence upon him and that position his stories comfortably in the gray area between "reality" and staged artifice.

TRADITIONS OF DISBELIEF

Historically, folklorists have defined *legend* in terms that suggest that both tellers and audiences must agree that the content of the legend is true. Yet, given the complexity of the belief-disbelief continuum (or conduit) cited above, it should be clear that very little would qualify as legend under such a definition (Dégh and Vázsonyi 1976, 100). Rather than concerning themselves with whether or not a supposed "legend" meets the qualifications to be classified in that generic construct, folklorists since the late 1960s have followed Dégh's lead in focusing more upon the range of beliefs that are borne out in the legend-telling (and tripping) event.

One of the most exciting developments in legend scholarship in the last quarter century has been not only this shift away from the shared belief in the veracity of legends, but also the growing focus on the methods skeptics employ to counter them. Linda Dégh and Bill Ellis may have co-pioneered this angle of exploration, but the work of folklorist David Hufford has done the most to theorize and conceptualize it. Hufford has noted that the stories and explanations intended to discredit legends (which Dégh and Vázsonyi [1976, 112] terms "negative legends" and Ellis [2001, 85–86] calls "anti-legends") feature a mixture of commonality and variation comparable to the legends themselves. These legends comprise what Hufford calls "traditions of disbelief," traditional in the sense that they too contain all the requisite characteristics of the designation. Traditions of disbelief assume that all supernatural legends are patently false and, as Hufford notes, in doing so are "necessarily ethnocentric in the most fundamental sense . . . [They say] over and over again: 'What I know I *know*, what you know you only *believe*—to the extent that it conflicts with my knowledge'" (Hufford 1982, 47–48). Rather than the tradition arising from a foundation of belief, these counter legends often claim that the supernatural traditions condition individuals' experiences, which in turn seem to supply supporting evidence for the tradition (49). This view is ignorant of cross-cultural parallels which confirm that experiences more profoundly shape tradition rather than vice versa (50).

It is also the case, Hufford contends, that legends discrediting legends contain no *greater* cultural logic than the legends themselves—only a *different* logic. That is, those who offer legends of disbelief begin from the foundation that all ostensibly supernatural phenomena are explainable through science or through other means that attempt to prove the legends' "irrationality." The supernatural legends, on the other hand, stem from a no less "logical" base that states that there is a realm of activity that humans cannot explain, even through the supposed omniscience of the scientific world. It then becomes an issue of the locus of *one's faith*: whether in the supernatural or in the books and journals of the scientific academy. It is a difference, to use Dégh and Vázsonyi's (1976, 112) term, of "reality values." In this sense, "born sceptics, searchers for truth, and knowledgeables are recognized folk characters" (113). The point is that all legends—"positive," "negative," or apathetic—make a statement. They want us to believe that there *are* ghosts, that there are *no* ghosts, that *allegedly* there are ghosts, and all possibilities in between (119).

Pseudo-scientific explanations are found throughout the genre of supernatural legends, and in the case of "the ghost down at the railroad bed" in Brooklet, they are employed by both believers and nonbelievers. These tell of the tragedy that suggests an encounter with the supernatural, but they release this tension by explaining it away through a "rational" scientific interpretation (Dégh and Vázsonyi 1976, 113). Over their many years of interaction with the supposed revenant, the residents along Railroad Bed Road have picked up scientific explanations—not fully understood and in themselves folkloric—that attempt to untangle the mystery. Many people now believe the light to be caused by a "gaseous substance" that forms naturally under appropriate conditions.[8] Truman Page, another Railroad Bed Road resident, explains what he knows of the process:

> We was visiting at Okefenokee Swamp a few years back, and one of the guides down there was telling us about these gases. In fact, he took a stick

and some of the soft ground, and he pushed down there and there was water, and it was just bubbly, and he claims that was gases coming out of there. Gases down there had formed, and it made not like a bright light, but there was a light burning those gases. And when you got close to it, just a vibration or a breath or any little thing would cause it to go off and on. A breeze could come out and blow it out and then it'd come back on later.

Jesse Wise offers a bit more elaboration:

What I believe we were actually seeing was something like decaying matter which was phosphorous or something that would come out. Something like this would glow at night . . . We used to have all these trees. Well, the trees have been cut now so we don't have the litter on the ground—the composition of all that swampy land, leaf matter, and undergrowth. And see, that's what generates this phosphorous gas that comes up out and it drifts off, and of course you can see it. See, I can understand *that*. That's my theory. See, I don't believe in ghosts at all, but I do know there are phenomenons out there that you can't explain. That's what makes things exciting.

We could surmise from these inchoate explanations of my friends in Brooklet that the tour guides at the Okefenokee State Park had an uncertain understanding of the "scientific" reasoning themselves. It is a weak—and common—explanation to merely suggest that the "supernatural" is actually a natural agency that is not yet fully understood or perhaps even known to exist, but which will eventually dispel all "superstition" (Hufford 1982, 54).

But even given all the scientific reasoning of the times, one must accept that the correct explanation for the lights may indeed lie in the supernatural realm. Georgia Southern University students may be the most cynical of all, considering that many of them likely wander out of psychology and chemistry classes just hours before visiting the property surrounding Railroad Bed Road. But Georgia Southern student Samantha Blake likely speaks for most in her remarks concerning her frustration and confusion over not knowing what to believe when it comes to the phantasmal.[9] "In the back of my mind, I know it's something else. I know it's probably gases that mix together and there's a light that appears, but I can just see it and I will hit the floor and start screaming my head off. I mean, it's just pure fear because my first thought is, 'Oh my gosh, there's a man, he's coming after me, he wants my head because he can't see.'"

Blake echoes author and fellow Georgian Margaret Wayt DeBolt, who quotes an anonymous author in her book *Savannah Spectres*, "I do not believe in ghosts, but I am afraid of them" (1984, 1). Likewise, Brooklet denizen Joann Tyson is at a loss for what to believe, and she feels she will always have to balance both the fascination and frustration this story engenders, a sentiment she elegantly captures in her statement, "Shame old roads can't talk, isn't it?"

Another explanation often advanced in the rhetoric of traditions of disbelief is that those who experience what is incorrectly perceived as the supernatural are merely hallucinating; that is, they are literally "under the influence of psychotropic substances ranging from alcohol to the opiates and alkaloids such as LSD" (Hufford 1982, 49). Ellis lends credence to this notion as well: "It is, however, impossible to distinguish . . . legend-focused behavior [as ostension amid supernatural interpretation] from other kinds of activity that form part of the trip, such as illegal drinking and marijuana smoking, After surveying 218 accounts of Ohio legend-trips, I concluded that trying to experience the supernatural was like such recreational drug use in that both are 'trips'—deliberate escapes into altered states of being where conventional laws do not operate" (Ellis 2004, 116).

Indeed, Georgia Southern University students lend support to this interpretation as well; as one student told me, he and his friends are "sometimes drunk, sometimes stoned, sometimes drunk *and* stoned" when they adventure out to the site. But though Ellis's quote has much to say about the power of the legend-trip to engender an altered social reality, he too seems to adhere to traditions of disbelief in his suggestion that alcohol and drugs are, literally by definition in his case (Ellis 1996, 439), essential to the legend trip. It is only a small step from this point to infer that one's perceptions and thus beliefs are shaped by the use of these mind-altering substances.[10]

CONCLUSION

Traditions of both belief and disbelief have perhaps had no more fertile ground in which to flourish than they do in the current cultural landscape. To many, ghost stories seem anachronistic in a global world of scientific discovery, lavish technology, and instantly available, free-flowing information. Like the word *folklore* itself, traditional narratives concerning the supernatural are erroneously thought to be of a bygone era, sepia-toned in the "primitive" ways of life of our ancestors. Given the reinforcement and validation these flawed notions of residual culture find in the popular media and in the academy, traditions of disbelief promise to continue to expand and emerge in opposition to supernatural belief. Ironically, however, those very beliefs that they arise to overthrow are intensified by the forces of modernity that seem to contradict them. In truth, like all folklore, legends of supernatural belief are forever emerging, evolving, and undergoing processes of modification so as to have them make cultural sense in the milieu of our current existence—a feat achieved only through narrative *and* experience. We must acknowledge this fact if we hope to maintain even the illusion of reality.

NOTES

1. This fascination of O'Connor's formed the basis of her grotesque novel *Wise Blood*, a symbolic excursion into the animalistic nature of human beings.

2. The analogy could apply, too, to the shift in folklore scholarship from a focus on the primitive "folk" separated from the educated observer to the view—now common in folkloristics—that all people qualify as "the folk."

3. The names of the students interviewed remain anonymous in this essay as requested on release forms.

4. For an in-depth exploration of this phenomenon specifically, see Bird 1994.

5. Brooklet resident Joann Tyson, who worked in the post office with her husband, longtime Brooklet postmaster Alvis Tyson, has always thought "the old railroad bed" was a sort of "lovers' lane" for teenagers and college students. "I've heard 'em say, 'Let's go to the old railroad bed.' And then it didn't take me but twice to find out what the old railroad bed was"—quite literally "a railroad *bed,*" Alvis Tyson jokes.

6. Similarly, Bill Ellis recalls an informant telling him, "This is not a story, this is some*thing* that happened to me" (Ellis 2001, 134).

7. Bateson's helpful explanation of this complicated sentence is his example: "The playful nip denotes the bite, but it does not denote what would be denoted by the bite."

8. The same justification is found in Saratoga, Texas, where, on Bragg Road (also known as Ghost Road), an almost identical story involving a headless railroad worker exists to explain mysterious globes of light that hover in midair (http://www.qsl.net/w5www/bragg.htm [accessed April 3, 2003]).

9. My interview with Blake was conducted with her aunt, Vivinea Page, and her uncle, Truman Page. Thus, she is the only student who consented to the use of her name in my future applications of our interview.

10. To be fair, however, Ellis's scholarship demonstrates that he would never claim that adolescents' beliefs are insignificant based on traditions of drug use.

7

Ostensive Healing
Pilgrimage to the San Antonio Ghost Tracks

Carl Lindahl

As Linda Dégh and Andrew Vázsonyi explain in their essay "Does the Word 'Dog' Bite?" (Dégh and Vázsonyi 1983), people enact legends through ostension. Bill Ellis's essay "Legend-Trips and Satanism" (Ellis 1991) explores adolescents' ostensive behavior in the context of the "Satanic panic" of the 1980s. Dégh, Vázsonyi, and Ellis discuss ostensive behavior that authorities perceive as dangerous and possibly criminal. Considering ostension in a new way, Carl Lindahl explains that it can inspire a sense of wonder. For those who participate in a legend trip to a place where something wondrous happens, the trip may seem more like a pilgrimage by reverential travelers than a jaunt by rebellious thrill seekers.

The kind of ostension that happens during legend trips has a close connection to the age of the trip's participants. For teenagers who sneak out together late at night, rebellious activity can seem very appealing. For the legend trippers Lindahl describes—members of families who belong to San Antonio's Hispanic community—there is no need to defy adult norms. Older and younger family members come together with a common interest in watching something miraculous take place. If they watch very closely, they may see their car move uphill when its gearshift is in neutral—and if they are very lucky indeed, they may see the handprints of small spectral children appear on their car's rear windshield.

The search for something amazing at the San Antonio train tracks is part of the "gravity hill" phenomenon that exists across the United States. On Sweet Hollow Road in New York and on Spook Hill near Lake Wales, Florida, as well as at numerous other locations, people claim that their cars go uphill when the gearshift is in neutral. The movement of an unpowered car goes against our understanding of science and suggests the presence of a supernatural or religious power. More specifically, tiny handprints on the car's rear windshield suggest that spirits of the dead have visited the living.

DOI: 10.7330/9781607328087.c007

According to Lindahl, this kind of experience can "transcend horror and inspire a sense of wonder in those who bring legends to life." As legend trippers take on various roles to explore a haunted place, they feel excited and expectant. Whether or not they believe that something miraculous has happened in such places, they may derive great satisfaction from participating in the "sacred dimensions of ostension."

L<small>INDA</small> D<small>ÉGH INTRODUCED FOLKLORISTS TO OSTENSION</small>, the sincerest form of imitation: the process through which people live out legend, making it real in the most palpable sense. Dégh's landmark essay "Does the Word 'Dog' Bite?" (Dégh and Vázsonyi 1983) examined ostension primarily as a criminal process, most relevant to such monstrous events as one that occurred in Houston in 1974 when Ronald "Candy Man" O'Bryan used legends of tainted Halloween candy as a cover to poison his own son on Halloween night (Grider 1984; Sauke 2003). Subsequent studies (e.g., Ellis 1989a) have dwelt upon the horrors that result when legends become scripts for people compelled to personify the frightening forces that intrude upon the innocence of everyday life and drag away victims who never return.

Ostension may be calculatingly conscious, as in the case of Candy Man O'Bryan, or the result of an unconscious, delusional compulsion, as dramatized on April 18, 1986, when Juana Leija performed her fatal imitation of La Llorona. The best-known Hispanic legend in Houston, La Llorona concerns a married woman who, betrayed by her husband, flies into a rage and kills her own children by tossing them into a river. Juana Leija now recalls that "she had no idea what would happen next" (Ruiz 2001, 30A; see also Axtman 2001; Tolson 2001) when she gathered her seven children, put them on a bus, rode with them to downtown Houston, walked them to a bridge spanning Buffalo Bayou and, in plain sight of the city's central police station, picked them up one by one and threw them into the water. Six children had hit the water and two had drowned by the time passers-by managed to save the remaining four. The great majority of the residents of Houston's Hispanic neighborhoods may be unfamiliar with the term *ostension*, but they are fully familiar with its underlying concept. Hispanic students entering my folklore classes in the days following the Leija murders brought reports from their families and friends about the distraught mother who had "turned into La Llorona." Through such headline-making crimes, folklorists have come to recognize ostension as the most terrifying evidence imaginable of the negative potential of folk narrative.

Despite scholars' concentration on criminal imitations, there is ample evidence that ostension can transcend horror and inspire a sense of wonder in those who bring legends to life. Like role-playing criminals, would-be saints create for themselves a scripted world infected with violence, but the saint enters that world ostensively as the victim rather than the villain, and in the process of death is transformed into a spiritual hero.[1] Similarly, pilgrims to shrines such as Saint Patrick's Purgatory in Ireland pass through a ritualized death and resurrection, mortifying themselves into another world that they regard as far better, not far worse, than the world they have temporarily left behind (Turner and Turner 1978, 104–139).

Unlike many of those influenced by her work, Dégh has always recognized the complex implications of her concept and has continually spoken about the potential for more innocent forms of ostension inherent in the actions of those who set out on nighttime quests to "induce the reenactment of [a] tragic event from the past" (Dégh and Vázsonyi 1983, 20; see also Dégh 2001, 422–428). Such legend quests constitute a sort of *ostensive play*, an improvised drama in which the players, visiting the site of a haunting or the scene of a crime, take on, by turns, the roles of legend villains and victims as they both re-create the storied events and simultaneously expand the tale by adding their experiences to the core narrative (Lindahl 1993). Yet at certain times these imitations transcend play and open windows to another world, creating occasions for both terror and pious rapture.[2]

In the same Houston neighborhoods where stories of Juana Leija melted together with legends of La Llorona in the 1980s, there also thrive accounts of a tragedy, distant in both time and place, and of its persisting supernatural echoes. These accounts are so compelling that many who hear and retell them undertake long journeys to live momentarily inside the legend. In the process, these legend-trippers express an extraordinary range of ostensive action, from thrill-seeking play to humbled reverence. I explore here this phenomenon through the accounts of one young woman, Lydia Z., a twenty-two-year-old student at the University of Houston who spent only a few minutes at the legend site but for whom the legend of the San Antonio ghost tracks realizes all the playful, scary, and sacred dimensions of ostension.

THE LEGEND OF THE GHOST TRACKS

Among the most popular legend-tripping destinations in Texas is an isolated railroad crossing at the southern extreme of San Antonio. I have yet to meet a San Antonio Hispanic who has not heard the legend of the train tracks. More than a hundred Hispanics from the San Antonio area have shared with me accounts of a school bus crushed by a train and of the lingering presence of the spirits of the children slain in the crash. All but three of these tellers have visited the crossing to test for themselves the validity of the claims that the dead children will reveal themselves to those who seek them.

At the core of the train tracks legend is a "gravity hill" phenomenon: people who visit the scene by car drive slowly (and at least seemingly) upward along a gradual incline toward the tracks. Stopping short of the rails, the driver shifts the car into neutral, and the car seems to roll uphill and over the tracks in defiance of gravity. There are many similar gravity hill sites in the United States, and many of the people (especially non-Hispanics) who visit the San Antonio train tracks from afar do so simply for the thrill of defying gravity without any prior knowledge of a legend associating the site with the mass death of children. Legends told outside the Hispanic community often dwell first and foremost on the gravity hill dimensions of the site and treat the story of the bus secondarily, if at all.[3] Many non-Hispanic versions of the legend tend to treat the children cursorily.

If we seek a normal form for the San Antonio train tracks narrative, perhaps we can do no better than the dry version that I found posted more or less verbatim, as follows, on several different currently accessible Internet sites:

Once, there was a tragic accident on a set of train tracks: A busload of children was crossing the tracks, and could not get out of the way in time to avoid the approaching train. The train smashed into the bus, killing most of the children and the driver survived. Now, if your car stalls out on the tracks, it will be pushed over the tracks to safety before the train hits you. The ghosts of the children have saved you, and sometimes you can see their small handprints in the dust on your car. The most well known example of this urban legend are the haunted train tracks in San Antonio, Texas. [This account differs from those known to Lydia in only one major detail: in Lydia's version there were no survivors; the female driver died along with the children.][4]

Except for the last few words identifying San Antonio, this text is exceedingly spare, unrooted in either time or place. Lacking the specificity that gives life to legends when they are actually told, this skeletal narrative imparts an almost Märchenesque air of distance and abstraction. It begins "Once, there was" and proceeds to read like one of the short summaries familiar to those acquainted with *The Types of the Folktale* (Aarne and Thompson 1961). The text's most legendary trait is a string of thirteen

Ostensive Healing

Figure 7.1. The "Ghost Tracks," San Antonio, Todos Santos 2003. As night falls, carloads of adults and children gather along the ghost tracks after crossing them to compare their experiences. Photo by Carl Lindahl.

words that present the all-important evidence to validate its supernatural claim: "sometimes you can see their small handprints in the dust on your car."

The legend may simply be a "type" when told on the Internet, but when told in Houston it is fundamentally a Hispanic legend—and a very important one.[5] Hispanic legend-trippers tend to seek and feel more at the train tracks than non-Hispanics do; many come to the site essentially as pilgrims. In June of 2001, I spoke with a vanload of girls, all dressed in their Catholic school uniforms, who had driven 275 miles that night from Brownsville, Texas, simply to drive over to the tracks and then back home; on Todos Santos (All Saints Day) 2003, one couple drove 200 miles from Houston and a second couple came 150 miles from Corpus Christi to be at the tracks at that special time; all these pilgrims were Hispanic. Similarly, Lydia traveled in a party of thirteen, ranging from six months to more than fifty years of age, who drove from Houston to park their rented van at the desolate stretch of tracks for the purpose of experiencing both a thrill and a miracle.

Lydia's account of the train tracks is not merely a narrative but a continually relived experience in which legend embraces legend-tripping; both blend into ostension, and ostension inspires both terror and reverent wonder. I know nobody who lives more thoroughly with, or more complexly and animatedly through, legendry than Lydia. She can move into "legend mode" at the slightest suggestion; Lydia's recorded words, which dominate this article, are a case in point. As a full-time mother, dutiful daughter, full-time student, and part-time employee, Lydia had trouble finding the time to sit down with me to tell her stories of and reflections on the train tracks. Finally, we found a brief time slot that allowed her to visit my university office between dropping her daughter off at a day-care center and driving her mother to the dentist. All of the remarkable quotations that follow are taken from this ninety-minute session. I find it embarrassing that many of us who are paid richly and full-time to study, catalog, and (too often) discredit legends do not ultimately tell half as much about why we should study them as Lydia—stopping to catch her breath between her child's crisis and her mother's needs—told me in just over an hour.

Lydia is an animated narrator. Her words revisit her fears so effectively that in listening I did not merely share the excitement she felt when she first visited the train tracks, but also felt as if I had been there before. Once into her story, Lydia often speaks with breathless speed, stringing together as many as four or five sentences with no hint of a pause between them. She sometimes punctuates these bursts of narration by stopping suddenly to dwell with startling emphasis on a single word, which she then repeats to intensify the effect. Dialogue repeatedly breaks into her narration. As in classic ballads, she presents actors without introducing them. Her voice simply shifts to impersonate her fellow participants—sometimes as individuals (her boyfriend Lonnie, her baby Danielle, the unnamed driver of the van), but more often as a kind of chorus: the *we* who drove to the tracks together, or the *they* who do not share her beliefs.

I have never heard Lydia tell the train tracks legend simply, in a discrete linear narrative sequence, largely because nearly everyone to whom she talks has heard numerous previous accounts. Like many legend-ritual complexes, the San Antonio train tracks tale possesses a relatively thin etiological core but an extraordinarily rich ritual component, which generates resonant experiences for those who visit the site; these visitations in turn give rise to narratives far more elaborate than the core story, which becomes secondary in the telling. Lydia's initial description of the legend-trip is relatively undramatic and only marginally narrative:

> Well, when I went I was still with my ex-boyfriend [Lonnie], so we went (. . . just like . . . a family outing thing), and . . . we were in a *huge* van, and, we happened to be in the very back, back seat of the van . . . We didn't *see*

anything, but when we got out, you know, we saw the little prints and all that. That was really cool. And we felt it being pushed and all that. The guy that was driving: *"I swear I didn't touch anything. I didn't touch anything. I swear! I swear! It wasn't me"* [laughing] . . . He had . . . it in neutral. And we were sitting there, and all of a sudden this *huge* . . . I guess it must have been like a fifteen-passenger van . . . You could feel it being pushed over, like it was nothing. It was really cool. It was something else. It really was.[6]

In Lydia's life with this legend, there was a long and intermittent prototext to the visit itself. Even in relating her earliest recollections, Lydia tells little of the story, but instead visits the tracks in her imagination: she emphasizes the physical setting of the train wreck and focuses on the experience of those who went to the tracks before her. Her memories of the first train tracks stories she heard flow naturally into her recent experience as a legend-tripper:

I remember hearing it as far as I can remember. When I was in elementary school. We all always used to talk about it, about the kids and the train tracks and how sad it was, and how spooky it would be to see the little handprints—and then of course there would always be somebody: "Oh yeah. I went and did that and it's true." And—but the thing that I found consistent throughout the years was that it was always where you couldn't see around the corner, like . . . the train was coming this way [gesturing to the left] you couldn't see that side. And you *couldn't*. It was true when we got there. There's a—I want to say, kind of a wall, but it's just huge trees and bushes and . . . if you go farther there's like a baseball field and that's like the *only* light that's out there. But . . . it's weird, because . . . you can't really see around that corner till you get right on top of it . . . Like at night. It's really spooky to do that at night [laughter].

On Lydia's trip and in her later narrations, the legend—and the trippers' experiences of the supernatural—extended far beyond the simple core of the story as it is normally told. In Lydia's account, not only the railroad crossing, but the entire surrounding region, was suffused with the supernatural, and there were other spirits nearby besides those of the children. Here Lydia describes a narrative and experiential dimension of her trip that does not factor in any of the hundreds of accounts I have heard orally or collected on the Internet:

There're supposed to be two bridges that . . . you pass before you get there, and I don't know the story behind it. All I know is there's supposed to be like these ghostly dogs with red eyes that are supposed to be haunting these bridges, right? So, you know . . . we're ready to do stuff. We're waiting to see the dogs, driving back and forth, looking around. And we didn't see . . . them on the bridge at least. But when we went up and over the railroad tracks . . . we turned [on] this long road that . . . goes alongside the tracks: a *long* like dirt road. Well, in this huge van, there's like nowhere to make a U-turn . . . to come back. So we ended up turning about . . . a mile down the road . . . and we were coming back, and . . . I was looking . . . out my side of the window, looking at the trees, and *I see these* like glowing things—it was like [whispering], "What's that?" And I touched the person in front of me, and I was like, "What's that? What's that? Tell me I'm not seeing something." And everyone was . . . pressing against the windows, and the driver was like, "What? What? What's the matter? What's the matter? What's wrong?" And by now we're all spooked out, we're scared. Everybody has goose bumps. We see, we *see*, these four red glowing things . . . staying steady with the van, and as we get up to the train tracks, you know, we don't see them anymore. And we're like [whispering], "Sssh! Be quiet. Be quiet. Do you hear any barking? Do you hear any barking?" We couldn't hear it, but we saw that there were . . . four glowing things. We assumed that those were the dogs. But you know. We don't *know* that. And . . . there wasn't any reason for anyone to be in there—unless, you know, they were trying to play a prank or whatever: "Oh, these are tourists. Let's scare them"—or whatever. But that, that was really weird.

We really got scared. We didn't get out of the van until, I think, we stopped at a gas station right . . . after we got onto the freeway, and that's where we saw the handprints.

[I asked Lydia: "So you didn't get out of the van to look right after you crossed the tracks?"]

No! We were like [breathless and half laughing], "No, we're not going to get out of the van! No. They're going to follow us, they're going to do something—the ghosts are going to do something bad to us because we were—we were acting stupid . . . I know they're going to hurt us."

Lydia and her friends had driven 200 miles to visit this special site, but they never set foot outside their van.

To this point, Lydia's extended account could have been told similarly, if not as dramatically, by any number of college-age legend-trippers. The first major difference signaling the special nature of Lydia's community is that this band of trippers numbered not only teens, but also grandparents, parents, and a baby:

The driver was in . . . his late thirties . . . I have to think of how we were sitting . . . the girl . . . in the passenger seat . . . was . . . about twenty-four, and then the next row back was . . . Lonnie's mother and his aunt. His mother . . . was in her mid-forties and her sister . . . was in her fifties. And there was some older people, and then there was some of us that were younger and then there was people that were younger than us—like, teens—and, then, my daughter was with us.

It is when Lydia begins talking about her infant daughter's presence in the van that her story deepens.[7] The baby's vulnerability requires special precautions at the tracks. The baby's father must use a blessed object to protect her:

Danielle was with us too. I was . . . still kind of like, "I don't want to take her, Lonnie. . . . I want to go, but I don't want to just leave her with your uncle." He was like, "Well, let's just take her." And . . . I guess it was me being superstitious or whatever, because I mean—you grew up listening to everything—and then you have certain things that you stick to regardless of how silly it sounds. Well, it just so happens that my grandmother had given Lonnie this . . . when you make your first Communion, you get like this little . . . I want to say it's like a flint-kind-of-material necklace, and it's got the Sacred Heart on one side and then a picture of Jesus on the other. Well, she had it. Before my grandmother got sick, she used to go to Mexico a lot, and go to the churches and get things blessed and everything. Well, she got a blessing. At that point in time she really liked Lonnie, and you know, she wanted us to make it, so she gave this to him as a present from her . . .

And he kept it wrapped up in a plastic bag so it wouldn't get messed up, and he gave it to my little girl and he told the baby, "Hold this, while we go over the train tracks, okay?" And [in a singsong baby voice] you know, she's just sitting there going "ah-ah-ah-ah-ah"—and so she's hanging on to it. So you know, we gave her that kind of like to protect her—because she's still a little kid. And then, from what *we* believe in . . . that negative energy [can] gravitate towards . . . the younger children, because they haven't hit that point to where they cross over to being, like, a young adult. You know, children and adolescents, they are still like, kind of *stuck*. So the spirits or whatever it is—gravitate towards them. That's why the little kids can see the ghosts, or they can see things, and you're like, "No, that's not there." And they say [exuberant childlike voice], "Yes, it's right there." So it makes you wonder if the little kids are really telling you the truth when [people] say they have *imaginary* friends . . . That kind of explains that a little bit.

So we gave her that [Sacred Heart], and she held on to it, and she was fine, but we gave it to her . . . to protect her, because I didn't want anything to happen to her. I don't know what . . . other [people do] . . . But I was just a little bit more cautious.

The way in which Lydia described taking her baby to a site where children had died suggested a special notion that children—both living and dead—serve in some way or another to guide their mortal elders in matters of the spirit.[8] I had to ask Lydia more about this, especially about how Lydia attributes this belief to a number of people in her community and particularly about whom she was referring in saying "we believe." She answered,

> It's something that we've always thought of . . . I know my family, and . . . Lonnie's family too, the way he was brought up—I mean—to *me*, that explains a lot. I mean, not everybody believes that. [With] kids, some people are just like, "Uh, crazy"—and you know, seeing things . . . imaginary playmates, or whatever. You know, "Child's unhappy," but—I think that that's true. I really do. That's just the way I was brought up . . .
>
> They're so innocent that they don't *know* they're not supposed to see that . . . They haven't been taught you're not supposed to see things like that. They really don't know . . . You know, my little girl—my uncle died not too long ago. And . . . he had lived with her for a couple months, so she had become close to him, and she liked him a lot. And his name is Daniel. And her name is Danielle . . . I didn't intend *to do* that when I named her, but when . . . he found out what her name was, he told me that he—even though he knows that she wasn't named after him, that he was just very honored that I gave her that name. And so, she got to be close to him and stuff, and then, you know, he *died*. He died of a heart attack, and it happened that . . . Danielle was with her dad that weekend. And when I got Danielle back . . . I didn't tell Danielle. And we were at home, and she told me, "Mommy, where is Uncle Daniel?" I said, "What do you mean, 'where's Uncle Daniel?'" Because—I mean, she's going through that stage where she can talk very well, but she can't put the right words in order, you know. She can get her point across, but sometimes it's out of order.
>
> And she said, "Mommy, I saw Uncle Daniel yesterday."
>
> And I said, "You *did? Where?*" And I wasn't telling her anything.
>
> She says—"He was at my Grandma Mercy's house, and he sat on the couch, and he said, he said he had to tell me bye."
>
> I said, "Are you sure, Baby? Were you asleep?"
>
> "No. No. I was sitting there and my daddy wasn't there, and *he* walked into the room, Mommy. He was there. I saw him."
>
> And [laughing nervously] it really kind of gave me the creeps. I was like, "Oh, no." It was like, "No—my child, do not . . . don't tell me things like that, because I don't know whether to cry, or"—I mean, I *believed* her, because I mean, she has no reason to make something up like that. And she didn't *know* what happened. So—and then when I told my mom that, *oh, my gosh*, my mom bawled her eyes out. She was just crying, crying, crying . . . that was her closest [brother]—she was very, very close to him. And so, you know, when I told her that, it, it, it made her cry, but then she felt,

Ostensive Healing

Figure 7.2. The "Ghost Tracks," San Antonio, Todos Santos 2003. Many who cross the tracks bring their children and ask them to sit outside, in the backs of their vehicles, to see if they will sense the presence of the ghosts pushing them over the tracks. Photo by Carl Lindahl.

well, at least he told her "bye." You know, at least she got a chance to see him, he got a chance to see her, because he really liked her. He did . . . He just thought she was something else. So—like that's, the kids seeing things and all that.

When a child dies very young it's really sad, because they didn't get to live their whole life . . . I think it does have some sort of connection, for some reason . . . What I've always believed is that if a child dies young, or even if an adult dies at a young age . . . that they go on to be like a guardian angel or something. And . . . I think it makes people feel *safe* that the kids are just so innocent. And they don't know any kind of wrongs, and all they want to do is, you know, when something like that happens, is they do become a guardian for somebody. They just want to protect and make sure that the person's okay. I've always heard that growing up and maybe it's just our culture that, you know, they teach us that . . . it explains a lot of things.

This reference to the sanctity of the children reminded me of another account of a visit to the train tracks that Lydia had told me earlier that day. This story had rushed into Lydia's mind—and apparently into the minds of the others at the tracks—at the moment they had reached the peak of the fear:

> I remember hearing . . . that, a group of friends, they went, and they were just in a regular car, and they did the whole powder thing [that is, they dusted the trunk of their car with talcum powder in order to see the handprints of the ghostly children once the car crossed the tracks], and they waited, and they got pushed over. And one of the people in the car said [dismissive tone], "No, no, it's not true." Whatever. Whatever. "It's . . . nothing . . . there's got to be an explanation." Well, they did it again. You know, they re-powered the car—and this time, along with the little kids' prints, there was big handprints, too! So that really spooked them out, they were like, "No. Don't make fun of it. Don't make fun of it. Just let is happen and just don't say anything bad, because . . . it could come back and get you . . . You know. We played around. You better watch it, because it'll come back and get you."

In Lydia's view, if the task of the youngest dead is to protect the living, the task of the elder dead is to protect the ghostly children:

> I think maybe they saw it as like a warning . . . I've always heard about the . . . small handprints, and then over the years I've heard about . . . the larger handprints, and . . . I've always just thought of it as . . . the adult that died with them, the bus driver, is protecting them, you know, they couldn't protect the kids . . . when it happened, but that's maybe their way of . . . protecting the children from being exposed to too much . . . You know. A little bit is okay . . . and everyone wants to experience the supernatural thing, but if you push it, and you make fun of it . . . It's like, "Okay, well fine, you don't believe it. Go away. You don't need to be here. No. *I'm, I'm* protecting these children."

This particular point in the group's journey signals a sort of climactic clash of the two sets of understandings and expectations that the family had brought with them to San Antonio that night. Undoubtedly, most or all of the family had come looking for thrills and terror—and they had encountered more than enough of both to satisfy themselves. Equally, most had brought with them a sense of pious awe—a conviction as palpable as the holy object that Lonnie had placed in his baby's hand—that there was something spiritual about this journey. Listening to Lydia's voice and story leap back and forth between the poles of frisson and faith, I was filled with an often confusing sense of two supernatural worlds opening up simultaneously, as if I were watching a horror film projected on a church altar screen as Mass was in progress.

Repeatedly throughout her account, Lydia portrayed in identical terms the taboo thrills of legend-trippers and the miracles effected by the sacred nature of children: "spooky," "creepy," and "weird" are the most common words to describe both sorts of experience. Furthermore, whether describing the thrill or the miracle, she used the same vocal style, performing both with a breathlessness underpinned by an ever-present hint that nervous laughter might erupt, as it often did. There was an undertone of barely containable hysteria—even joyous hysteria—that continually put a haunting edge on her voice.

In performance, Lydia seemed to give both kinds of supernatural experience equal validity and approval. But at—and only at—the point in her telling where she described the peak of her fear did she choose between them. This is the moment:

> We were like [breathless and half laughing], "No, we're not going to get out of the van! No. They're going to follow us, they're going to do something—the ghosts are going to do something bad to us because we were—we were acting stupid . . . I know they're going to hurt us, because we didn't *believe* that they were there—and now we see that they *are* and, no, we're not going to get out of the van."

At no other time, in more than a year of intermittent prior reports and performances, had Lydia ever hinted that she or her companions harbored the slightest doubt about the existence of the child ghosts.

I immediately asked her, "So none of you believed it?"

Lydia quickly retracted the notion of disbelief, but even her retraction offers a greater intimation of doubt than she had revealed at earlier times.

> Oh, we all thought . . . we knew it was going to happen. It's just that—we knew, but still, we hadn't gone through it. You know, we knew it would happen, because we'd heard from so many people that it's real . . . and we even all saw it on TV that one time when they profiled it on the news. And we were like, "Okay, well, yeah, it happens. Let's go see if it—" When you *actually* go through it, it's different . . . You feel a little adrenaline rush, you get all tense and you: "Oh my God, this is actually happening." It's an experience. It really is . . . I liked it. It was fun. But I wouldn't want to do it by myself . . . I would have to have people around me.

This, in greatly abridged form, is Lydia's account of her legend-trip to the San Antonio train tracks.

ON THE BORDERS OF OSTENSIVE HEALING AND OSTENSIVE PLAY

Lydia's intense and varied experience of the ghost tracks legend challenges us to deepen our thinking about legend in general. I, for one, would like to see more and deeper examinations of legend as pious thrill, because such experiences constitute a rich part of both Lydia's and her community's lives with legend. Apparently, most of the people in Lydia's party regarded their legend-trip as a religious experience through which they sought not to test their faith but to use it. Nevertheless, most experienced more immediately the thrill of a good scare, and only later a deeply spiritual sense of well-being. For Lydia and her boyfriend's family, the journey to the train tracks was an exercise in both positive and negative ostension. The family went to the train tracks to play the roles of the victims, the children who died there. The sense of connection the family felt with the children was deep indeed, a fact conveyed by Lydia's previously quoted words about the spiritual nature of children. The connection grows even stronger when we consider Lydia's mother's reflections on *why* the children's spirits appear at the tracks at all. She has never been to the site, but she has heard the story most of her life:

> [People] who have witnessed it, they have never said . . . that it's scary . . . It just sends chills through them because it's kind of a scary *feeling*, but if it is their spirits . . . I would want to see them, because I would want to say a prayer for them. I don't know if that area has ever been blessed in any way, but I'm sure that the spirits are there trying to reach out to people who have some kind of a faith to say a prayer for them . . . that they are with God.[9]

According to Lydia and her mother, one visits the tracks not only to step into the roles of the dead children but also to perform a kind of ostensive healing of their ghosts. A trip to the tracks may fill the need of the children's souls to save others, an act through which the pilgrims in turn help save themselves.

> [I asked Lydia if it would be too much to suggest that their journey was a pilgrimage. She answered:] We traveled a long way to go there, and that was the intended place to go. And we stayed there for a little bit . . . when we left, we were . . . praying [laughs]. We were like, "God, I hope we didn't do anything bad. Please don't punish us for this." We just wanted to . . . to see if . . . it was going to happen. Because . . . I heard sometimes that it *didn't* happen . . . And like [whispering], "Please, don't, don't punish us for all this—we're sorry. We didn't do anything bad, we just—" I guess maybe you could call it a pilgrimage, and not like great, great distances traveled, but I mean we went from here to San Antonio with the intention of seeing that.

Evidently, Lydia has a paradigm for pilgrimage against which she measures the San Antonio trip. The one criterion that fits least well is that, to her, 200 miles might not constitute a distance sufficient for the standards of a pilgrimage. Keep in mind that her grandmother would travel hundreds of miles into Mexico to obtain sacred objects or have them blessed. Lydia realizes that the prayers of her group fall in their proper structural slot, but she maintains a humble and comic awareness that these prayers were failures because the group was praying for themselves and not for the dead children. On one level, however, the prayers may not be indicative of failure, a point to which I shall return.

Simultaneously, perhaps equally, and—Lydia might say—as the inevitable result of the flawed nature of humans older and less innocent than the children who haunt the tracks, the group that gathered there was at least potentially there to hurt the children—even against their will—through their otherwise innocent delight in a good scare. They approached the haunted site a little too enthusiastically, with attitudes a bit too irreverent to suit the tragic circumstances that they were commemorating in their nighttime ritual. This polar experience—of thrill and miracle—forms a kind of dialectic in the daily lives of Lydia and her community. This is not the dialectic of belief and disbelief that Dégh (Dégh and Vázsonyi 1973; Dégh 1995b) has so compellingly described, because here both poles are positive—both affirm belief and project that "what if" quality upon which the most powerful legends feed.

Furthermore, this dialectic of scary belief and pious belief only rarely embodies the tensions that emerge in the dialectic Dégh describes. Of all the narrations and evaluations Lydia shared with me, it was only at the violent crux at the train tracks that scary and godly beliefs at least *seemed* to come into conflict. Perhaps the reason for this is that the scary and the holy occupy different, if overlapping and interdependent, places in the lives of Lydia and her community. The scary is dramatic, the pious meditative. Lydia loves her thrills and at certain moments, as at the scariest point of the pilgrimage, the thrill is all, but it soon vanishes. Almost immediately afterward the thrill is gone. The thrill is a thing in itself, and a good thing, but the point of the thrill is to transcend it, to reach a point where the adrenaline diminishes and a person can reflect on the intimations of the sacred that the thrill has opened up.

DIALECTIC, DOUBT, AND HEALING IN MAL OJO AND AT THE TRACKS

My second observation concerns the legend dialectic as it is generally understood. There is no greater affirmation of the importance of Dégh's characterization of legend as debate than the fact that even those narrators who consider themselves dyed-in-the-wool believers often internalize the debates swirling around their beliefs. As Lydia's climactic description affirms, the numinous is the numinous precisely because it almost always lies beyond our experience. We may live day in and day out buoyed by thoughts of miracles, but miracles would not be miracles if they happened every day. The thrills of the scare relieve the pattern of everyday life, but the revelations that follow deepen that pattern. In her narratives, Lydia tests her own belief as much as others test it. Her ritual activities and later narrated recollections are both ways of simultaneously expressing doubt and overcoming it. Both the group outing to the tracks and Lydia's narrated memories of that trip serve Lydia's community as bonding mechanisms, ways of enhancing relationships within families and among friends as the group works through doubts to express its convictions.

Another dimension of Lydia's internalized doubt is that, since entering college, she has been exposed to diverse people—cultural outsiders—who question, rather than take for granted, her beliefs and rituals. The dialectic that Lydia presents in performing for me has been conditioned by the expectation that outsiders like myself will have doubts. I find it difficult to generalize about someone so undeniably and masterfully *herself* as Lydia—but anyone who listens to her at length will note that she persistently refers to her beliefs and convictions as things that are shared within a certain group. When speaking of her personal beliefs, she invariably extends them to larger worlds, using such terms as "we" and "our community." Because Lydia does sometimes refer specifically to "my family" and "Lonnie's family," we might too quickly infer that she is speaking solely about the family of her birth and her boyfriend's family when she says "we" or "us." But she also talks about "my race"—in most contexts, a "politically incorrect" term from which many of us shrink. Among Texas Mexicans, "race" is the English cognate of the Spanish *raza*, and one of the most common terms of cultural pride in Texas is *La Raza* (The Race). La Raza carries a special, positive meaning for Mexican Americans, for whom it signifies a culture born from the coming together of colonial Spanish and colonized Native American populations—people who were considered tainted by miscegenation and judged imperfect because of their "mixed" race. It is an act of defiance for Mexican Americans to seize upon the term that condemned them to marginality and then apply it to themselves: rather than being trapped between races, "We, the Hispanics, are *the* race." In Lydia's legend dialectic, she sometimes characterizes the believers as "Catholic," "my family," or "Lonnie's family," but the major field is "Hispanic." Most of the believers are Hispanic, and most of the doubters are not.[10]

In her narrations of the supernatural, Lydia capitalizes on doubt to effect conversion. In our conversations, she has described her family rituals to neutralize the effects of evil eye, or *mal ojo*, a tradition widespread among Mexican Americans in Houston—but also very particularly described by Lydia as a means through which parents bond with their children. Mal ojo is most often caused inadvertently when strangers admire or envy someone; the affliction can be averted if the stranger touches the victim before the illness sets in; otherwise, relatives or friends of the victim must employ a domestic religious ritual to drive the illness out of the victim's body and into an egg.[11]

> Blessing the egg, right? . . . I do that all the time with my daughter . . . take the egg—start blessing her. And then you're supposed to put it on a windowsill where the moonlight's supposed to hit it and her guardian angel or whoever protects her, her protector—is supposed to take all the . . . evil that people wished on her, intentionally or unintentionally—supposed to take it away and it's supposed to cook the egg . . . It's *really weird*, because I've seen it work. I really have . . . You know, some people are like, "Well," you know, or "Whatever—the kid got over whatever she, whatever happened." You know? They don't believe in it, but I mean, it was done to me when I was a child, and I do it for my daughter. It was done to my mother when she was a child, and she did it to me, so . . . it's something we've always done.
>
> And it's weird, because like when my daughter starts crying . . . I'll take an egg and I'll bless her. And you're supposed to start at the top of the head and work your way down . . . The way I do it, I'll tell my daughter, "Okay, kiss the egg, and that will make it better." . . . That's just something *I* added . . . And *she* . . . stops crying, she calms down, and I don't know if it's maybe a psychological thing or not, but all I know is that it works . . . And sometimes when she's not feeling good, *she'll* go to the refrigerator and get an egg out: "Mommy, I want you to *do the egg on me* because I don't feel good." And I'll do it on her, and then she's fine. I've always believed in that. I think it works. It's just like when they give you a placebo, and they tell you that . . . it's medicine and it'll make you better, [but] it's just a [fake] pill, that's all it is, and you know, people believe . . . and then they get better . . . That would explain it scientifically, but—you know, if you're brought up . . . believing in it all your life, you know, *that's not going to cut it* [laughing].
>
> Now that I'm getting closer to finishing school, I'm getting to be friends with people that are a little bit older than me, and they have kids. And they're not Hispanic . . . they don't know . . . my cultural background or whatever, and . . . a lot of them happen to be either white or black . . .

you know, with my daughter going to day care . . . Some of the mothers talk and they're like, "I don't know what's wrong with her, but she's just acting up and she's running a fever."

And I say, "What religion are you?" You know, they're not Catholic. Like, okay, well. "I can tell you something that you can try," and I recommend doing the blessing of the egg.

And they'll come back to me, "Oh, my gosh, Lydia, that totally works. It calmed her down . . . I did what you said . . . and it was just something else, to see that."

And then I would say to them what ojo means.

By way of explanation: mal ojo is understood in one particular way far more than any other among my Mexican American students. If you see a baby and are thrilled and delighted by the sight, you can do that baby harm simply through the sheer force of the instantaneous surge of your often loving, sometimes envious or possessive feelings. The only way you can undo the harm before illness sets in is to touch the child. Mexican Americans are fully aware that this belief makes little sense to most outsiders. Thus, believers who are struck with a sudden, potentially hurtful ojo-causing admiration of gringo babies work out subtly nonthreatening strategies to touch the infant and thus ensure its safety. My most recent experience of this phenomenon occurred in May 2001 at a Mexican restaurant in Houston. I was sitting with a woman and her five-month-old baby. Many workers passed by and looked affectionately at this baby. As we were finishing the meal, our waitress came up and asked if she could hold the child. With the baby in her arms, she asked, "Can I take her back and show her to the girls in the kitchen? They think she's really cute." The waitress then carried the child safely out of the mother's eyeshot where the entire kitchen staff could touch her, to protect her.

I linger on this point because I see a direct parallel between mal ojo and Lydia's interpretation of what happened at the climactic moment of her visit to the tracks. Both in ojo and at the tracks, you can feel a great *rush* (to use Lydia's term) of feeling over what you've seen or sensed. That rush may be in many ways a good thing, innocent and *unconscious* (again, Lydia's word). But if you are (quoting Lydia) *stupid* or *don't believe* or forget that you believe, you can bring harm to the living baby or to the children's ghosts. Back to Lydia's narrative:

And then I would say to them [the gringos] what ojo means, and they're just like [awestruck, quivering voice], "Oh, you know what? Somebody *did*, like, 'that's a pretty little girl.' And they didn't touch her . . ."

"And if it works for you, keep doing it, you know, if you want to do it. I mean, it works for me because I've tried it."

"Thank you so much. Thank you, because we didn't know what was wrong with her, and we didn't want to take her to the *therapist*. Thank you so much."

Both at the tracks and in ojo, a sort of double salvation takes effect. The perpetrator of the unintentional harm crosses an emotional line and then takes steps to save her accidental victim. In ojo, the surge of feelings toward the child leads to a moment of realization that such emotional excess can cause harm. In touching the child, the perpetrator cures both the child and herself. At the train tracks, the process of double salvation becomes more complex: as the children rescue the pilgrims in their cars, the pilgrims give the children a chance to save themselves, or at least to exercise their need to do good. Further, in playfully saving the children, the pilgrims experience a thrill that takes them to a point beyond piety, at which they must penitently save themselves. The emotional rush—the frisson of recognition that they have entered the presence of the supernormal—is both a spiritual transgression and an instrument of salvation.

OSTENSIVE ACTION AT THE LEGEND SITE

Lydia's articulation of the miracle at the tracks, forceful and unique, is echoed in many aspects by the actions of those who visit the site, demonstrating that much of what Lydia says and believes is broadly representative of the shared faith and experience of many in her Texas-Mexican Hispanic community. Within that community, the truth of the tale of the ghostly children and the efficacy of ritual treatments for ojo are both subjects of some debate. The Catholic Church sanctions neither the ritual cure nor the "pilgrimage" to the train tracks; yet the folk Catholicism of South Texas continually reinforces the special religious dimensions of motherhood, infancy, and healing. Perhaps the three most popular pilgrimage sites in the region are the shrines consecrated to the Virgin of San Juan (San Juan, Texas) and to the Santo Nino, or "Blessed Infant" (San Antonio), as well as the unconsecrated shrine of the folk healer Pedro de Jaramillo (Los Olmos). This constellation—mother-child-healing—is central to Lydia's accounts of both mal ojo and the ghost tracks. Just as Mexican American women more commonly attend church and visit shrines than the men do, they also tell the story of the ghost tracks more often. Mark Glazer's research in the Lower Rio Grande Valley indicates that the ghost tracks tale is not only more popular among Hispanics than among non-Hispanics, but also more commonly told by and to Hispanic females than Hispanic males. Glazer reasons that the "motif of child ghosts" is a major cause of its popularity among women (Glazer 1989, 172).

Those choosing to visit the ghost tracks will not find themselves alone. In each of my three journeys to the tracks—taking place at varied times of day, from twilight to midnight—I was joined by at least a dozen cars full of people who crossed the tracks and then lingered on the downhill side to check each other's car bumpers for ghostly handprints and to share their current and past experiences. Two crucial dimensions of Lydia's account—the special spiritual nature of children and the sense of legend as pious thrill—were plainly apparent in the words and actions of these pilgrims.

Many adults come to the tracks with their own children, ranging in age from toddlers to young adults. At my second visit, a woman told me how she had first brought her child with her to the crossing when he was two years old. As unseen hands pushed her car over the tracks, her child grew suddenly wide-eyed and pointed to the windshield: he saw a child lying on the car's hood. The mother could not see the spirit, but the child could—and now, as a six-year-old, the boy still remembers what he saw that night. On my third visit, I met a woman who had just crossed the tracks with her child: she felt nothing particularly strange, but her son "felt something; he *really* did." Parents look to their children to see and feel *for them* things that they can no longer see and feel themselves.

The legend of the ghost tracks is a tale straining for wholeness. As Dégh has stated, "The greater the popularity of a legend within a group . . . the more and more conspicuous its incompleteness becomes" as it passes from teller to hearer to teller; this "fragmentary character of the modern legend is clearly related to its collective nature." Legend sharers "put together their pieces of knowledge" in communal gatherings (Dégh 1971, 62–63).

Searchers, restless as the ghosts they seek, revisit the shrine again and again, in hope of reaching an even deeper realization of some indefinable presence they already deeply feel. They share their quest with and ultimately pass it on to their children, through whom they hope to make a more direct contact with the other world. Those who came as children with their parents will likely return some day with their own children in tow.

In the space of one hour (5 to 6 p.m.) straddling sundown on November 1, 2003, I watched as thirty-three carloads of people performed the ritual of the tracks. The great majority of riders experienced the momentary thrill of feeling their cars being pushed over the rails. After stopping on

Ostensive Healing

Figure 7.3. The "Ghost Tracks," San Antonio, Todos Santos 2003. A father and daughter at the tracks. The father, who has been to the site many times and has sensed the presence of "something strange" while rolling over the tracks, asked his daughter to sit on his car trunk and tell him if she felt anything unusual. She did not. Photo by Carl Lindahl.

the other side to search for the miraculous ghostly hand- and fingerprints on the trunks of their cars, the pilgrims freely shared their stories and their faith with all interested parties. Most impressive to me was the testimony of one man who had brought his teenage daughter with him to the tracks. Dressed in the bright orange "trick or treat" T-shirt of a thrill seeker, he was simultaneously searching for something deeper. He told me that he had first been brought to the tracks by his parents, and he had felt something then. Later, as a teenager, he often revisited the tracks with friends. Once he spent the entire night there. Again, he felt something, but he could not explain what. Tonight—on Todos Santos (All Saints Day)—he was bringing his daughter to see what she would feel. As he placed his car in neutral, waiting for the ghostly push, he had his daughter sit on the car's roof, facing backward (toward the ghosts) with her feet on the trunk, to find out whether she could sense something miraculous. This father and many like him are pilgrims whose shrine is immanent, yet intangible, at the exact place where (and time when) their car tires touch the shoulder of the railroad tracks and they feel themselves pushed from behind. So they visit and revisit, hoping to achieve for even one second the complete communion of the living and the dead.

Among the hundreds of thousands who have visited the train tracks south of San Antonio, there are many who come simply to experience the thrill of a gravity hill; such legend-trippers have no particular knowledge of or interest in the tales of ghostly children.[12] For many Hispanics, however, the train tracks mark a semi-sacred site that verifies a constellation of culture-specific beliefs. What happens at the tracks both parallels and overlaps what happens at other cruces in Hispanic culture in which children, spirits, supernatural afflictions, and healing rituals converge. Hispanic pilgrims bring an entire constellation of beliefs and practices with them to the tracks, and they discover a pattern of intertwined social messages alongside the handprints left by the ghostly children on their cars.

NOTES

I would like to thank a number of people who contributed to this essay, especially Lydia Z. herself, who generously shared with me her words and experiences, granting me full permission to interview her and use that interview in the first version of this chapter, which I presented at the annual meeting of the International Society for Contemporary Legend Research in San Antonio, June 2001. Lydia has now apparently left the University of Houston, and I have been unable to show her the final version of the essay; I thus find it necessary to preserve a certain measure of anonymity for her by withholding her surname. Thanks as well to Mark Glazer and Sylvia Grider, who contributed important information, and to Diane Goldstein, Janet Langlois, Libby Tucker, and an anonymous *JAF* reviewer, who critiqued earlier versions of this work. Finally, my thanks, with fond memories, to the folklorists—Diane Goldstein, Elissa Henken, Cathy Preston, and Jeannie Thomas—who accompanied me in *communitas* on my first visit to the ghost tracks in June 2001.

This article is dedicated, with gratitude, to Linda Dégh, who has been the most important influence on my academic life. In my writing, I have tried not only to recognize her extraordinary contributions to legend theory but also to imitate (ostensively, if you will) her equally important practice of placing the narrator squarely at the center of folk narrative studies. Nothing a folklorist attempts to do is more vexing or more important than the search to discover how best to vocalize a folk artist—the most efficacious ways of stepping back or moving aside to help tradition bearers speak to those who would otherwise never have a chance to hear them. Great folk performers are often known for the humility and selflessness with which they share their arts. Almeda Riddle, for one, said that the best thing she could do for her singing was to let it interpret itself: "Get behind the song. If you get behind it, they'll see it. If you get in front of it, they'll just see you and get disgusted" (quoted in Lindahl 1997, 335). A great folklorist is no less humble than the folk artists she studies. She can receive no higher honor than having introduced us to a traditional artist who, largely through her efforts, is now as well known as she is. Thus it is through Linda Dégh (1989, 1995a, 1995b) we know Zsuzsanna Palkó, one of the outstanding narrators of twentieth-century European oral tradition, a woman of art and piety whose magic tales blessed the dead during night-long wakes and whose ritual treatments helped failing infants reach old age.

Thus, in this essay, I have spoken about ostension principally by seeking ways to let one young woman speak for herself. Lydia Z. is, like Zsuzsanna Palkó, both a narrator and a healer. Palkó—both the master storyteller and master healer of her village—was approaching seventy when Dégh (1995b) began to collect her stories. In contrast, when I first met Lydia, she was twenty-two years old, less than one-third the age of Aunt Zsusza, and just beginning to realize the potential of her narrating and healing. Neither as a storyteller nor as a healer can Lydia sound Palkó's depth of experience, yet I hope that in her words you have sensed, as I have, the presence of a future master of both media.

1. Without referring to the term *ostension* (which Dégh had not yet introduced to folklore studies), Victor Turner (1974) described the last acts of legendary Archbishop Thomas Becket and made a strong argument for the proposition that Becket crafted his own death as part of an ostensive drama.

2. Ostensive play is, fortunately, a much more common form of legend imitation than is ostension itself. Playful trips to haunted sites or ritualized play (as in the "Bloody Mary/Mary Whales" enactments that take place during adolescent sleepovers) are among the most common forms of legend performance. During the past twenty-three years, more than two-thirds of my University of Houston folklore students have reported that they have participated in such acts of ostensive play. For a discussion of another legend complex that moves beyond play to combine terror and pious rapture, see Lindahl 2004b.

3. Folklorist Sylvia Grider of Texas A & M University reports that, in more than twenty-five years of teaching in College Station (some 150 miles from the San Antonio train tracks), she has heard many of her students talk about San Antonio's gravity hill; she adds that a substantial number of them have made the 300-mile round trip to test the crossing for themselves. Among these students, the story of the school bus and the ghost children is seldom mentioned.

4. The text appears here as it does on the website Prophet31 (2004) with the exception of the term "train tracks," which I spell as two words; Prophet31 runs them together into "traintracks." Among the many web citations of the San Antonio ghost tracks, several involve research aimed at establishing what is "true" and "false" about the legend. None of these inquiries has been able to establish that a train-bus accident ever took place at the site or anywhere else in San Antonio (see, for example, Mikkelson 1998–2003, which asserts that horrific news accounts of an actual train-bus wreck that killed twenty-six schoolchildren in Utah in 1938 became the inspiration for the San Antonio story; see also Allen 2003). Other websites refer to experiments that have been conducted to test whether the cars are actually pushed uphill and over the tracks. One such site reports that "despite an *illusionary* appearance of a level, or even slightly inclined road, the street surface was actually at a two-degree declination as it approached the railroad track crossing" (Wagner 2017).

5. The keeper of one legend website (Obiwan 1998) conducted a survey to assess the relative popularity of four well-known "ghostly urban legends": "Bloody Mary," "The Vanishing Hitchhiker," "La Llorona," and the "Haunted Train Tracks." I quote: "Here are the results of the vote for January 1998 . . . There were 144 responses total . . . Almost 90% of the respondents, have heard of the legend of Bloody Mary. Wow! The Vanishing Hitchhiker story ran a close second . . . 78% . . . 42% have heard about some Haunted Traintracks. Only . . . 25% [of these] people have heard the story of La Llorona. This is to be expected, since the story is fairly restricted to the southwestern U.S."

This survey is of relevance to Lydia because in her community the relative popularity of these four legends exactly reverses the national results. I have not conducted a formal survey, but on the basis of twenty-four years of teaching folklore in Houston, I rate the legends known to my Mexican American students in the following order: La Llorona and the apparition of the Virgin of Guadalupe to Juan Diego are known to nearly all of them. The legend of the Devil in the Dancehall is known to about three-quarters. In the past five years, various accounts of the Chucacabra have vied with the Devil in the Dancehall in popularity. These are the only Mexican American legends currently better known that the Haunted Train Tracks. For similar findings on the popularity of "the Devil at the Dance," see Glazer (1984); for detailed studies of the popularity of "Gravity Hill" and other relevant legends in the Rio Grande Valley of South Texas, see Glazer (1985, 1986, 1989, and 1990).

In interviewing six Houston folklore classes about the legend of the train tracks, I have discovered that it was known to all of my Hispanic students and to one of my non-Hispanic students. Although many of my Hispanic students had not been to the site itself, all were able to situate it in San Antonio, and all knew people who had visited the tracks. Although Houston is 200 miles from San Antonio, the legend of the ghost tracks is a local legend for Houston Hispanics.

6. This and all other quotes from Lydia are transcribed from an audio-recorded interview conducted by the author on May 18, 2001. The quotes repeat Lydia's words exactly as spoken. No translation was necessary, for Lydia spoke in English almost exclusively and used Spanish only when referring to illnesses (such as *ojo* and *susto*) or concepts (*La Raza*) that are difficult to translate into English. For example, *ojo* is the equivalent of English "eye," but when used by Lydia, it refers to a supernaturally induced illness also called *mal ojo* ("evil eye") or *mal de ojo* ("eye ailment"). The great majority of Hispanic Houstonians I have interviewed, like Lydia, tend to retain the Spanish terms *ojo*, *susto*, and *La Raza* when speaking in English.

The transcription principles used here are identical to those employed and explained in Carl Lindahl's (2004a, xxxvii–xliv) *American Folktales from the Collections of the Library of Congress*. Ellipses indicate that words spoken by Lydia have been deleted from the transcription. The great majority of these deletions were repeated words and phrases such as "you know" and "like" that did not, in my opinion, contribute to the meaning of Lydia's performance. In oral performance such repetitions are often innocuous; in certain cases, they may even add to the effect of a performance. It is my judgment, however, that when they appear in written form, these expressions distract the reader; thus, convinced that it would be an injustice to Lydia's eloquence to include them, I deleted them.

7. As Lydia tells this account in May 2001, she is separated from her boyfriend Lonnie, the father of her daughter Danielle; but the two were still together when they drove to the train tracks.

8. The train tracks legend seems to resonate particularly for Lydia in her roles as woman and young mother. Some degree of corroboration for this suggestion can be seen in the statistical analyses of Mark Glazer (1990, 82), who has found that, when told among the Mexican American inhabitants of the Lower Rio Grande Valley, the San Antonio "Gravity Hill" legend is significantly more popular among females than among males, and that it is most often performed in informal conversations rather than in more formally structured "storytelling situations." In another analysis of the same legend, Glazer writes, "The fact that it tells of the deaths of small children and features ghosts who are children accounts for its strong feminine appeal" (Glazer 1989, 176).

9. Quoted from Lydia's student fieldwork project, in which she interviewed her mother for an assignment in my Introduction to Folklore class at the University of Houston, spring 2000.

10. Americo Paredes (1993a, 1993b) and William Madsen (1973, 70–71) have both noted divisions in the Texas Chicano community over issues of belief revolving around such ritual practices as the diagnosis and treatment of mal ojo. Madsen sees the divisions falling principally along class lines. The staunchest believers tend to be lower-class members of the community; nonbelievers are more likely to be middle-class Hispanics with a desire to assimilate. Madsen also discusses the concept of La Raza (17–25; see also Paredes 1993b).

11. Among Texas Mexicans, rituals for treating mal ojo may take many forms. Robert Trotter and Juan Antonio Chavira describe the ailment as it is typically understood and treated in the Rio Grande Valley of South Texas: *"Mal ojo* . . . is caused by persons with 'strong vision' admiring a child, a grown person, or an object. If these persons fail to touch whoever or whatever they are admiring, their strong vision causes that person to be ill or that object to be damaged. The symptoms in children are usually irritability, fever, headaches, vomiting, and drooping eyes. *Mal ojo* is treated by having the child lie down and sweeping him three times with an egg. The sweeping is done by forming crosses (*crucitas*) with the egg, on the child's body, starting at the head and going to the feet. While sweeping, the healer recites the Apostle's Creed three times, making sure that he sweeps both the front and the back. The egg is cracked and dropped into a glass or jar filled with water. The jar may then be placed on the child's head, and another Creed recited. The jar is then placed under the child's bed, usually under the place where the child rests his head. The next morning at sunrise the egg may either be burned or cast away" (1981, 92). There are numerous variations on this basic pattern, particularly in the way in which one "reads" the results of the ritual through the condition of the egg that has been passed over the child's body. Madsen states, "The formation of the egg indicates whether the diagnosis of evil-eye sickness was correct and the cure successful. The significance of the egg formation is interpreted in different ways. Some say that if the yolk rises to the center of the glass, it is a sure sign that the evil-eye sickness has been drawn out of the body. Others say that the egg white must form the shape of an eye on the surface of the water to indicate a successful cure. Still others maintain that the egg must look as though it has been cooked for a little while if the treatment has been effective" (1973, 78–79). Lydia's family uses the "cooked egg" diagnosis in their ritual, which differs from other rituals mentioned in the cited literature by having the egg placed on a windowsill rather than under the child's bed.

12. Although I saw non-Hispanic visitors at two of my three visits to the tracks—including African, Asian, and European Americans—some three-quarters of the visitors were Hispanic. There are two ways in which the behavior of Hispanic visitors both strongly echoes Lydia's accounts and differs markedly from the behavior of non-Hispanic visitors. First, all twelve of the carloads carrying two or more generations of pilgrims to the tracks were Hispanic families. Second, all of the seven adults who talked about their children's special power to sense the presence of the ghosts were Hispanic. In these two dimensions, the legend of the ghost tracks seems to be powerfully and perhaps uniquely Hispanic in nature.

8

Contemporary Ghost Hunting and the Relationship between Proof and Experience

Lynne S. McNeill

Since the turn of the twenty-first century, ghost hunting has appealed to an increasingly large number of people. The easy availability of related technology and the popularity of movies and TV shows about the supernatural have encouraged legend trips. Finding a variety of technological devices on the Internet, ghost hunters can plan to investigate an allegedly haunted place with maximal information and minimal expense.

As noted in our introduction, TV shows about ghost hunting drew huge audiences in the United States and the United Kingdom after the turn of the millennium. Since YouTube began in 2005, anyone with a video camera and a computer has been able to upload a video of a ghost hunt for others to watch. Certain ghost-hunt videos have attracted large numbers of viewers, inspiring some of them to make their own investigations of haunted places.

Of course, this form of entertainment is not new; the ancient Greeks explored haunted bathhouses, and the Victorians tramped around old mansions in England, hoping to find evidence of something spooky taking place. The British Society for Psychical Research, founded in 1882, gave ghost hunting a philosophical foundation and considerable prestige. Among the best-known early presidents of this society were William James, Andrew Lang, Henri Bergson, and Gilbert Murray.

Lynne McNeill's chapter chronicles the efforts and beliefs of early twenty-first century ghost hunters who use technological devices in their searches for supernatural evidence. EMF (electromagnetic filed) meters, cameras, tape recorders, night-vision scopes, and walkie-talkies are among the key devices that members of the American Association of Electronic Voice Phenomena use; so are dowsing rods, although these are less generally accepted. The purpose of this organization is to record ghosts' voices in order to provide "objective evidence" of life after death.

Surveying North American ghost hunters' methods of conducting their research, McNeill finds that "objective evidence" discovered through the use of scientific methods matters greatly to participants. Examining traditions of belief and disbelief, she asks key questions. Which tools will facilitate the most objective results, and how can people best use those tools? Can psychics assist in ghost hunts, or do they diminish objective validity? Do photographs provide reliable proof, or do voice recordings offer better evidence? And how do personal-experience narratives, sometimes called memorates, contribute to this process? This last question is of particular interest to folklorists. Finding that personal-experience stories enhance the persuasive power of ghost hunters' websites, McNeill notes that skeptical comments also appear on the sites, facilitating debate.

McNeill suggests that objective evidence is only part of ghost hunting's appeal; also very important is the "lure of the numinous," which comes from oral tradition and friendship networks. Telling memorates encourages more people to experience this lure. To what extent does belief rely upon proof? This essay supports discussion of multiple questions and opens the door for further study of ghost hunting.

ACCORDING TO THE FOUNDER of the American Association of Electronic Voice Phenomena, an organization built around the practice of recording phantom voices, the association was created "to provide objective evidence" of life after death (Butler and Butler 2001). This is a commonly expressed goal for many contemporary ghost hunters, enthusiasts who seek, with the aid of modern technology, to gather evidence of ghosts. Ghost hunting can take many forms and its practitioners espouse many different methods but, in general, ghost hunting consists of going out in teams to places reported, by tradition or by witnesses, to be haunted, and attempting to record, photograph, or otherwise detect supernatural presences. Todd Roll from the Wausau Paranormal Research Society explains his procedures of a basic ghost hunt by summarizing:

> If the case warrants further investigation based on our historical findings we will set up a date to visit the location and have a second interview with the witnesses. At this time we will bring along all of our equipment which includes, a Nightshot camera to film in infra red, EMF meters to measure electro-magnetic and geomagnetic fields, temperature gauges to detect changes in temperature, a Geiger counter to measure ionizing radiation, a standard 35mm camera to photograph the location and a tape recorder for EVP (electronic voice phenomena) to record sounds that cannot be heard at the time of the investigation. (Roll 2004)

Figure 8.1. Typical ghost-hunting equipment as displayed on the Ghostly Activities blog (https://www.ghostlyactivities.com/).

Each group has its own method, but there are some similarities. Stephen Weidner, founder of the American Association of Paranormal Investigators, explains his group's thorough method when entering a potentially haunted space:

> Once the preliminary is completed, two separate groups (team "Alpha" and team "Beta") should be assigned to the location. Team "Alpha" (consisting of the team lead, researcher, security, tools manager and medium) will enter the site first from the front. Team "Beta" (consisting of the team lead, researcher, security, tools manager and medium) will start their investigation of the site from the opposite end. Once the teams meet in the middle, it is okay to break for a few minutes. DO NOT DISCUSS ANY FINDINGS TO ANY OTHER TEAM during this time. The findings will match at the end of the investigation. Continue through the investigation to the end and meet up at the "Home Base" to finish up field paperwork. At this point the investigation is finished at the location site and will continue at the Investigation Headquarters for evidence gathering and discussion.
>
> Now the fun part begins with comparison of data and examinations of photos and recordings. DO NOT disregard any evidence, recordings, or findings. Keep everything. Create a back up report or computer disk of all information and reports.

As the investigation data is reviewed again and again, it is important to do a follow up if applicable. Once all data is completed and a report is designed and executed, send a complimentary report to all parties involved at the location. They will appreciate any and all courtesies. (Weidner 2004)

The level of technological reliance, professional attitude, and rigorous assessment described in these examples is common. Even before the existence of more modern tools like night-vision cameras and EMF meters, a reliance on scientific tools was typical for ghost hunts. In 1920, Harry Price, a member of the Society for Psychical Research, itemized his ghost-hunting kit: "Felt overshoes; measuring tape; tape, electric bells, lead deals, and other items for making motion-detecting tools; dry batteries and switches; cameras; notebooks and drawing pads; bell and string, chalk; basic first-aid kit; mercury for detecting vibrations" (Brown 2006, xviii).

Alan Brown, in his study of ghost hunters from the American South, enumerates the contemporary evolution of this kit: "Notebook and pen or pencil; flashlight; watch; compass; EMF meter; still cameras; video cameras; tape recorders; infrared meters; digital thermometers; night vision scopes; motion detectors; walkie-talkies; dowsing rods; Geiger counters; ion particle counters; thermal scanners; oscilloscopes" (xxi–xxiii).

With the exception of dowsing rods (which Brown notes are a controversial tool among ghost hunters), all of these items are used for the purpose of bringing a "luster of respectability" (2006, xx) to the endeavor. As will be discussed in a moment, objectivity is of the utmost importance in ghost hunting, and technology is often considered the best means to that end. But there is also an intriguing tendency among ghost hunters to share memorates—undeniably subjective experience narratives—as evidence, a practice that might seem to contradict the explicit and at times aggressive adherence to objective scientific methods. By taking a closer look at how the relationship between proof and experience is constructed and used by ghost hunters through their chosen modes of presentation, this article aims to shed some light on this situation.

Before beginning an in-depth examination of ghost-hunting practices, one thing that should be made clear is that ghost hunters and folklorists are not always on the same page with reference to conceptions, definitions, and theories as to the nature of ghosts and other supernatural creatures. For a start, the ghost hunters' goals of proving or disproving the existence of something are not necessarily in line with those of a folklorist, who, while perhaps being personally interested in such a matter, would probably be more professionally interested in the cultural patterns expressed or dramatized by the beliefs. But along with that general divide, the incredible preponderance of ghost-hunting information in the popular media—television shows, ghost tours, Internet sites—has also managed to irk some folklorists, who feel it demeans or trivializes the supernatural.

Gillian Bennett, for example, criticizes the media's love of the "Haunted Inns of England" phenomenon, where "ghosts are tourist attractions, a specialty of the house" (Bennett 1999, 1), and contrasts such "synthetic" thrills with genuine reported memorates. These "Haunted Inns of England" are often the stomping grounds of ghost hunters, especially in their televised materials, as they often pursue both well-known hauntings and new, individually reported cases. But judging from the ghost hunters I have spoken with, they would probably be surprised to find out a folklorist would feel their efforts were "trivializing" the supernatural.[1] On the contrary, ghost hunters generally feel that they are the stalwart few who are giving the supernatural genuine consideration in a world of doubters. When ghost hunters look at the field of folklore, on the other hand, it is often for more practical and less theoretical purposes: to find out about haunted places. Ghost hunters will often consider local tradition in order to validate a claim of a haunting. One hunter even supported his own belief in the supernatural by deferring to the authority of tradition and pointing out that "all the old folklore stories . . . mention things of a nonhumanly manner." Several hunters I contacted also spoke of looking to folklorists to find out what is "just an urban legend" and what is not.

So ghost hunting and folklore do not always match up in their approaches to ghosts. While a story may kick off or inspire a ghost hunt, hunters almost unanimously explain that what they are looking for is much more scientific and much less narratable than traditional ghost descriptions. While a ghost hunter may indeed find a human-shaped apparition in a photograph or record a human voice, the most common findings are photographs of orbs and vortices, light sources that appear on film but that were not visible to the human eye while a picture was being taken. Hunters also make recordings of EVP, or electronic voice phenomena, phantom voices captured on tape when none of the people present were speaking. They also look for instances of instrumental transcommunication; similar to EVP, these are messages sent through other electronic media such as radios, fax machines, computers, and telephones. Different ghost hunters may specialize in only one or in many of these techniques, but in general the emphasis on science, apparent in the terminology and the technology used, is the same across the board.

This emphasis relates back to the idea of objective evidence. As the main web page of the American Association for the study of EVP states,

Figure 8.2. A ghostly orb in the swimming pool on the famous haunted *Queen Mary* ship. Photo by Chris Poppleton.

the organization was "established in 1982 to provide objective evidence that we survive death in an individual conscious state." It later notes that "members understand that this 'objective evidence' must be based on good science, [and] as such, you will see that great care is taken by the members to maintain an objective view of the phenomena" (Butler and Butler 2001). Such proclamations are common on ghost-hunting websites. A brief survey of the science of parapsychology, the more generalized umbrella field for ghost hunting and often a basis for the scientific methods of ghost hunting, provides some illumination. According to Robert Thouless, author of *From Anecdote to Experiment in Psychical Research*, "The quality of mind required of a psychical researcher is not an inclination to believe in stories of the marvelous or an inclination to reject them, but a willingness to allow the degree of his belief or unbelief to be determined by the evidence and not by his prejudices or by his wishes, or by current fashions of thought" (Thouless 1974, 3). As is evident in this statement and in the rest of his work, Thouless is aware of the reputation of psychical research as a home for those who perhaps believe only because they want so badly to do so.

Debates between those with "an inclination to believe in the marvelous" and "those with an inclination to reject them," as Thouless puts it, or to use Gillian Bennett's terms, traditions of belief and traditions of disbelief, are common to this field. Bennett defends the somewhat unlikely description of the scientific rationalist perspective (the disbelievers) as "traditional" by observing that the same rationalist explanations of supernatural phenomena in use today—psychosis, psychological desire, drugs and alcohol, delirium, dreams, overactive imaginations, etc.—have been used since at least the sixteenth century (1999, 33). The tradition of belief, on the other hand, involves those who "have faith in human perception and trust other people to see accurately and interpret correctly what happens in the world around them" (37). The debate, embedded in many authoritative traditional notions on both sides, creates an impasse. For the believers, empirical evidence external to an individual's experience is not necessary; for the disbelievers, a reliance on subjective impressions is seen as unprofessional and naive. It is surely in part to overcome this reputation of irrationality that psychical researchers in general and ghost hunters in particular spend so much time emphasizing "good science." It is as though there is an assumed, ever-present heckler in the imagined audience whom they must placate with assurances of proper scientific methods at every turn. Alan Brown described what some paranormal researchers are up against, when even other parapsychologists are aware of the obstacles: "In 1963, Dr. Jule Eisenbud, a psychiatrist at the University of Colorado Medical School, published an article in which he presented the keystone argument against the existence of the paranormal. If paranormal phenomena are genuine, then scientists should be able to replicate them in strict laboratory conditions. Therefore, the findings of paranormal investigators cannot be accepted as valid proof without undermining the very foundations of the scientific method" (Brown 2006, 348).

Of course, as Todd Roll notes, "ghosts cannot be made to appear in laboratories under scientific conditions" (Roll 2004). The opportunity to create long-term, empirically revealing studies would require more time, money, and acceptance from the establishment than most ghost hunters have, and other discrediting factors—especially the prevalence of fakery—combine to stagnate many extended studies.

Richard Wiseman and Robert L. Morris, in their *Guidelines for Testing Psychic Claimants* (Wiseman and Morris 1995), offer three separate chapters on the subject of dealing with possible fakers, acknowledging that being taken in by cheats has cost more than one otherwise respected parapsychologist to lose credibility. In many books on psychical research, there is an almost obsessive focus on how to eliminate cheaters and fakers. Ghost hunting shares this concern, and many serious ghost hunters deride

Figure 8.3. Two Utah State University students ghost hunting with a cell phone and divining rods on the haunted fourth floor of the Ray B. West building. Photo by Lynne S. McNeill.

those they consider to be amateurs for polluting the pool of evidence. As Dr. Dave Oester, co-founder of the International Ghost Hunters Society, explains, "So many novices are photographing dust particles as ghost orbs, that any photo with multiple orbs [is] almost always [a photo of] dust orbs" (Oester 2004). Another group states, "The Internet has become a dump of sorts for all sorts of tales ranging from places wrought with strange noises to face-to-face confrontations with the supernatural. Our project is geared towards objectively investigating sites of these reports and conveying to the wondering public what OUR experience was like and how it compares to those reports" (COPA-Group 2009).

It seems that indicating awareness of the weaknesses of the competition serves to heighten one's own air of trustworthiness; many ghost-hunting websites even feature a section devoted to fakery for comparative purposes. By examining and debunking *some* submitted images, the impact of the remaining images is strengthened. The open acknowledgment of fakery implies that the images being offered as proof have undergone similar scrutiny, and been judged authentic.

The ghost hunters themselves, outside of the media in which they present their materials, articulate the need for scientific methods quite often. When I surveyed ghost hunters from around North America about the ways in which they conduct their research, I found a consistent focus on the use of tools that would allow for the most objective results. Robert Hunnicutt, founder and director of the Georgia Ghost Society, shares his method:

> Almost every situation will require the use of environmental measuring, such as the use of E.M.F. (electro-magnetic frequency) meters, geiger counter for low level radiation and the use of portable and stationary digital thermometers. I use two different types of thermometers, a hand held laser sighted thermometer for instantaneous readings and wireless thermometer with digital probes left in significant locations. Last, but not least is the set up and use of multiple infrared video cameras set up in key locations. We use 3 Sony camcorders with Night-Shot and 2 Panasonic low lux closed circuit video cameras. I also use an infrared nightvision monocular in conjunction with the video recorders, which I carry with me throughout the night. In some situations we will also use both audio monitors to allow us to listen to remote locations of the site and digital audio recorders to record any ambient sounds that may be recorded during the investigation. We also have portable fm transceivers to allow every investigator to stay in contact with each other. (Hunnicutt 2004)

The emphasis on scientific evidence gathering in these situations is supported not only by the techniques investigators approve of, but also by those they disapprove of. New forms of technology can come under fire, as the Utah Ghost Hunters webpage indicates when it proclaims, "As ghost hunters it is physical proof that we seek. If you manage to take a picture of a ghost with a digital camera it will never be accepted as proof of anything" (Utah Ghost Hunters 2004). And while some ghost hunters consider the testimony of purported psychics to be of value in an investigation, many are vehemently against such a practice, as it only encourages subjectivity. Vancouver Paranormal's website sums this idea up nicely: "Since the beginning of mankind, people have claimed that certain people possess certain powers. For hundreds, if not thousands, of years people have been trying to prove this. In all that time, not a single piece of PHYSICAL evidence has been produced to support the claim. Therein lies the problem. In gathering physical evidence of ghosts and hauntings, psychic evidence means nothing" (2006). Dr. Oester agrees: "Scientific evidence is more convincing since people who experience physical or emotional sensation are often self induced. We have found from our 1,000 field investigations that psychic sensations are generally more active in front of a camera than without a media audience. We shy away from psychics or mediums as they seem to have an overactive imagination. They never validate their visions or feelings with physical evidence" (Oester 2004).

Even those who do believe in psychics personally still recognize the general lack of credibility they have in the greater scientific community. Stephen Weidner notes that "having been a scientifically tested medium myself, I do believe some psychics are valid. The problem is the pool is so polluted, it takes learning how to sort out the bad from the good" (Weidner 2004).

So where in all this focus on hard science is there room for more subjective expressions such as personal-experience narratives or memorates? Interestingly, despite the incredibly pervasive emphasis on the filter of technology and the insistence on objective proof, in almost all manifestations of ghost hunting in popular culture—the Internet, televisions shows, ghost books—personal-experience narratives and memorates abound. Television shows, such as the Discovery Channel's *Real Ghosthunters* and Living TV's *Most Haunted*, regularly use people's own retellings of the events that have prompted the more scientific investigation as a means of introducing their topic, offering dramatic reenactments of the events as the original participants tell the story in a voice-over, emphasizing subjective details along with the common reality-testing assurances. Mikel Koven, in his examination of the folkloric nature of the mass-mediated narratives presented in *Most Haunted*, explains that, for this show, the investigative team is not limited to scientists and skeptics:

> The *Most Haunted* team is led by former children's television presenter Yvette Fielding and is supported by a number of experts, including a historian (Richard Felix), a parapsychologist, and at least one psychic medium. These four investigators fulfill very specific roles in the investigation: the medium's presence is to facilitate contact with any spirits or ghosts at the location; Felix, as the show's resident historian, is present to verify any historical information generated by the medium; and the parapsychologist is present to ensure as "scientific" an investigation into the purported haunted site as possible and to attempt to debunk any immediate claims that the phenomena experienced are paranormal. (Koven 2007, 187)

The combination of both official and unofficial means of knowing are represented and, as Koven points out, the debate between them is encouraged for both the experts and the viewing audience.

Lest we think this is peculiar to televised ghost hunts, and perhaps a calling card of televised media, ghost-hunting websites and discussions in online message boards regularly relate subjective experiences with the supernatural. Hunters will describe both physical and mental sensations—sudden chills, emotional vibrations—that they experience during the technology-driven hunts. Sharon Raines, co-founder with Dave Oester of AAPI [American Association of Paranormal Investigators], explained, "While doing the interview, we try to get a 'feel' of the area in question: hot or cold spots, impressions, intuitions, empathic impressions" (Raines 2004). Still more descriptive are the longer narratives describing particular ghost encounters like the ones on the Utah Ghost Hunters' page, an Internet site that emphatically stands by the importance of objective proof. A woman named Andie contributed the following story:

> The door was wide open and I saw something that caught my eye it was like a hazy white ball of light but just bright enough to see. Well then all of a sudden this ball of light turn into a human figure, it was a little girl and she was dressed in a plaid dress. She started to come closer to the room and she was look at me. I quickly laid down and told myself I was just imaging it. But to prove it to myself I sat back up at first nothing was there. Then there she was and again she started coming toward the room. (Utah Ghost Hunters 2004)

It appears that these experiences are shared in an effort to enhance the impact of the scientific findings as valid proof, but when they appear alongside the adamant, and at times vehement, discrediting of subjective experience, it begins to create an interesting conflict. How do these two ideas reconcile within the same field?

One issue that becomes very important when looking at the phenomenon of ghost hunting is the idea of proof, not simply in terms of evidence but in terms of proving something to others, convincing them that a certain thing does or does not exist. All the ghost-hunting websites I looked at and all the people I surveyed who are involved in ghost hunting spoke in some way about proof. The question then becomes proof for whom? For oneself? For others? The consensus was divided when I asked hunters directly. Most hunters I came across, like Bob Hunnicutt, were clear in their assertion that the investigation is never aimed at convincing another person: "One of the most important rules we have is do not attempt to convince anyone of the existence of the supernatural. Most people already have a preconceived notion of whether or not they believe" (Hunnicutt 2004). As another investigator put it, anonymously: "I never try to convince anyone of anything . . . I found out many years ago that it can get me into trouble."

Others, such as Stephen Weidner, espouse the opposite point of view: "Our reports are designed to show our scientific methods of analysis and are made public to other Paranormal Investigators around the world . . . It's time to provide evidence of [spirits'] existence to any skeptic" (Weidner 2004). As I touched on before, it is always possible that the goals of ghost hunters and the goals of the media that so often project their work are different—it could be that ghost hunters indeed do not have the goal of proving anything about the subject they study to anyone else, and it is the television producers who add in the stance of persuasion. But it does appear, when we take a closer look at ghost hunters' websites—the content and design of which they have control over—that, for many, convincing others is at least in part the goal. If there were no anticipated audience, there would be no *need* to display one's findings on a website—the use of the Internet implies an assumed audience. Even if hunters do not feel the need to try to seek out skeptics and forcibly change their minds, the information they provide to everyone who comes across their sites is unmistakably presented *as evidence*. The appearance of the websites alone—occasionally austere and professional looking but most often evoking a sense of the supernatural through graphics, fonts, and colors—is an important implicit statement in favor of belief. In the content of the sites, evidence such as photographs, EVP recordings, and video stills are provided for the possibility of the existence of ghosts, and while most professional sites do make it clear that they are remaining skeptical, they also do not provide much of the evidence they have gathered that supports *non-supernatural* explanations for their own investigations.

Considering this—that there is some unavoidable aspect of persuasion to these websites—the intersection of objective "good science" and subjective personal-experience narratives makes for an interesting commentary on what we consider to be adequate proof for belief in the supernatural. We are a society that trusts facts and figures, yet, as Erving Goffman has observed, when a performer believes in what he or she is performing, "[o]nly the sociologist or the socially disgruntled will have any doubts about the 'realness' of what is presented" (Goffman 1959, 17). Does a reading on a Geiger counter convince a skeptic more than an investigator's animated personal description of sensing a presence in an empty room? The easy answer is the logical one—most people assume we are a culture that likes provable, testable facts.

The ghost hunters themselves, at least the ones I spoke with, were divided on which constitutes better proof, but it seems that most investigators take the stance of desiring objective proof while personally recognizing the persuasive power of personal-experience narratives and memorates as a rhetorical tool. Todd Roll explains: "I find both types of evidence convincing. For me seeing a ghost would mean more than getting a spike on my EMF meter, but I am also aware that our sense can play tricks on us and what we might think is a ghost could just be a draft, or a reflection of light" (Roll 2004).

Sharon Raines concurs, explaining her stance on science versus perception in cases where more than one person has perceived something paranormal:

> If we can prove there is no anomalous natural cause such as elevated CO^2, elevated O^2, geomagnetic anomaly, hazardous materials which could cause mental impairment, radiation, etc., and we still all agree on what we saw or heard or felt, then that's 20–50% proof. If someone recorded the voice as well, add another 20–50%. I don't think we have the equipment to go further. The last 20–30% always boils down to belief. No one has been able to capture and hold the ghost for filming, interview, and scientific testing in a lab situation, and that is what our society believes is necessary in general. It would probably be easier to catch ET because at least he would be in our current space-time. Look how many decades it took the scientific community to accept the theory of Continental Drift! Better still, how many centuries was the earth flat, even after the Egyptians and Greeks proved otherwise? Have you ever tried to pet Schrödinger's cat? While I believe in the scientific method in general, I also believe what we are learning about the quantum universe has thrown a wrench into the works and requires that we re-think much of our standard methodology. (Raines 2004)

The stance on the side of scientifically verifiable evidence would seem to be born from the defensive position against the reputation with which psychical research is regularly branded—that of being swayed by a tradition of belief. The staunch refusal to wholly trust psychic evidence, even when many ghost hunters describe their own psychic experiences during hunts, is a recognition of the same possibility of loss of credibility that psychical researchers fight so hard to avoid in the books that teach their techniques.

Working in tandem with this desire to appear as rational as possible in order to preempt criticism of methodology and motivations is the unavoidable lure of the numinous. Ghost hunters may not be forcing their proof on their audiences, but they are conceivably looking to draw in undecided audiences, and the bait needs to be good. As Rudolph Otto says in his introduction to the English edition of his work *The Idea of the Holy*, the "non-rational" is of profound import to metaphysical issues, and yet is difficult to articulate. Because of this, his work "attempt[s] to analyze all the more exactly the feeling which remains where the concept fails" (Otto 1958, xxi). That feeling is the numinous. As Otto explains, when we take the moral element from the concept of the "holy," we are left with an "unnamed something" (6), the "unique original feeling-response" that is, as he says, an object of "search and desire and yearning" (32). Otto describes a journey through the "feelings of horror and shudder and spectral haunting in order . . . to *break through the hard crust of rationalism* and bring into play the feelings buried deep down in our religious consciousness" (194; my emphasis). It is perhaps this desire to break through rationalism that motivates the sharing of memorates, which articulate the numinous so much better than do empirical facts and calculations and figures.

A thing cannot really be said to be supernatural if it conforms in all ways to natural, scientific expectations and regulations. And if it is the *supernatural* element that provides that lure of the numinous, then objective evidence alone will not be a successful draw. Narrative carries with it the weight of tradition and the lure of the numinous, and offers a friend-of-a-friend kind of assurance. Retaining a sense of the numinous through memorates allows the numinous to remain a lure, perhaps inviting more people to join the tradition of belief and then to continue from that perspective into the realm of more scientific proof, where the objective evidence will be a complement to some preexisting state of inclination rather than an isolated calculation. Robert Hunnicutt sums up this dual treatment of the traditions of belief and disbelief when he notes: "The general rule is: if someone believes, no proof is necessary. If they don't, no proof is enough. When I do discuss a case, I will usually discuss what [I've] witnessed along with the instrument readings" (Hunnicutt 2004).

When faced with potential rejection from both the tradition of belief and the tradition of disbelief—each simply inviting the criticism of the other—the practice of ghost hunting has padded itself with ample cushions of two types; though the resulting approach might at times contradict itself, detractors from both camps will ideally be met with, at least according to their own standards, potentially satisfying proof.

NOTE

1. I do not mean to imply that all folklorists hold this opinion, or that those who do are inflexible on the point. For an excellent consideration of commodified belief traditions, see Goldstein 2007.

9

"There's an App for That"
Ghost Hunting with Smartphones

Elizabeth Tucker

Most legend trips are spontaneous and quite casual—the participants usually aren't bringing the tools of ghost hunting along with them. But who goes anywhere without their phones these days? The ubiquity of smartphones has led to the common scenario—inconceivable just a few decades ago—of almost every member of a social outing having with them at all times a reliable camera, audio recorder, video recorder, encyclopedia, dictionary, newspaper, notebook, calendar, and telephone, all in one small device. Not to mention a whole host of ghost-hunting tools, too, as Elizabeth Tucker explains in this essay about the use of smartphones in legend tripping.

There is almost no aspect of contemporary life that it not in some way permeated by technology. While many people associate the idea of "folklore" and the specific genre of "legend" with the past, with old-fashioned beliefs and customs, we see technology in these realms just as much as anywhere else. As this volume has shown, legend telling and legend tripping occur whenever and wherever people come together to explore their environments and muse about the possibilities of reality. Folklorists began studying communications technologies as a setting for the exchange of folklore as early as 1990, when John Dorst wrote about the use of email and discussion groups to share jokes. Given that the Internet didn't achieve what most people would consider to be widespread use until the mid-1990s, it seems that folklorists were on the front lines of the study of digital culture!

Tucker points out that new smartphone apps are being created daily that address a variety of our practical needs; it makes sense that apps would be developed that would address spiritual or supernatural needs as well. The trend of using technology to seek out paranormal presences has a strong continuity over time, as Tucker describes in the Spiritualist movement of the mid-nineteenth century. People have long been interested in using whatever tools are available—whether rapping on tables, flipping tarot cards, moving the planchette on a Ouija board, recording into a record or cassette, or opening up a smart-

phone app—to attempt contact with the other side. Tucker uses the phrase "hypermodern ostension" to describe today's use of consumer technology and media to pursue legend tripping, highlighting the "accessible excess" that the equipment allows.

Contemporary technology isn't involved in legend tripping only at the evidence-gathering level, either—it can also provide a new avenue for the spread of legends and legend-trip rituals. Tucker describes how the students featured in her essay not only used a ghost-hunting app to seek ghosts but also filmed their adventure with another cell phone and uploaded the video to YouTube. Michael Kinsella (2011), in his book Legend-Tripping Online, talks about the new role that the Internet plays in helping legend trips reach new audiences and potential participants. "Sites such as YouTube . . . bring multimedia presentations of the supernatural back into the corpus of oral or text-based storytelling and supply environments for entire legend complexes to spawn and thrive in the face of previous spatial and/or temporal confines" (39). The audiovisual record of Tucker's students' legend trip is available for anyone to view, and will likely serve as the catalyst that inspires another group to make the same trip in the future, using the newest apps that have come out.

Almost everywhere we go these days—airports, subways, highways, stores, and classrooms—we see people using cell phones. Many of these qualify as "smartphones": tiny computers that perform an amazing variety of functions. With smartphones we can send and receive messages, check the Internet, take pictures, and make videos. Because of their fantastic versatility, smartphones have their own kind of magic. Jeff Stahler's widely circulated cartoon shows the wicked queen from "Snow White" holding a smartphone on a selfie stick and gazing at its surface, asking, "Smartphone, smartphone on a stick, who has the fairest profile pic?" (Stahler 2015). This cartoon wryly recognizes the smartphone as an arbiter of status and places it in the long tradition of oracle consultation that scholars have documented for many years (Stoneman 2011).

If the smartphone is a source of magic, its applications, downloadable programs for mobile devices known colloquially as "apps," provide a cornucopia of wondrous possibilities. Apps, obtainable from "app stores," offer delicious food, comfortable hotels, quick transportation, and other pleasing commodities. Unstinting in their provision of choices, they remind us of the genie that emerges from a bottle in the *Arabian Nights*. There are apps for courtship, weddings, pregnancy, and other life crises. In 2010 the Apple Corporation registered a trademark for its slogan "There's an app for that," which appeared in its 2009 commercials. Gradually, this slogan has proved its validity. In June of 2016, Apple's app store offered 2 million apps and Android's app store offered 2.2 million ("Number of Apps" 2016).

Besides satisfying people's practical needs, apps respond to their spiritual needs and interests. A few examples of spiritually oriented apps are Archangel Oracle Cards, Buddha Mantra, Wicca Spells, and Dialing God. Ghost hunting is one of the many expressions of interest in life after death. A broad range of ghost-hunting apps—Ghost Radar, Phantom Radar, Spirit Story Box, Ghost Hunter, and others—makes ghost hunting easier than ever for those who want to take legend trips to haunted places.

This chapter will explore how smartphone apps have influenced legend trips during the second decade of the twenty-first century. Since the late 1960s, folklorists have recognized that visitors to legend-related sites tend to follow a certain sequence: telling stories during travel to the site, participating in ritualistic, possibly rebellious behavior, and telling stories during travel home (Dégh 1969a; Thigpen 1971; Ellis 1982–1983). When smartphone technology becomes dominant, does this sequence change in any way? Because it seems important to consider both long-established and more recent aspects of legend-trip behavior, both will receive careful consideration here.

All of the four legend trippers whose adventure I will analyze in this chapter are college students. In *Haunted Halls: Ghostlore of American College Campuses* (2007), I explore reasons why late adolescents who are attending college may have a strong interest in taking legend trips. Intensely interested in learning, both in and outside the classroom, they may choose to enter "a mysterious realm filled with sensory stimulation and ambiguity" (182). Older adolescents' reasons for visiting legend sites include "desires to understand death, probe the horror of domestic violence, confront racism, and express the uneasy relationship between humans and technology" (182). But of course college students' legend trips are not just attempts to learn; they also combine fear with excitement, allowing for thrills under safe circumstances.

Important insight into late adolescents' legend trips comes from Simon J. Bronner (2012), whose *Campus Traditions: Folklore from the Old-Time College to the Modern Mega-University* analyzes college students' folklore in depth and detail. In the "Legend Quests" section of his chapter about "Legendary Locations, Laughs, and Horrors," Bronner notes, "On these playfully framed trips, students talk to one another about frightening scenarios under the cloak of legend, and they experience for themselves the reality of the spooky sites, even as they confront their own cloudy fears and doubts" (323). Emphasizing the centrality of late adolescents' own fears and uncertainties, Bronner reminds us that play provides a frame for trips to legendary locations. Like other forms of play that late adolescents and young adults enjoy, legend trips are spontaneous, exciting, creative, and fun. After graduating from college, people tend to cherish their memories of legend trips, as Bronner does in recalling his trip to visit a rural graveyard with friends from Indiana University on a foggy summer night (319). Both playful and meaningful, these trips offer intriguing ambiguities that provoke reflection long after the experience ends.

HYPERMODERN OSTENSION

As Linda Dégh and Andrew Vázsonyi explain in their article "Does the Word 'Dog' Bite? Ostensive Action: A Means of Legend-Telling," ostension is "presentation as contrasted to representation" (Dégh and Vázsonyi 1983, 6). Dégh and Vázsonyi identify three forms of ostension: pseudo-ostension (hoaxing), proto-ostension (appropriating a legend as one's own experience), and quasi-ostension (misunderstanding something that happens in a legend) (18–20). In relation to Slender Man, the fictive bogeyman created on the Internet in 2009, Jeffrey A. Tolbert identifies reverse ostension, which "weav[es] together diverse strands of 'experience' (in the form of personal encounters with the creature, documentary and photographic evidence, etc.) into a more or less coherent body of narratives" (Tolbert 2013, 3). Tolbert's recognition of reverse ostension on the Internet shows that this medium of communication is making further forms of ostension possible.

According to sociologist Avery Gordon, author of *Ghostly Matters*, some of the most "dominant and disturbing" aspects of American culture are "the commodification of everyday life, the absence of meaning and the omnipresence of endless information" as well as "the relentless fascination with catastrophes" (1997, 14). Gordon characterizes our information-overload era with eerie precision; during the years since her book was published, we have seen the rise of fake news and other phenomena documented by Russell Frank (2011) in his study *Newslore*. The ubiquity of Internet rumors and legends about politics, health, and other important subjects makes ostension even more meaningful than it might be otherwise.

For legend trips involving significant use of smartphone and Internet technology, a new kind of ostension emerges. In *Putting the Supernatural in Its Place: Folklore, the Hypermodern, and the Ethereal*, Jeannie Banks Thomas (2015, 7–8) introduces the term *hypermodern folklore*: "lore that emerges from, deals with, or is significantly marked by contemporary technology and media (including the omnipresent Internet) or consumerism (with all its accessible excesses and its ability to generate pleasure mixed with anxiety)." This term works very well for folklore related to digital technology. During legend trips influenced by smartphone apps, hypermodern ostension takes place. Presentation of legends during these trips relies upon smartphone technology and popular media as well as consumerism.

"Accessible excesses" of consumerism appear during hypermodern ostension. People who want to use their smartphones to find ghosts can choose among a dizzying array of ghost-hunting apps, including Phantom Radar, Ghost Radar, Ghost Hunter, Haunted House, Ghost Locator, Ghost Communicator, Ghost Detector, Ghost Observer, Spirit Story Box, and many others. App stores generally offer multiple versions of ghost-hunting apps that have become popular. Because such apps tend to cost very little, it is easy for people to download multiple apps to try out. Many ghost-hunting apps cost 99 cents, and many are free. Evaluative articles on the Internet such as "We Tested Every Ghost-Hunting App in the Haunted Buildings of NYC" (Crowley 2014) encourage consumers to try out new apps. As a result of low prices and high praise of new products, experimentation with numerous apps has become very common. This experimentation involves both hunting for ghosts with apps and posting videos of ghost-hunting experiences on YouTube.

The first ghost-hunting app for smartphones was Ghost Radar, introduced by Spud Pickles in 2009. Ghost Radar Free, developed for iPhones, became known as Phantom Radar later; Phantom Radar was the app that the four students used in the ghost hunt analyzed in this chapter (Phantom Radar 2017). Ghost Radar has an "FAQ" (Frequently Asked Questions) page that gives consumers helpful information. The question "Is Ghost Radar real?" is followed by the reply, "It is as effective as an EMF detector or a KII [electromagnetic frequency detector]. The theory of what is happening is that intelligent energy can be made aware of their ability to influence the sensors of the device. You must decide for yourself if the readings are indicative of actual paranormal activity" (Ghost Radar®: LEGACY-Documentation 2016). It is important to note that the app developer encourages the consumer to trust his or her own judgment. As Linda Dégh and Andrew Vázsonyi demonstrate in *The Dialectics of the Legend*, a wide range of beliefs keeps legends alive; skepticism is one reaction that keeps both narratives and descriptions of legend trips circulating.

Ghost Radar's developer, Jack Jones, welcomes questions submitted online. When I asked him how successful his apps have been, he answered, "The apps have simply been more successful than we ever anticipated.

The Ghost Radar® apps have been downloaded tens of millions of times." Jones also mentioned that this app appeals to "people of all ages" (Jones 2016). He did not, however, answer my question about the role of stories in usage of Ghost Radar. Although his website does not emphasize app users' stories, the websites of a number of other-ghost hunting apps do. For example, Spirit Story Box's website encourages app users to submit stories about their own experiences. Spirit Story Box's homepage includes a running feed of users' personal-experience stories that describe their successes using the app (Spirit Story Box 2016). As Lynne McNeill notes in "Contemporary Ghost Hunting and the Relationship between Proof and Experience," placement of personal-experience stories on ghost hunters' websites can make the website seem more persuasive (McNeill 2006, 105).

No personal-experience stories appear on the download page for Phantom Radar, the app chosen by many college students I know. Available on iTunes and in other app stores at no cost, this app has been popular among young people. Its developer, Inner Four, Inc., understands the appeal of easy availability. Phantom Radar has received enthusiastic reviews in YouTube videos (e.g., Blast Process 2014).

There are, of course, other factors besides cost. How much does use of ghost-hunting apps depend upon narration of legends and personal-experience stories? Answers to this question vary according to the app and its user or group of users. People can use ghost-hunting apps anywhere, not just in places known through legends, but legends attract visitors to promising places and encourage hope for having a similar experience. In "The Commodification of Belief," Diane Goldstein observes that in belief tourism, "the *real* sought-after experience [is] the potential for one's own supernatural encounter" (Goldstein 2007, 197). Although using one's own smartphone to hunt ghosts is not the same as participating in belief tourism, the goal is the same: experiencing something supernatural that can become an exciting story to share with others.

ROOTS IN NINETEENTH-CENTURY SPIRITUALISM

Ghost hunting with smartphone apps derives from American Spiritualism, which began in the mid-nineteenth century. In 1848 two teenaged sisters, Margaret and Kate Fox, claimed that spirits were contacting them by making rapping noises in their home in Hydesville, New York. News of their claim spread rapidly through the media of that time period: telephone, telegraph, and newspaper. The Fox sisters gave many lectures and psychic readings, becoming international celebrities. Even though Margaret admitted in 1888 that the spirit rappings had been a hoax, she recanted her confession afterwards, and most of the sisters' followers remained loyal to them (Weisberg 2005, 1–4).

By the 1870s there were Spiritualist churches in both the United States and Great Britain. Members of the Spiritualist church believe that the dead can send messages to the living through psychic mediums and by other means. Lily Dale Assembly in western New York, founded in 1879, is one Spiritualist village that has remained active up to the present. Visitors to Lily Dale consult psychic mediums, attend lectures, and view paintings and writings said to have been generated by spirits. They also hear stories about the Fox sisters' experiences in Hydesville and see pictures of early mediums' contact with spirits through table tipping (Tucker 2015a).

The first efforts to record spirits' voices involved long-playing records in the 1940s; in 1982, Sarah Estes founded the American Association of Electronic Voice Phenomena. Frank Sumption created the Ghost Box, also known as Frank's Box, in 2002. This box generates white noise and captures bits of sound from an AM radio receiver. Smartphone apps that are supposed to respond to sound patterns and electromagnetic frequencies belong to the tradition established by Frank's Box. Through generation of words and symbols such as dots of different colors, these apps offer messages from nearby spirits.

LEGENDS OF OLD DICKINSON

Users of ghost-hunting apps tend to bring them to places that have a reputation for being haunted. Old houses and hotels make especially good legend-trip sites, as do cemeteries; so do hospitals, schools, colleges, and universities. Institutions whose existence began some time ago have an intriguing connection to the past. For college students, haunted places have a particular appeal. While pursuing their educations and preparing for future careers, students may feel a heightened sense of their environment's possibilities. Legends that tell of statues coming to life and students walking through a gate that marks the mouth of hell or flunking out because they have stepped on the wrong spot contribute to the impression that the college campus is a strange, enchanted place. Many campus legends tell of hauntings in residence halls, viewed as liminal places because students both study and sleep there. In the liminal zone between alertness and sleep, ghosts become nonliving residents of the campus environment. As I discovered when doing the research for my book *Haunted Halls* (2007), it is common for each campus to have its own haunted places. Simon J.

Figure 9.1. "Danger" sign welcomes visitors to the sub-basement. Photo by Geoffrey Gould.

Bronner's *Campus Traditions* documents an intriguing range of haunted locations on college campuses (Bronner 2012, 277–332).

A well-known haunted place on the campus of Binghamton University inspired the legend trip that four of my students took on May 2, 2014. Mike, Amy, Jack, and Simon, all of whom were residents of Newing College, decided to venture into the dark, semi-deserted sub-basement of Old Rafuse, a former residence hall that now holds administrative offices and a couple of classrooms. Old Rafuse is part of Old Dickinson, a complex of eight former residence halls that has gradually begun to serve other purposes. Across the street from Old Dickinson stand the current Dickinson Community and Newing College.

Old Dickinson no longer functions primarily as a residential area at Binghamton University, but it has an invisible network of legends about which students quickly learn. Many of these legends focus on the sub-basement, where a student supposedly hanged himself back in the 1970s. Students have told the story of this suicide with minor variations, including the names of two residence halls in which the suicide took place. In *Haunted Halls* I explore several variants of this legend, one of which describes a female student seeing the face of a male student in the mirror of her room. After going down to the sub-basement with a friend to try to figure out what she has seen, she realizes that this was the face of the student who committed suicide by hanging from a pipe many years ago (Tucker 2007, 98–99).

There have also been legends about a cleaning lady fainting in the sub-basement and refusing to clean there again. This legend is based on an upsetting experience that a member of the custodial staff actually went through. When she was reaching up to clean a light fixture, she fainted and fell off a stepladder. Upon awakening from the faint, she declared that she had felt the spirit of a student named Michael pass through her body. Both students and staff members were troubled by the report of this incident, but staff members did not worry about it for long. Students, however, found stories about what had happened to be very intriguing. Some of them brought Ouija boards down to the sub-basement to see if they could find any ghosts there. Once a small group of students tried to summon spirits in the sub-basement with a Ouija board and claimed that handprints of little baby ghosts had appeared on the surface of windows there. This claim would sound familiar to anyone who had heard a legend about a "gravity hill," including the one that Carl Lindahl (2005) examines in his "Ostensive Healing: Pilgrimage to the San Antonio Ghost Tracks." As Lindahl explains, legend trips to the San Antonio train tracks inspire a sense of wonder; similarly, students who explore Old Rafuse's sub-basement approach their destination with excitement and awe.

When Old Rafuse still functioned as a residence hall, the sub-basement contained a room full of washers and dryers. One legend tells of a demonic face appearing in the glass windows of washing machines, frightening students who had nervously come down to the sub-basement alone, late at night, to do their laundry. A small room that contained an incinerator did not inspire legends while students still lived in the building but gained a reputation for being haunted once the students moved out. When people perceive a building as abandoned or semi-abandoned, ghost stories tend to multiply. The comforting routines of daily life no longer make the place seem familiar, so legends about ghosts become more common. Such was the case at Mansfield University, when a temporarily abandoned building inspired a number of rumors and legends (Glimm 1983, 120–122).

DOWN TO THE DEPTHS OF THE SUB-BASEMENT

At the beginning of their adventure in Old Rafuse on May 2, 2014, Amy, Mike, Jack, and Simon felt excited and curious. Their first attempt to enter the building failed, because the doors were locked when classes were not

"There's an App for That"

Figure 9.2. Pipes covered with peeling paint remind students of the legend of an earlier student who committed suicide. Photo by Geoffrey Gould.

in session. On their second try, however, they entered the building holding two smartphones: one for making a video of the trip and the other for using the Phantom Radar app. Bright-colored dots appeared on the screen as they walked down the two flights of stairs that led to their destination, the sub-basement. Simon shouted, "We got a shiny blue dot and a big red dot! Oh, yeah! Red, that means something!" On Phantom Radar, red means a strong ghostly presence; yellow means the presence is less strong, and blue means it is weak. Going beyond those explanations, one of the male students wondered whether the color red showed how the ghost was responding to their visit: "Red on the thing, I saw it! Maybe it's angry!" His mention of anger coincided with their arrival in the dimly lit, shadowy sub-basement, where they saw pipes protruding from the walls. Mike said, "There's a story about a guy hanging himself on a pipe" and Simon replied, "Oh God, creepy!" Then they took a quick look at the laundry room, where students had seen scary faces. With these reminders of the building's invisible, inherited story structure, the legend quest moved forward.

As dots appeared on the screen, words also came up. The first two words, "Height" and "Introduce," got no reaction from the students, but the next, "Maria," fully engaged their attention. "Are there any stories about a ghost named Maria?" Amy asked. The others shook their heads as they entered one of the sub-basement's storage rooms, which contained old music stands, books, boxes of old clothes used by a group of performers, a few compact discs, and other castoffs jumbled together.

Mike plunged his arm into a box of women's clothes and blankets, shouting, "Oh, my God, it's some girl's bed stuff! It *smells*!" His reaction reminded me of a visit to the boys' unit of a camp with my Girl Scouts in the late 1970s in southern Indiana; the sights and smells of the boys' tents and bathrooms at the camp fascinated the girls. Although this group of students was much older, three out of four of them were young men who seemed eager to find clues about a mysterious female ghost, so gender was a factor in their quest.

One of the clues they discovered in the storage room was a video, *The Little Princess*, which Jack pulled out of the bottom of the box of clothes. Holding the video up, Jack asked, "Could this be Maria?" Amy had seen the movie, but the three male students hadn't. As I watched their video I remembered that the 1995 film *A Little Princess*, based on the 1905 novel by the same name by Frances Hodgson Burnett, shows the quasi-magical transformation of a dreary boarding-school bedroom into a luxurious, delightful place to live. To some extent, that transformation resembled the one that these four students were experiencing: a change from a dull basement to a space haunted by significant ghosts from the building's past.

The next two words that appeared on the screen were "July" and "Sunday." As soon as they heard "July," the students got excited. "I was born in July!" shouted Jack; Amy said, "So was I!" Mike commented in a sepulchral voice, "Jack, you're going to *die*." Amy added ominously, "It's really *cold*." With a little help from Phantom Radar, they were establishing the time frame of a possible story and predicting a grim denouement for their own legend trip. Their prediction may have been influenced by *The Blair Witch Project*, the 1999 film in which all three student filmmakers die, or, more generally, by the many horror films in which visitors to creepy places do not survive. One prototype for this expectation is the legend "The Fatal Initiation," in which a fraternity initiate spends a night in a graveyard and dies of fright.

Right after Mike's prediction of Jack's demise, the four students walked into the scariest room in Rafuse's sub-basement. They could see it was the scariest room, because a few years ago someone had written a message on its door: "Rumor has it that a ghost haunts this room." Maintenance staff kept the door closed, so anyone brave enough to go into the room had to push the door open. The room was small and did not contain much: just a pile of trash, a plug surrounded by soot, a dirty sink with a red spot that looked like blood, graffiti, and an incinerator. Part of the pile of trash was a heap of broken

Figure 9.3. Plug surrounded by soot in the "haunted room."
Photo by Geoffrey Gould.

glass. The room looked as if it had been abandoned and left to fall apart for many years, even though students had lived in the building a few years before.

No wonder someone had designated this creepy room with the closed door the haunted room! As Sylvia Ann Grider observes, basements of houses have a "subliminal association . . . with castle dungeons and torture chambers" (155). This association comes through even more strongly in the basements of residence halls, which belong to campus legend landscapes involving stories of suffering students who commit suicide, get possessed by spirits, and experience other kinds of misery. The longer a residence hall basement is left mostly unoccupied and the dirtier it gets, the better it works as a setting for a legend trip in which seekers confront decay, suffering, and the presence of a ghost. And a room within the basement that seems to be secret is particularly intriguing, as the well-known folktale "Bluebeard" suggests (Tatar 2006).

Figure 9.4. Sink in the "haunted room"; its red stain makes students wonder what happened there. Photo by Geoffrey Gould.

Who was the ghost in this strange, uncomfortable room? As they stood there, the four students saw two new words pop up on Phantom Radar: "Couple" and "Forget." At this point they did something they had not done before: they started talking to the smartphone as if it were a Ouija board. Jack asked, "What does Sunday mean, and who is Maria? Are you Maria? Do you have anything to do with a Sunday in July?" Mike asked, "What do you want us to forget? What does this word mean?"

No more words appeared on the smartphone, but something else happened: the students heard noises that scared them. Some of them heard water dripping, and others heard broken glass crunching on the floor. Maybe a ghost was signaling its presence, as it did in so many folktales, including those that contained the motif E402, "Mysterious ghostlike noises heard." "Run!" said Jack. "Run for your lives!" They scrambled up the two flights of stairs and exited the building.

Once they were safely outside, Mike summed up what had happened: "Looks like this was a pretty productive ghost hunt. We found out something about this girl, Maria, and a Sunday in July. It was probably in the sub-basement, where it said there was a ghost and something having to do with a couple. It could have been a summer program when they were in high school. Maybe Maria was a girlfriend with a boyfriend. That's all we know. There were a bunch of noises in that room. It sounded like water dripping, something on the floor. There was a lot of broken glass. We are *not* going back there!" Feeling good about having made it through their descent to Rafuse's sub-basement, he and the other students posted their video of the trip on YouTube (Old Dickinson 2014).

CONCLUSIONS

This exciting ghost hunt followed the classic legend trip sequence identified by Dégh, Thigpen, and Ellis in many respects. The four students discussed Dickinson legends before choosing Old Rafuse Hall and making their way down into its dark, spooky sub-basement. With some trepidation, they entered the laundry room, the storage room, and finally the furnace room that earlier students had identified as a haunted place. When they heard strange noises, they got scared and ran back up the stairs, exiting the building as fast as they could. Immediately after the hunt they told a story about what had happened; then they ambled across the street to their well-lit, comfortably furnished residential community.

There was, however, an important change in the older pattern. Besides recalling details from the stories they had learned from oral tradition, the students used a smartphone app as their guide for the hunt. Phantom Radar supplied a tantalizing series of colored dots that told them where ghosts might be; it also gave them words that became a story. To some extent, these words facilitated reverse ostension, defined by Jeff Tolbert as creation of a story through a combination of digital elements. The words that appeared on Phantom Radar's screen could be recognized as a narrative, although this narrative's disjointedness made it seem unlikely to become part of Old Dickinson's enduring legends.

The most significant change was the students' use of hypermodern ostension: representation of legend elements that demonstrates reliance on the contemporary era's "accessible excess" (Thomas 2015, 7). Using one smartphone to record their trip and another to run Ghost Radar, Amy, Simon, Jack, and Mike made constant use of digital technology. They used Ghost Radar as both a guide and an oracle to which they could speak directly, as people would speak to a Ouija board. They planned to upload their video to YouTube and did so immediately after their ghost hunt ended. Because of this plan, they were aware of performing for an audience throughout their search for ghosts. Their video might have "gone viral" and reached many viewers; most YouTube videos do not become that famous, but one never knows which way the fickle finger of fame will point.

Mike's summary of his group's hunt shows that he wanted it to be "productive." The students would have been disappointed if nothing much had happened and they had simply left the building. Using the Phantom Radar app helped them put together a scenario in which something exciting would take place. A name, a month, a day of the week, and other information gave them ingredients from which a narrative could grow.

Significantly, the story about mysterious "Maria" did not matter as much to the students as their own experience did. Mock-seriously predicting their own death, hearing scary sounds, and feeling uncomfortable in the dirty, haunted room scared them enough that they ran away from the basement. Although the dots and words on Phantom Radar intrigued them, what they saw, heard, and felt in the sub-basement affected them more deeply than messages received on the machine. They were proud of having experienced something frightening in that spooky place underground and enjoyed posting their video for others to view on YouTube.

Information flows constantly from Phantom Radar, Ghost Radar, Spirit Story Box, and other ghost-hunting apps that we can buy for low prices or download for free. These images and sounds not only offer guidelines for locating ghosts; they also represent our current era of semi-reliable electronic communication. At the center of each college ghost hunt stand young people whose eagerness to confront their own fears motivates them to move forward. As long as they keep daring to undertake such quests, their stories deserve to be told.

10

Living Legends
Reflections on Liminality and Ostension

Lynne S. McNeill

I RECENTLY TOOK A LEGEND TRIP—all by myself, a rare experience for me—to a famous local site known as St. Ann's Retreat or, more simply, "the nunnery." The nunnery has been a legend-tripping locale for many decades in northern Utah, but I'd never visited it myself, despite talking at length with my students every semester about the stories that surround it. As is true of so many legend-tripping sites, the stories told about the nunnery are cumulative and overlapping, and several folklorists have written about the legend complex. Lisa Gabbert's (2015) "Legend Quests and the Curious Case of 'St. Ann's Retreat'" and Anna-Maria Arnljots's (2000) "St. Anne's Retreat" are two informative works by local Utah folklorists. The main legend tells of pregnant nuns in the early 1900s being sent to St. Ann's to wait out their condition, and the story focuses on one young nun who discovers that the babies, rather than being given up for adoption as the nuns believed, were being drowned in the on-site swimming pool. When she attempts to run, the young nun is drowned along with her baby, usually at the behest of an evil priest or mother superior.

The empty swimming pool at the now-abandoned retreat is the central target for legend trippers, who go to see if they can hear the cries of ghostly babies emanating from within the pool as legend suggests. The young nun, sometimes cast as a *La Llorona* figure, weeping and seeking her baby by the river and in the woods surrounding the camp, is at other times conflated with stories of a local witch, Hecate (alternately spelled Heckada or Hekada), who can be seen moving through the trees with a glowing green lantern and two red-eyed Doberman pinschers (sometimes pitched as "hellhounds"). Linda Dégh, in her pioneering work cited in chapter 1, explained

Figure 10.1. The abandoned swimming pool at St. Ann's Retreat. Photo by Lynne S. McNeill.

that legend trips often involve stories of both the initial legend and the later experiences of legend trippers, and St. Ann's is no exception. In the mid-1990s, a group of teenaged legend trippers visited the nunnery and got more than they bargained for; two watchmen patrolling the private property went too far in their duties, tying the teens up in the swimming pool, harassing them, and holding them at gunpoint. The story of this event has joined the original stories of pregnant nuns, dead babies, and witches to produce a compelling legend complex.

Bill Ellis, in chapter 2 of this volume, proposes that most legend trips are taken by adolescents as a kind of ritual of rebellion, but my solo trip reminds us that people of all ages may go legend tripping for a variety of reasons. I visited at dusk, nervous about trespassing and yet undeniably excited to finally see for myself the site of so many narratives. I didn't experience anything particularly paranormal, but I was deeply impressed with the feeling of the place; its abandoned buildings, made of stone and wood, spoke to long-ago habitation at the same time that they clearly signaled current neglect. The sense that the space was *meant* to be inhabited gave me the eerie feeling that perhaps it still was, even though I didn't witness anything especially strange. When I stood by the swimming pool to get photos with my phone, thinking not only of the fictional story of the nuns but also of the very true story of the legend trippers from the 1990s, it wasn't hard to imagine that the ghosts of the past were pressing in. The river runs close to the camp, and the pervasive sound of rushing water resembled, as it so often does, the voices of distant children, reminding me not only of the St. Ann's legends but of stories of water babies and Cry Baby Bridges around the country. I didn't linger long, but the distinctive feeling of the nunnery stayed with me long after I left.

My legend trip to St. Ann's Retreat touched on almost all of the themes that legend trips and the research that folklorists have done with them highlight: landscape and place, age and gender, belief and disbelief, fear and wonder, past and present, rebellion and obedience. The essays compiled in this volume show that none of these themes are simple or obvious—there's no single type of landscape that makes a good legend-tripping site, just as there's no single age or gender that makes someone a legend tripper. Certain elements may be consistent from example to example; the abandoned basement described in Elizabeth Tucker's chapter 9 mirrors the derelict buildings I saw at St. Ann's and provides a similar atmosphere for legend trippers. But other examples may highlight differences; the stories of the nuns, untrue as they are, are disheartening rather than inspiring, standing in opposition to the experiences featured in Carl Lindahl's chapter on gravity hill, which affirmed and upheld the teller's faith. The contextual framing of a legend and a legend trip, as Tim Prizer explains in chapter 6, can determine many things, and folklorists are reminded not to make assumptions about who goes legend tripping and for what reasons. Questions of belief especially aren't straightforward either; despite the long relationship of the genre of legend to ideas about belief, legend trips show us that belief and disbelief are part of a complex, nuanced, and often contradictory spectrum. Linda Dégh's work reminds us that as much as we might want to infer a "profound" belief on the part of enthusiastic legend trippers, we can't assume it.

One overarching theme that emerges from the many examples of legend tripping that this volume includes is that of *boundaries*. Whether situated at the boundary between childhood and adulthood, between the city and the wilderness, or between belief and disbelief, legend trips highlight the liminal elements of our lives, and so become a way for us to articulate and negotiate that liminality. Add to this the fact that, as Elizabeth Bird reminds us, *doing* is often more important than *telling*, and we understand that the power of legend trips is decidedly distinct from the power of legends. Through ostension, legend trips aren't limited to the narration of a symbolically meaningful legend; we can actually act out the narrative ourselves, putting ourselves smack in the middle of the experiences and events about which we've heard others tell. By embodying multiple forms of liminality at once, we intensify—and share—the sensation of being betwixt and between.

Legend tripping, like any other form of folklore, wouldn't persist as a traditional activity if it weren't serving some implicit or explicit purpose for the people who do it. While legend trips are indisputably entertaining—one of the most common explicit functions of legend trips is to have fun!—the scholarship collected here indicates that enjoyment isn't the only motivating factor when it comes to the decision to take a legend trip. Discovery, experimentation, socializing, and pushing against both societal and personal limits all factor in to the ongoing appeal of legend tripping. As Patricia Meley notes in chapter 3 of this volume, motivations within a single legend trip can be as diverse as alleviating boredom and proving one's bravery. The genre of legend is above all defined by the question of *possibility*—the pursuit and debate of what is possible in this world is at the heart of these narratives. Folklorist Elliott Oring explains that legends often depict "the improbable within the world of the possible" (Oring 1986, 125), highlighting that legends press against the boundaries of our credulity. In many legend-tripping scenarios, we can see the question of possibility being pushed to its outer limits; legend tripping is the embodied, lived experience of investigating the possibilities that legends suggest to us. Even if the typical legend trip results in more questions than answers, we've benefited from submerging ourselves in a liminal state, from letting wonder and possibility suffuse a few hours of our lives.

Discussion Questions and Projects

INTRODUCTION (MCNEILL AND TUCKER)

- When you were growing up, did your neighborhood have a "haunted house"? Did people narrate legends about this house around Halloween? Why do American neighborhoods tend to have just *one* haunted house rather than several of them?
- Does a legend trip need to be far from home to seem exciting and intriguing? Discuss potential legend-trip sites located both close to your home and farther away.
- Which term works better, *urban legend*, *contemporary legend*, or simply *legend*? Why?
- Discuss parallels between the epic hero and the legend tripper. How important is it for both epic heroes and legend trippers to visit the realm of the dead, and how hard is it for both of them to go there?
- With a couple of friends, act out Dégh and Vázsonyi's "dialectics of the legend" while narrating a supernatural legend together. Each person can take one role: believer, skeptic, or a position in between.
- Legend self-survey: write down as many legends as you can remember from your childhood/adolescence and reflect upon their meaning. Linda Dégh gave this assignment to all of the graduate students in her legend classes.

CHAPTER 1 (TUCKER)

- Linda Dégh's early study of haunted bridges near Avon and Danville shows how richly symbolic bridges can be. Why are bridge legends especially meaningful for adolescents?
- As Clements and Lightfoot's article shows, there is a close connection between the history of a local cemetery and the ghost legends that people tell about it. Discuss the history and legends of cemeteries in your local area.
- Clements and Lightfoot quote descriptions of adolescent behavior that includes destruction of gravestones and mistreatment of dogs. How can we explain this kind of behavior?

- How does BarBara Lee's exorcism of Stepp Cemetery compare to other exorcisms of which you have learned in historical accounts and films?
- When the movie *The Exorcist* came out in 1973, it terrified many viewers. Is exorcism still a troubling subject now?
- Find two videos about Stepp Cemetery on YouTube and compare them to the descriptions of the cemetery in this chapter.

CHAPTER 2 (ELLIS)

- Like the haunted graveyard near Wheeling that Ellis mentions, many cemeteries have legends about a cursed grave marker/seat or a mysterious portrait on a tombstone. Have you heard about similar horrors in cemeteries of your hometown?
- Ellis suggests, "Many haunted locations seem to exist only in the minds of the participants: instructions on how to find them are unusually, perhaps deliberately, vague. At night, after a few beers and joints, doubtless any old house, bridge, or graveyard can be the 'right' one." What is the significance of these vague directions to haunted locations?
- Ellis notes, "Legends project social warnings about sex onto marginal figures like ghosts and lunatics whom the participants can defy in good conscience." Marginal or liminal figures are very prominent in folk legends. Why do teenagers, in the midst of this liminal age stage, need to tell stories about such figures?
- Ellis interprets the adolescents' car as both a "personal, mobile territory where they are free to make their own rules" and "a sanctuary from which conventional authorities can safely be challenged." Books such as Stephen King's *Christine* and films such as *Christine* (1983), *Maximum Overdrive* (1986), and *Super Hybrid* (2010) have developed cars' supernatural power in intriguing ways. Why are cars so meaningful and frightening to teenaged drivers?
- Ellis also suggests that legend trips constitute "ritual acts of rebellion." How common are such acts among teenagers today? Do parents and other adults tend to hear about their children's acts of rebellion?
- Using the appendix of Ellis's article as a frame of reference, make a list of local legends of your current hometown and consider taking a trip to visit one of them.

CHAPTER 3 (MELEY)

- Meley challenges Ellis's idea that legend trips are a kind of delinquent act, citing her informants' claims that while they may partake in delinquent behavior at times, it's not something that is tied to their visits to the Wall or to Haug's Road. From your experience, is legend tripping usually a type of delinquency? Why or why not?
- The legend trippers in this chapter are ambivalent about their hometown—they want both to defend it and to get out. What role do you think boredom plays in perpetuating legend-tripping traditions?
- It is noteworthy that this large group of friends lives in a small town. Do you think that small towns have more legend trips than large cities?
- Meley studies the legend telling and legend tripping of a group of friends in Pennsylvania for more than six months. How feasible would it be to do such an extensive study of teenagers' activities now? Consider the effect of human subjects laws on plans for a study of this kind.
- Unlike some earlier studies of legend tripping, Meley's includes both males and female legend trippers of diverse ethnic backgrounds. Does this diversity seem to make their legend tripping different from that of single-sex groups with more homogeneous backgrounds?

CHAPTER 4 (ELLIS)

- Discuss quasi-ostension (misperception of something that happens in a legend) and pseudo-ostension (deliberate pranks). Have you experienced either of these? How does it change the experience to know that an intentional prank has taken place?
- Note that there is some ambiguity in this essay: Ellis has not had a chance to meet the people who left "Satanic" artifacts, but he is confident that the artifacts resulted from teenagers' ostensive behavior. To what extent does this approach build upon his earlier work that is included in the casebook?
- Fear of Satan's influence grew rapidly in Puritan New England, culminating in the Salem witch trials of 1692. How has understanding of witches changed since then?

- Compare the "Satanic panic" of the early 1980s to the "clown panic" of the fall of 2016. What social and/or political conditions generated these two moral panics? Do such panics seem likely to continue?
- Find someone who went through the "Satanic panic" of the early 1980s and interview him or her about stories that circulated then.

CHAPTER 5 (BIRD)

- Does your community have a striking memorial like the Black Angel? If so, are there legends and legend trips associated with it? If not, where do people go to engage in the kinds of activities that Bird describes as taking place at the Black Angel: young people acting out various roles, testing themselves and each other?
- Think back to a time when you were expected to be brave (or cautious or scared) during a social gathering, and describe it. Did you feel social pressure to act a certain way? Did the expectations of your peers make you more or less likely to go along with the activities?
- Parts of the Black Angel legend don't seem very fair—especially the "test" element that says the statue will turn white again if a virgin touches it. Participants are set up to fail the test—why do you think this element persists?
- Bird explains that female and male participants behave differently during legend trips; males act tough, while females act scared. How do these contrasting roles correlate with contemporary norms for male and female behavior?
- Visit a cemetery in your community and pay attention to the gravestones. What patterns in form can you see? Are there any graves that stand out visually? Can you determine why some graves are distinctive?

CHAPTER 6 (PRIZER)

- Bill Ellis is one of the premier scholars of legend tripping, and Prizer disagrees with him on some points. Scholarly disagreement can be a wonderful source of intellectual stimulation—two highly informed people look at the same phenomenon and draw different conclusions. Can you think of other instances that you've encountered in your studies where scholars disagreed on something? Was the disagreement resolved, or does it still stand?

- Between Ellis and Prizer, with whom do you agree? Does Prizer convince you that Ellis's understanding of who goes legend tripping is too limited? Or do you think that overall Ellis is still right that it's mostly adolescents?
- Prizer points out that sometimes people who share legends are in an echo chamber—hearing their own stories given back to them by their peers. This is an increasingly common occurrence on social media. How does an understanding of legends and legend tripping apply to these other situations?
- Can you find an example of a local legend trip that has distinct audiences, like the Railroad Bed Road that Prizer writes about?
- Prizer's essay's illustrations remind us that photographs can convey the mystique of a legend-trip site. If you can, visit a legendary location on a famous road and photograph it from different angles.

CHAPTER 7 (LINDAHL)

- Lindahl distinguishes between "scary beliefs" and "pious beliefs." How does this distinction apply to beliefs from your own experience? Discuss the dialectic between these two kinds of beliefs, which differs from the dialectics of the legend delineated by Linda Dégh and Andrew Vázsonyi (see introduction).
- Lindahl argues that the children's souls need to help visitors to the site save themselves. To what extent does this process of salvation rely upon Christian beliefs?
- One of Lindahl's main points is that legend trips can inspire a sense of wonder, which may matter more than fright. Do you agree with this statement?
  - How much does it matter that "gravity hills" work? A number of websites explain what happens when people drive their cars to such places. Do some research to learn about the physics of this intriguing phenomenon.
- Drive to the closest "gravity hill" with a friend and ask the friend to make a video of what happens when you put your car in neutral. Compare your video to other "gravity hill" videos that you can find online.

CHAPTER 8 (MCNEILL)

- Visit a ghost-hunting website and look for the rhetorical clues it provides. Where do you see evidence that the site is attempting to persuade viewers to believe (or not believe) in ghosts? Consider the content of the site, but also the visual and tonal elements: is the website presenting a scientific or a numinous feel to visitors? What makes you say that?
- What would it take for you to believe that a ghost hunter had recorded genuine evidence of a real haunting? Imagine the scenario that would best convince you. What kinds of evidence would be required?
- Do you personally find the numinous to be alluring? Is the supernatural a draw or is it off-putting? Why?
- What kinds of equipment do ghost hunters use these days, and how much does it cost? Is it necessary to spend a lot of money to prove that you are ready to go ghost hunting?
- Look into a local ghost-hunting group and the sites its members tend to visit. Find a ghost hunter and ask whether personal stories or objective evidence have influenced him or her more.

CHAPTER 9 (TUCKER)

- This legend trip demonstrates commodification of belief; an inexpensive smartphone app demonstrates belief or potential belief in ghosts. How common are such apps now? Does it seem necessary to believe in ghosts to use a smartphone app of this kind?
- Old Rafuse is not a private home; it used to be a student residence hall, but now it holds administrative offices, and its sub-basement is run-down and semi-abandoned. Why does this decline capture students' interest, and why do abandoned buildings or parts of buildings appeal to ghost hunters in general?
- How does reliance on free-flowing information in ghost-hunting apps reflect the electronic era that we inhabit now?
- Try using a ghost-hunting app in several old buildings and keep a log of the words and color cues that come up. Do the patterns that emerge seem to suggest that ghosts are present? If so, how closely are these patterns related to legends?
- What other examples of "hypermodern folklore" or "hypermodern ostension" can you think of?

- Look for a legend-trip video that has been posted to YouTube. You can choose a video that has been filmed somewhere near you or an example made somewhere far away. Compare the experience of watching the video to the experience of actually going on a legend trip yourself. How is watching a filmed legend trip different from watching a scary movie?

CHAPTER 10 (MCNEILL)

- How does a solo legend trip differ from a group trip?
- Is there any legend-trip destination that you would not want to visit alone? Why?
- Take a legend trip (or reflect on a recent one) and look for the themes of this book's chapters in your own experience.

References

Aarne, Antti, and Stith Thompson. 1961. *The Types of the Folktale: A Classification and Bibliography*. Folklore Fellows Communication 184. Helsinki: Suomalainen Tiedeakatemia.

Abrahams, Roger D. 1969. "The Complex Relations of Simple Forms." *Genre (Los Angeles)* 2 (2): 104–128.

Allen, Paula. 2003. "Utah Bus Crash, Front-Page Coverage Launched S. A. Legend." *San Antonio Express*, January 26, 2003.

Allen, William R. 1986. "The Cage of Matter: The World as Zoo in Flannery O'Connor's *Wise Blood*." *American Literature* 58 (2): 256–270. https://doi.org/10.2307/2925818.

Alphonso, Patricia. 1981. "'We Don't Wanna Hear the Scientific Reason': Teenage Lore of St. Bernard Parish." *Louisiana Folklore Miscellany* 1:31–32.

Andreas, Brian. 1993. *Mostly True: Collected Stories and Drawings*. Decorah, IA: StoryPeople.

Aries, Philippe. 1974. *Western Attitudes toward Death*. Trans. Patricia M. Ranum. Baltimore: Johns Hopkins University Press.

Arnljots, Anna-Maria. 2000. "St. Anne's Retreat." *Digital Collections, Utah State University Libraries*. Accessed September 12, 2017. http://digital.lib.usu.edu/cdm/landingpage/collection/p16944coll20.

Axtman, Kris. 2001. "Why Juries Often Spare Mothers Who Kill." *Christian Science Monitor*, July 9, 2001.

Baker, Ronald L. 1969. "The Face in the Wall." *Indiana Folklore* 2:29–46.

Baker, Ronald L. 1970. "Legends about Spook Light Hill." *Indiana Folklore* 3:163–189.

Baker, Ronald L. 1972. "'Monsterville': A Traditional Place-name and Its Legends." *Names* 20 (3): 186–192. https://doi.org/10.1179/nam.1972.20.3.186.

Baker, Ronald L. 1982. *Hoosier Folk Legends*. Bloomington: Indiana University Press.

Bateson, Gregory. (Original work published 1955) 1972. "A Theory of Play and Fantasy." In *Steps to an Ecology of Mind*, 177–193. New York: Ballantine.

Bauman, Richard. 1977. *Verbal Art as Performance*. Prospect Heights, IL: Waveland.

Ben-Amos, Dan. 1972. "Toward a Definition of Folklore in Context." In *Toward New Perspectives in Folklore*, ed. Americo Paredes and Richard Bauman, 3–15. Austin: University of Texas Press.

Bennett, Gillian. 1988. "Legend: Performance and Truth." In *Monsters with Iron Teeth: Perspectives on Contemporary Legend III*, ed. Gillian Bennett and Paul Smith, 13–36. Sheffield: Sheffield Academic Press.

Bennett, Gillian. 1989a. "Belief Stories: The Forgotten Genre." *Western Folklore* 48 (4): 289–311. https://doi.org/10.2307/1499544.

Bennett, Gillian. 1989b. "Playful Chaos: The Anatomy of a Story-Telling Session." In *The Questing Beast: Perspectives on Contemporary Legend IV*, ed. Gillian Bennett and Paul Smith, 193–212. Sheffield: Sheffield Academic Press.

Bennett, Gillian. 1999. *Alas, Poor Ghost! Traditions of Belief in Story and Discourse*. Logan: Utah State University Press. https://doi.org/10.2307/j.ctt46nwwn.

Best, Joel, and Kathleen A. Bogle. 2014. *Kids Gone Wild: From Rainbow Parties to Sexting; Understanding the Hype over Teen Sex*. New York: New York University Press.

Bird, S. Elizabeth. 1983. "The Black Angel: Interpreting an Iowa City Legend." Paper presented at the annual meeting of the American Folklore Society, October 27, 1983, Nashville, TN.

Bird, S. 1994. "Playing with Fear: Interpreting the Adolescent Legend Trip." *Western Folklore* 53 (3): 191–209. https://doi.org/10.2307/1499808.

Blank, Trevor J. 2013. "Hybridizing Folk Culture: Toward a Theory of New Media and Vernacular Discourse." *Western Folklore* 72 (2): 105–130.

Blank, Trevor J. 2015. "Faux Your Entertainment: Amazon.com Product Reviews as a Locus of Digital Performance." *Journal of American Folklore* 128 (509): 286–297. https://doi.org/10.5406/jamerfolk.128.509.0286.

Blank, Trevor J. 2016. "Giving the 'Big Ten' a Whole New Meaning: Tasteless Humor and the Response to the Penn State Sexual Abuse Scandal." In *The Folkloresque: Reframing Folklore in a Popular Culture World*, ed. Michael Dylan Foster and Jeffrey A. Tolbert, 179–204. Logan: Utah State University Press.

Blank, Trevor J., and David J. Puglia. 2014. *Maryland Legends: Folklore from the Old Line State*. Charleston: History Press.

Blank, Trevor J., and Lynne S. McNeill. 2015. "Boiling Over: Creepypasta, Slender Man, and the New Face of Fear in Folklore." *Contemporary Legend*, series 3, 5: 1–13.

Blankenhorn, Stewart. 1983. "Pitcarin." Unpublished manuscript, Penn State Harrisburg Folklore Archives, accession #83-024.

BlastProcess. 2014. "App Review: Phantom Radar the Ghost Detector." March 24, 2014. Accessed November 26, 2016. https://www.youtube.com/watch?v=zJGyShMdF4w.

Blom, Thomas. 2000. "Morbid Tourism—A Postmodern Market Niche with an Example from Althorp." *Norsk Geografisk Tidsskrift* 54 (1): 29–36. https://doi.org/10.1080/002919500423564.

Bourget, Dominique, Andre Gagnon, and John M. W. Bradford. 1988. "Satanism in a Psychiatric Adolescent Population." *Canadian Journal of Psychiatry* 33 (3): 197–202. https://doi.org/10.1177/070674378803300307.

Bowman, Marion. 1987. "Contemporary Legend and Practical Joke." In *Perspectives on Contemporary Legend II*, ed. Gillian Bennett, Paul Smith, and J. D. A. Widdowson, 171–175. Sheffield: Sheffield Academic Press.

Boyes, Georgina. 1984. "Belief and Disbelief: An Examination of Reactions to the Presentation of Rumor Legends." In *Perspectives on Contemporary Legend*, ed. Paul Smith, 64–78. Sheffield: Sheffield Academic Press.

Bronner, Simon J. 1988. *American Children's Folklore*. Little Rock: August House.

Bronner, Simon J. 1990. "Left to Their Own Devices: Interpreting American Children's Folklore as an Adaptation to Aging." *Southern Folklore Quarterly* 47:101–115.

Bronner, Simon J. 2009. "Digitizing and Virtualizing Folklore." In *Folklore and the Internet*, ed. Trevor J. Blank, 21–66. Logan: Utah State University Press. https://doi.org/10.2307/j.ctt4cgrx5.5.

Bronner, Simon J. 2012. *Campus Traditions: Folklore from the Old-Time College to the Modern Mega-University*. Jackson: University Press of Mississippi. https://doi.org/10.14325/mississippi/9781617036163.001.0001.

Brown, Alan. 2006. *Ghost Hunters of the South*. Jackson: University Press of Mississippi.

Bruner, Edward M. 1984. "The Opening Up of Anthropology." In *Text, Play, and Story: The Construction and Reconstruction of Self and Society*, ed. E. M. Bruner, 1–16. Washington, DC: American Ethnological Society.

Brunvand, Jan Harold. 1981. *The Vanishing Hitchhiker*. New York: Norton.

Brunvand, Jan Harold. 1984. *The Choking Doberman*. New York: Norton.

Brunvand, Jan Harold. 1986. *The Mexican Pet*. New York: Norton.

Brunvand, Jan Harold. 1993. *The Baby Train*. New York: Norton.

Butler, Tom, and Lisa Butler. 2001. "About the AA-EVP." *AssociationTransCommunication*. https://atransc.org/about-aaevp/. Accessed August 9, 2018.

Carey, James W. 1977. "Mass Communication Research and Cultural Studies: An American View." In *Mass Communication and Society*, ed. James Curran, Michael Gurevitch, and Janet Woolacott, 409–425. London: Edward Arnold.

Chadwick, Nora Kershaw, and Viktor Zhirmunsky. (Original work published 1968) 2010. *Oral Epics of Central Asia*. Cambridge: Cambridge University Press.

Christiansen, Reidar Th. 1958. *The Migratory Legends*. Folklore Fellows Communication 175. Helsinki: Suomalainen Tiedeakatemia.

Clasen, Mathias. 2012. "Monsters Evolve: A Biocultural Approach to Horror Stories." *Review of General Psychology* 16 (2): 222–229. https://doi.org/10.1037/a0027918.

Clements, William M. 1980. "The Chain on the Tombstone." In *Indiana Folklore: A Reader*, ed. Linda Dégh, 258–264. Bloomington: Indiana University Press.

Clements, William M., and William E. Lightfoot. 1972. "The Legend of Stepp Cemetery." *Indiana Folklore* 5 (1): 92–135.

COPA-Group. 2009. Description. *AboutUs.org*. Accessed October 11, 2009. https://www.aboutus.org/Copa-Group.com.

Crowley, Matt. 2014. "We Tested Every Ghost-Hunting App in the Haunted Buildings of NYC." *Daily Dot*. Accessed November 23, 2016. www.dailydot.com/debug/ghost-hunting-apps-haunted-nyc/.

Davis, Judy. 1975. "Exorcist: Gosport Woman Claims to Drive Out Unwanted Spirits." *Bloomington Herald-Telephone*, April 15, 13. Bloomington, Indiana.

DeBolt, Margaret Wayt. 1984. *Savannah Spectres and Other Strange Tales*. Norfolk, VA: Donning.

Dégh, Linda. 1969a. "The Haunted Bridges Near Avon and Danville and Their Role in Legend Formation." *Indiana Folklore* 2 (1): 77–81.

Dégh, Linda. 1969b. "The House of Blue Lights." *Indiana Folklore* 2 (2): 11–28.

Dégh, Linda. 1971. "The 'Belief Legend' in Modern Society: Form, Function and Relationship to Other Genres." In *American Folk Legend: A Symposium*, ed. Wayland D. Hand, 62–66. Berkeley: University of California Press.

Dégh, Linda. 1980a. "The House of Blue Lights Revisited." In *Indiana Folklore: A Reader*, ed. Linda Dégh, 179–195. Bloomington: Indiana University Press.

Dégh, Linda, ed. 1980b. *Indiana Folklore: A Reader*. Bloomington: Indiana University Press.

Dégh, Linda. (Original work published 1969) 1989. *Folktales and Society: Story-Telling in a Hungarian Peasant Community*. Bloomington: Indiana University Press.

Dégh, Linda. 1995a. *Hungarian Folktales: The Art of Zsuzsanna Palko*. Jackson: University Press of Mississippi.

Dégh, Linda. 1995b. *Narratives in Society: A Performer-Centered Study of Narration*. Folklore Fellows Communications 255. Helsinki: Suomalainen Tiedeakatemia.

Dégh, Linda. 2001. *Legend and Belief*. Bloomington: Indiana University Press.

Dégh, Linda, and Andrew Vázsonyi. 1971. "Legend and Belief." *Genre* 4:281–304. Also in *Folklore Genres*, ed. Dan Ben-Amos, 93–123. Austin: University of Texas Press, 1976.

Dégh, Linda, and Andrew Vázsonyi. 1973. *The Dialectics of the Legend*. Bloomington: Indiana University Folklore Institute.

Dégh, Linda, and Andrew Vázsonyi. 1976. "Legend and Belief." In *Folklore Genres*, ed. Dan Ben-Amos, 93–123. Austin: University of Texas Press.

Dégh, Linda, and Andrew Vázsonyi. 1978. "The Crack on the Red Goblet; or, Truth and Modern Legend." In *Folklore in the Modern World*, ed. Richard M. Dorson, 253–272. The Hague: Mouton. https://doi.org/10.1515/9783110803099.253.

Dégh, Linda, and Andrew Vázsonyi. 1983. "Does the Word 'Dog' Bite? Ostensive Action: A Means of Legend-Telling." *Journal of Folklore Research* 20:5–34.

Dégh, Linda, and Andrew Vázsonyi. 1995. "The Crack on the Red Goblet, or Truth and Modern Legend." In *Narratives in Society: A Performer-Centered Study of Narration*, ed. Linda Dégh, 170–172. Folklore Fellows Communications. Helsinki: Suomalainen Tiedeakatemia.

Dorfman, Celia A. 1985. "Too Close for Comfort: A Look at Witchcraft in Lucas County." *Toledo Metropolitan*, October, 46–49.

Dorson, Richard M. 1974. *America in Legend*. New York: Pantheon.

Dorst, John. 1990. "Tags and Burners, Cycles and Networks: Folklore in the Teletronic Age." *Journal of Folklore Research* 27 (3): 179–190.

Dundes, Alan. 1971. "On the Psychology of Legend." In *American Folk Legend: A Symposium*, ed. Wayland D. Hand, 29–31. Berkeley: University of California Press.

Dundes, Alan. 1988. *Cinderella: A Casebook*. Madison: University of Wisconsin Press.

Einarsson-Mullarky, Magnús. 1968. "The House of Blue Lights." *Indiana Folklore* 1 (1): 82–91.

Ellis, Bill. 1982. "Headless Hattie: Archetype and Legend in Adolescent Horror." Paper delivered at the annual meeting of the American Folklore Society, Minneapolis, MN, October 17, 1982.

Ellis, Bill. 1982–1983. "Legend-Tripping in Ohio: A Behavioral Study." In *Papers in Comparative Studies 2*, ed. Daniel Barnes, Rosemary O. Joyce, and Steven Swann Jones, 61–73. Columbus: Center for Comparative Studies in the Humanities, Ohio State University.

Ellis, Bill. 1983. "Adolescent Legend-Tripping." *Psychology Today*, August 1983.

Ellis, Bill. 1988. "The Fast Food Ghost: A Study in the Supernatural's Capacity to Survive Secularization." In *Monsters with Iron Teeth: Perspectives on Contemporary Legend III*, ed. Gillian Bennett and Paul Smith, 37–78. Sheffield: Sheffield Academic Press.

Ellis, Bill. 1989a. "Death by Folklore: Ostension, Contemporary Legend, and Murder." *Western Folklore* 48 (3): 201–220. https://doi.org/10.2307/1499739.

Ellis, Bill. 1989b. "When Is a Legend? An Essay in Legend Formation." In *The Questing Beast: Perspectives on Contemporary Legend IV*, ed. Gillian Bennett and Paul Smith, 31–54. Sheffield: Sheffield Academic Press.

Ellis, Bill. 1990. "The Devil-Worshippers at the Prom: Rumor-Panic as Therapeutic Magic." *Western Folklore* 49 (1): 27–49. https://doi.org/10.2307/1499481.

Ellis, Bill. 1991. "Legend-Trips and Satanism: Adolescents' Ostensive Traditions as 'Cult' Activity." In *The Satanism Scare*, ed. James I. Richardson, Joel Best, and David G. Bromley, 279–295. New York: Aldine de Gruyter.

Ellis, Bill. 1996. "Legend Trip." In *American Folklore: An Encyclopedia*, ed. Jan Harold Brunvand, 439–440. New York: Garland.

Ellis, Bill. 2001. *Aliens, Ghosts, and Cults: Legends We Live*. Jackson: University Press of Mississippi.

Ellis, Bill. 2004. *Lucifer Ascending: The Occult in Folklore and Popular Culture*. Lexington: University Press of Kentucky.

Ellis, Bill. 2015. "The Haunted Asian Landscapes of Lafcadio Hearn: Old Japan." In *Putting the Supernatural in Its Place: Folklore, the Hypermodern, and the Ethereal*, ed. Jeannie Banks Thomas, 192–220. Salt Lake City: University of Utah Press.

Erikson, Erik. 1968. *Identity: Youth and Crisis*. New York: Norton.

Evans, Chris, and Ted Wendling. 1985a. "Hunt Near Toledo Fails to Find Human Sacrifices." *The Plain Dealer*, 1. June 21. Cleveland, Ohio.

Evans, Chris, and Ted Wendling. 1985b. "Bedeviled Searchers Call It Off." *The Plain Dealer*, 1. June 22. Cleveland, Ohio.

Fine, Gary Alan. 1983. *Shared Fantasy: Role-Playing Games as Social Worlds*. Chicago: University of Chicago Press.

Fisher, Douglas. 1975. "The Four-Mile Desert: A Horror Story." *North Carolina Folklore Journal* 23:23–25.
Foster, Michael Dylan. 2015. *The Folkloresque: Reframing Folklore in a Popular Culture World*. Logan: Utah State University Press. https://doi.org/10.7330/9781607324188.
Frank, Russell. 2011. *Newslore: Contemporary Folklore on the Internet*. Jackson: University Press of Mississippi. https://doi.org/10.14325/mississippi/9781604739282.001.0001.
Gabbert, Lisa. 2015. "Legend Quests and the Curious Case of St. Ann's Retreat: The Performative Landscape." In *Putting the Supernatural in Its Place: Folklore, the Hypermodern, and the Ethereal*, ed. Jeannie Banks-Thomas, 146–169. Salt Lake City: University of Utah Press.
Ghost Radar®: LEGACY-Documentation. 2016. *Spud Pickles*. Accessed November 24, 2016. https://spudpickles.com/help/ghost-radar-legacy/.
Glazer, Mark. 1984. "Continuity and Change in Legendry: Two Mexican-American Examples." In *Perspectives in Contemporary Legend: Proceedings of the Conference on Contemporary Legend, Sheffield, July 1982*, ed. Paul Smith, 108–127. Conference Paper Series 4. Sheffield: Center for English Culture, Tradition, and Language.
Glazer, Mark. 1985. "The Traditionalization of the Contemporary Legend: The Mexican American Example." *Fabula* 26 (3/4): 288–297. https://doi.org/10.1515/fabl.1985.26.3-4.288.
Glazer, Mark. 1986. "The Mexican-American Legend in the Rio Grande Valley: An Overview." *Borderlands* 10:143–160.
Glazer, Mark. 1989. "Gravity Hill: Belief and Belief Legend." In *The Questing Beast: Perspectives on Contemporary Legend IV*, ed. Gillian Bennett and Paul Smith, 171–205. Sheffield: Sheffield Academic Press.
Glazer, Mark. 1990. "The Contexts of the Contemporary Legend: 'The Vanishing Hitchhiker' and 'Gravity Hill.'" In *A Nest of Vipers: Perspectives on Contemporary Legend 5*, ed. Gillian Bennett and Paul Smith, 77–87. Sheffield: Sheffield Academic Press for the International Society for Contemporary Legend Research in association with Center for English Culture, Tradition, and Language.
Glimm, James York. 1983. *Flat-Landers and Ridge-Runners*. Pittsburgh: University of Pittsburgh Press.
Goffman, Erving. 1959. *The Presentation of Self in Everyday Life*. New York: Doubleday.
Goffman, Erving. 1974. *Frame Analysis: An Essay on the Organization of Experience*. Boston: Northeastern University Press.
Goldstein, Diane E. 2007. "The Commodification of Belief." In *Haunting Experiences: Ghosts in Contemporary Folklore*, ed. Diane E. Goldstein, Sylvia Ann Grider, and Jeannie Banks Thomas, 171–205. Logan: Utah State University Press. https://doi.org/10.2307/j.ctt4cgmqg.11.
Goldstein, Diane E., Sylvia Ann Grider, and Jeannie Banks Thomas, eds. 2007. *Haunting Experiences: Ghosts in Contemporary Folklore*. Logan: Utah State University Press.
Gordon, Avery. 1997. *Ghostly Matters: Haunting and the Sociological Imagination*. Minneapolis: University of Minnesota Press.
Grider, Sylvia Ann. 1973. "Dormitory Legend-Telling in Progress: Fall, 1971–Winter, 1973." *Indiana Folklore* 6 (1): 1–32.
Grider, Sylvia Ann. 1984. "The Razor Blades in the Apple Syndrome." In *Perspectives in Contemporary Legend*, ed. Paul Smith, 128–140. Sheffield: Sheffield Academic Press for the International Society for Contemporary Legend Research, in association with Center for English Culture, Tradition, and Language.
Grider, Sylvia Ann. 1999. "The Haunted House in Literature, Popular Culture, and Tradition: A Consistent Image." *Contemporary Legend*, n.s. 2:174–204.

Grider, Sylvia Ann. 2007. "Haunted Houses." In *Haunting Experiences: Ghosts in Contemporary Folklore*, ed. Diane E. Goldstein, Sylvia Ann Grider, and Jeannie Banks Thomas, 143–170. Logan: Utah State University Press.
Grimm, Jacob. 1883. *Teutonic Mythology*. Vol. 3. Trans. James Steven Stallybrass. London: George Bell and Sons.
Grimm, Jacob, and Wilhelm Grimm. (Original work published 1891) 2006. *Deutsche Sagen*. Cologne: Anaconda Verlag.
Guinee, William. 1987. "Satanism in Yellowwood Forest: The Interdependence of Antagonistic Worldviews." *Indiana Folklore and Oral History* 16:1–30.
Gutowski, John A. 1970. "Traditions of the Devil's Hollows: Relationship between a Place Name and Its Legends." *Indiana Folklore* 3:190–213.
Hall, Gary. 1973. "The Big Tunnel." *Indiana Folklore* 6:139–173.
Hall, Gary. 1980. "The Big Tunnel." *Indiana Folklore: A Reader*, ed. Linda Dégh, 225–257. Bloomington: Indiana University Press.
Haring, Lee, and Mark Breslerman. 1977. "The Cropsey Maniac." *New York Folklore* 3 (1–4): 15–28.
Harling, Kristie. 1971. "The Grunch: An Example of New Orleans Teenage Folklore." *Louisiana Folklore Miscellany* 3 (2): 15–20.
Hawthorne, Nathaniel. (Original work published 1851) 1999. *The House of the Seven Gables*. New York: Dover Thrift Editions.
Hearn, Lafcadio. (Original work published 1894) 2012. *Glimpses of an Unfamiliar Japan: First Series*. Auckland, NZ: Floating Press.
Hicks, Robert. 1989. "Satanic Cults: A Skeptical View of the Law Enforcement Approach." In *Satanism in America: How the Devil Got Much More Than His Due*, ed. Shawn Carlson, and Gerald Larue, with Gerry O'Sullivan, April A. Mashe, and D. Hudson Frew, A1–A35. El Cerrito, CA: Gaia.
Hinson, Glenn. 2000. *Fire in My Bones: Transcendence and the Holy Spirit in African American Gospel*. Philadelphia: University of Pennsylvania Press.
Hoffmann-Krayer, Edouard, and Hanns Bächtold-Stäubli. 1931–1932. *Handwörterbuch des Deutschen Aberglaubens*. Vol. 4. Berlin: Walter de Gruyter.
Honko, Lauri. 1962. *Geisterglaube in Ingermanland*. Helsinki: Suomalainen Tiedeakatemia.
Honko, Lauri. 1984. "Empty Texts, Full Meanings: On Transformal Meaning in Folklore." *Arv: Scandinavian Yearbook of Folklore 40*, ed. Bengt R. Jonsson, 94–125.
Howard, Robert Glenn. 2008. "Electronic Hybridity: The Persistent Processes of the Vernacular Web." *Journal of American Folklore* 121 (480): 192–218. https://doi.org/10.1353/jaf.0.0012.
Hufford, David J. 1982. "Traditions of Disbelief." *New York Folklore* 8 (3–4): 47–55.
Hunnicutt, Robert. 2004. *Information About Ghost Hunting*. Email communication to Lynne McNeill, July 9, 2004.
Hyde, Lewis. 1998. *Trickster Makes This World: Mischief, Myth and Art*. New York: Farrar, Straus and Giroux.
Johnson, Donald F. 1984. "Black Angel Data Notebook." Unpublished research project. Iowa City: Department of Anthropology, University of Iowa.
Jones, Jack. 2016. Personal interview with Elizabeth Tucker online, March 14, 2016.
Kalmre, Eda. 2013. *The Human Sausage Factory: A Study of Post-war Rumour in Tartu*. Tallinn, Estonia: Rodopi.
Kimball, Solon T. 1960. "Introduction." In *The Rites of Passage* by Arnold van Gennep, translated by Monika B. Vizedom and Gabrielle L. Caffee, v–xx. Chicago: University of Chicago Press.
Kinsella, Michael. 2011. *Legend-Tripping Online*. Jackson: University Press of Mississippi. https://doi.org/10.14325/mississippi/9781604739831.001.0001.

Kitta, Andrea. 2011. *Vaccination and Public Concern in History: Legend, Rumor and Risk Perception.* New York: Routledge.

Kitta, Andrea. 2015. "'What Happens When the Pictures Are No Longer Photoshops?' Slender Man, Belief, and the Unacknowledged Common Experience." *Contemporary Legend,* series 3, 5: 62–76.

Knox, Mark. 1971. "The Moss Man." Unpublished manuscript, Indiana University Folklore Archives, accession #71-321.

Koske, Mary. 1981. "An Annotated Bibliography of the Theory of Angels." Unpublished manuscript, Indiana University.

Koven, Mikel J. 2007. "*Most Haunted* and the Convergence of Traditional Belief and Popular Television." *Folklore* 118 (2): 183–202. https://doi.org/10.1080/00155870701337403.

Koven, Mikel J. 2008. *Film, Folklore, and Urban Legends.* Lanham, MD: Scarecrow.

Langlois, Janet. 1980. "'Mary Whales, I Believe in You': Myth and Ritual Subdued." In *Indiana Folklore: A Reader,* ed. Linda Dégh, 196–224. Bloomington: Indiana University Press.

Lanning, Kenneth V. 1989. "Satanic, Occult, Ritualistic Crime: A Law Enforcement Perspective." In *Satanism in America: How the Devil Got Much More Than His Due,* ed. Shawn Carlson and Gerald Larue, with Gerry O'Sullivan, April A. Mashe, and D. Hudson Frew. B1–12. El Cerrito, CA: Gaia.

Lassen, Henrik R. 1995. "'The Improved Product': A Philological Investigation of a Contemporary Legend." *Contemporary Legend* 5:1–37.

Leach, Edmund. 1984. "Further Thoughts on the Realm of Folly." In *Text, Play, and Story: The Construction and Reconstruction of Self and Society,* ed. E. M. Bruner, 356–364. Washington, DC: American Ethnological Society.

Lee, BarBara. 1975a. Interview with Linda Dégh. May 14.

Lee, BarBara. 1975b. Radio interview on "Cross-Talk," WFIU, Bloomington, Indiana. May 14.

Licht, Michael. 1974. "Some Automotive Play Activities of Suburban Teenagers." *New York Folklore Quarterly* 30:51–52.

Lindahl, Carl. 1993. "Ostensive Play." Paper delivered at the annual meeting of the International Society for Contemporary Legend Research, Bloomington, IN, June 10, 1993.

Lindahl, Carl. 1997. "The Oral Aesthetic and the Bicameral Mind." In *Gilgamesh: A Reader,* ed. John Maier, 328–336. Wauconda, IL: Bolchazy-Carducci.

Lindahl, Carl. 2004a. *American Folktales from the Collections of the Library of Congress.* 2 vols. Armonk, NY: M. E. Sharpe.

Lindahl, Carl. 2004b. "Thrills and Miracles: Legends of Lloyd Chandler." *Journal of Folklore Research* 41 (2–3): 133–171. https://doi.org/10.2979/JFR.2004.41.2-3.133.

Lindahl, Carl. 2005. "Ostensive Healing: Pilgrimage to the San Antonio Ghost Tracks." *Journal of American Folklore* 118 (468): 164–185. https://doi.org/10.1353/jaf.2005.0023.

Lowney, Kathleen S. 1995. "Teenage Satanism as Oppositional Youth Subculture." *Journal of Contemporary Ethnography* 23 (4): 453–484. https://doi.org/10.1177/089124195023004003.

Lüthi, Max. 1976. "Aspects of the Märchen and the Legend." In *Folklore Genres,* ed. Dan Ben-Amos, 17–34. Austin: University of Texas Press.

Lyons, Arthur. 1989. *Satan Wants You: The Cult of Devil Worship in America.* New York: Mysterious Press.

Madsen, William. 1973. *The Mexican-Americans of South Texas.* New York: Holt, Rinehart and Winston.

Magliocco, Sabina. 1985. "The Bloomington Jaycees' Haunted House." *Indiana Folklore and Oral History* 14:19–28.

McIver, Tom. 1988. "Backward Masking and Other Backward Thoughts about Music." *Skeptical Inquirer* 13:50–63.

McNeill, Lynne S. 2006. "Contemporary Ghost Hunting and the Relationship between Proof and Experience." *Contemporary Legend* 9:96–110.

McNeill, Lynne S. 2012. "Real Virtuality: Enhancing Locality by Enacting the Small World Theory." In *Folk Culture in the Digital Age*, ed. Trevor J. Blank, 85–97. Logan: Utah State University Press.

Meley, Patricia M. 1991. "Adolescent Legend Trips as Teenage Cultural Response: A Study of the Lore in Context." *Children's Folklore Review* 14:5–25.

Mikkelson, Barbara. 1998–2003. "Helping Hands." Accessed September 2004. https://www.snopes.com/horrors/ghosts/hndprint.htm.

Mitchell, Carol A. 1969. "The White House." *Indiana Folklore* 2:97–109.

Moss, James C. 1979. "The Barrens of Southern Chester County and Their Role in Story Formation, Transmission and Maintenance." *Keystone Folklore* 23:1–27.

Mullen, Patrick B. 1972. "Modern Legend and Rumor Theory." *Journal of the Folklore Institute* 9 (2/3): 95–109. https://doi.org/10.2307/3814160.

Nicolaisen, W.F.H. 1984. "Modern Legend and Rumor Theory." In *Perspectives on Contemporary Legend*, ed. Paul Smith, 167–177. Sheffield: Sheffield Academic Press.

"Number of Apps Available in Leading App Stores as of June 2016." 2016. *Statista: The Statistics Portal*. Accessed November 21, 2016. https://www.statista.com/statistics/276623/number-of-apps-available-in-leading-app-stores/.

Obiwan. 1998. "Voting Center-Vote Results . . . for Ghostly Urban Legends." *Obiwan's UFO-Free Paranormal Page*. Accessed September 2004. http://www.ghosts.org/results/198res.html.

Oester, Dave. 2004. "Information about Ghost Hunting." Personal communication to Lynne McNeill, July 6, 2004.

Old Dickinson. 2014. *YouTube*, May 2, 2014. https://www.youtube.com/watch?v=_DJlPR30a2g&feature=youtu.be.

Oman, C. C. 1944. "The English Folklore of Gervase of Tilbury." *Folklore* 55 (1): 2–15. https://doi.org/10.1080/0015587X.1944.9717702.

Omvedt, Gail. 1966. "Play as an Element in Social Life." *Berkeley Journal of Sociology* 11:1–13.

Oring, Elliott. 1986. *Folk Groups and Folklore Genres: An Introduction*. Logan: Utah State University Press.

Orso, Ethelyn G. 1989. "The Mona Lisa of New Orleans' City Park: The Making of a Legend." Paper presented at the annual meeting of the American Folklore Society, Philadelphia.

OSUFA. n.d. The Ohio State University Folklore Archives, Columbus. Patrick Mullen, archivist.

Otto, Rudolph. (Original work published 1923) 1958. *The Idea of the Holy*. Trans. John W. Harvey. London: Oxford University Press.

Page, Truman, Vivinea Page, and Samantha Blake. 2003. Interview by Tim Prizer. April 3, 2003.

Paredes, Americo. (Original work published 1968) 1993a. "Folk Medicine and the Intercultural Jest." In *Folklore and Culture on the Texas-Mexican Border*, ed. Richard Bauman, 49–72. Austin: Center for Mexican American Studies, University of Texas.

Paredes, Americo. (Original work published 1977) 1993b. "On Ethnographic Work among Minority Groups: A Folklorist's Perspective." In *Folklore and Culture on the Texas-Mexican Border*, ed. Richard Bauman, 73–93. Austin: Center for Mexican American Studies, University of Texas.

Pentikäinen, Juha. 1968. "Grenzprobleme zwischen Memorat und Sage." *Temenos* 3:136–167.
Peuckert, Will-Erich. 1965. *Sagen: Geburt und Antwort der mythischen Welt*. Berlin: Schmidt.
Phantom Radar. 2017. "The Ghost Detector." *Cnet*. Accessed March 18, 2017. https://download.cnet.com/Phantom-Radar-The-Ghost-Detector/3000-2094_4-75186987.html.
Posen, I. Sheldon. 1974. "Pranks and Practical Jokes at Children's Summer Camps." *Southern Folklore Quarterly* 38:299–309.
Prizer, Tim. 2004. "'Shame Old Roads Can't Talk': Narrative, Experience, and Belief in the Framing of Legend-Trips as Performance." *Contemporary Legend* n.s. 7: 67–97.
Prophet31. 2004. "Haunted Train Tracks." *Urban Legends*. Accessed September 2004. https://www.geocities.com/area51/cavern/3987/traintracks.html.
PSUHFA. n.d. The Pennsylvania State University Hazleton Campus Folklore Archives, Hazleton. Bill Ellis, archivist.
Raines, Sharon. 2004. "Information about Ghost Hunting." Email communication to Lynne McNeill, July 22, 2004.
Raphael, Ray. 1988. *The Men from the Boys: Rites of Passage in Male America*. Lincoln: University of Nebraska Press.
Röhrich, Lutz. 1988. "The Quest of Meaning in Folk Narrative Research." In *The Brothers Grimm and Folktale*, ed. James M. McGlathery, 1–15. Urbana: University of Illinois Press.
Roll, Todd. 2004. "Information about Ghost Hunting." Email communication to Lynne McNeill, July 6, 2004.
Rudinger, Joel D. 1976. "Folk Ogres of the Firelands: Narrative Descriptions of a North Central Ohio Community." *Indiana Folklore* 9:52–62.
Ruiz, Rosanna. 2001. "Woman Who Threw Children in Bayou Is Mending Her Life." *Houston Chronicle*, July 4, 2001, 29A–30A.
Samuelson, Sue. 1979. "The White Witch: An Analysis of an Adolescent Legend." *Indiana Folklore* 12:18–37.
Sauke, Kim. 2003. *Death of Halloween*. Indianapolis: Cork Hill.
Simpson, Jacqueline. 1973. *The Folklore of Sussex*. London: B. T. Batsford.
Sparks, Beatrice. 1979. *Jay's Journal*. New York: Times Books.
"Spirit Story Box: The Spirits Are Telling Their Stories." 2016. Spirit Story Box. Accessed November 23, 2016. www.spiritstorybox.com/.
Stahler, Jeff. 2015. "Smartphone, Smartphone on a Stick, Who Has the Fairest Profile Pic?" *Sizzle*. Accessed March 6, 2017. https://onsizzle.com/i/smartphone-smartphone-ona-stick-stahler-2015-jeff-stahler-dist-by-universal-uclick-2550175.
Stoneman, Richard. 2011. *The Ancient Oracles: Making the Gods Speak*. New Haven: Yale University Press.
Tatar, Maria. 2006. *Secrets Beyond the Door: The Story of Bluebeard and His Wives*. Princeton: Princeton University Press.
Thigpen, Kenneth A. 1971. "Adolescent Legends in Brown County: A Survey." *Indiana Folklore* 4 (2): 141–215.
Thomas, Jeannie. 2003. *Naked Barbies, Warrior Joes, and Other Forms of Visible Gender*. Urbana: University of Illinois Press.
Thomas, Jeannie Banks. 2015. *Putting the Supernatural in Its Place: Folklore, the Hypermodern, and the Ethereal*. Salt Lake City: University of Utah Press.
Thouless, Robert H. 1974. *From Anecdote to Experiment in Psychical Research*. London: Routledge.
Toelken, Barre. 1975. "Folklore, Worldview, and Communication." In *Folklore: Performance and Communication*, ed. Dan Ben-Amos and Kenneth S. Goldstein, 265–286. The Hague: Mouton. https://doi.org/10.1515/9783110880229.265.

Toelken, Barre. 1979. *The Dynamics of Folklore*. Boston: Houghton Mifflin.
Tolbert, Jeffrey A. 2013. "'The Sort of Story That Has You Covering Your Mirrors': The Case of Slender Man." *Semiotic Review* 2 (November). Accessed November 23, 2016. http://www.semioticreview.com.
Tolson, Mike. 2001. "What Now for Andrea Yates?" *Houston Chronicle*, July 1, 2001, 1A, 16A.
Trotter, Robert T., and Juan Antonio Chavira. 1981. *Curanderismo: Mexican American Folk Healing*. Athens: University of Georgia Press.
Tucker, Elizabeth. 1975. "The Exorcist of Gosport." Unpublished graduate student paper, Folklore 404, Indiana University.
Tucker, Elizabeth. 2005. *Campus Legends*. Westport, CT: Greenwood.
Tucker, Elizabeth. 2007. *Haunted Halls: Ghostlore of American College Campuses*. Jackson: University Press of Mississippi.
Tucker, Elizabeth. 2008. "Houses of Horror." *Voices: The Journal of New York Folklore* 32 (3–4): 27.
Tucker, Elizabeth. 2011. *Haunted Southern Tier*. Charleston: History Press.
Tucker, Elizabeth. 2015a. "Messages from the Dead." In *Putting the Supernatural in Its Place: Folklore, the Hypermodern, and the Ethereal*, ed. Jeannie Banks Thomas, 170–191. Salt Lake City: University of Utah Press.
Tucker, Elizabeth. 2015b. "Waiting for Slender Man." *Contemporary Legend*, series 3, 5: 124–129.
Tucker, Elizabeth. 2016. "'There's an App for That': Ghost Hunting with Smartphones." *Children's Folklore Review* 38: 27–38.
Turner, Victor. 1974. *Dramas, Fields, and Metaphors*. Ithaca: Cornell University Press.
Turner, Victor. 1992. "Death and the Dead in the Pilgrimage Process." In *Blazing the Trail*, ed. Edith Turner, 29–47. Tucson: University of Arizona Press.
Turner, Victor, and Edith Turner. 1978. *Image and Pilgrimage in Christian Culture: Anthropological Perspectives*. New York: Columbia University Press.
Tyson, Alvis, and Joann Tyson. 2003. Interview by Tim Prizer, March 31, 2003.
Utah Ghost Hunters. 2004. Accessed July 5, 2004. http://www.ghostwave.com.
Vancouver Paranormal. 2006. Letters. *Vancouver Parnormal*. Accessed December 1, 2008. http://usersites.horrorfind.com/home/ghosts/phantomphive/lettersfromfolks.html.
Van Gennep, Arnold. (Original work published in 1908) 1960. *The Rites of Passage*. Translated by Monika B. Vizedom and Gabrielle L. Caffee. Chicago: University of Chicago Press.
Victor, Jeffrey S. 1990. "Satanic Cult Rumors as Contemporary Legend." *Western Folklore* 49 (1): 51–81. https://doi.org/10.2307/1499482.
Victor, Jeffrey S. 1993. *Satanic Panic: The Creation of a Contemporary Legend*. New York: Open Court.
Von Sydow, Carl Wilhelm. (Original work published 1934) 1948. "Kategorien der Prosa-Volksdichtung." In *Carl Wilhelm von Sydow: Selected Papers on Folklore*, 60–85. Copenhagen: Rosenkilde and Bagger.
Wagner, Stephen. (Original work published in 2001) 2017. "The Haunted Railroad Crossing." *ThoughtCo*. Accessed August 9, 2018 (original access date, September 2004). http://paranormal.about.com/od/hauntedplaces/a/The-Haunted-Railroad-Crossing.htm.
Weidner, Stephen. 2004. *Information about Ghost Hunting*. Email communication to Lynne McNeill, July 21, 2004.
Weisberg, Barbara. 2005. *Talking to the Dead: Kate and Maggie Fox and the Rise of Spiritualism*. New York: HarperOne.

Williams, Juanita H. 1978. "Woman: Myth and Stereotype." *International Journal of Women's Studies* 1:221–247.

Williamson, Tom, and Liz Bellamy. 1983. *Ley Lines in Question: Kingswood.* Tadworth, UK: World's Work.

Wise, Eleanor, and Jesse Wise. 2003. Interview by Tim Prizer, April 7, 2003.

Wiseman, Richard, and Robert L. Morris. 1995. *Guidelines for Testing Psychic Claimants.* Hatfield, UK: University of Hertfordshire Press.

About the Authors

S. ELIZABETH BIRD is Professor of Anthropology at the University of South Florida.

BILL ELLIS is Professor Emeritus of English at Pennsylvania State University in Hazleton.

CARL LINDAHL is the Martha Gano Houstoun Research Professor of English at the University of Houston.

LYNNE S. MCNEILL is Assistant Professor of English at Utah State University.

PATRICIA M. MELEY is an instructor in English and Humanities at Thaddeus Stevens College of Technology.

TIM PRIZER has taught anthropology at the University of North Carolina at Chapel Hill.

ELIZABETH TUCKER is Distinguished Service Professor of English at Binghamton University.

SPECIAL THANKS TO:

WILLIAM M. CLEMENTS is Professor of English at Arkansas State University.

LINDA DÉGH, who passed away in 2014, was Distinguished Professor of Folklore at Indiana University.

GARY HALL has taught folklore at Indiana University.

WILLIAM E. LIGHTFOOT, who passed away in 2016, was Professor Emeritus of English at Appalachian State University.

KENNETH A. THIGPEN is Associate Professor Emeritus at Pennsylvania State University Lehigh Valley and has been that campus's Director of Academic Affairs.

Index

Aeneas, 20–21
Albino Farm (Ohio), 71
alcohol, 64, 86
American Association of Electronic Voice Phenomena (AAEVP), 179
Amityville Horror, The (film), 24
Amityville Horror House (New York), 25
angels, 116–17
Anson, Jay, 25
apps, smartphone, 3, 192–206

Baughman, Ernest, 31
Bauman, Richard, 131
belief, 162, 167, 174, 179–91
Bennett, Gillian, 182, 184
Best, Joel, 8
Big Tunnel (Indiana), 10, 52–53
Bird, S. Elizabeth, 12, 112–13, 209
Black Angel statue (Iowa), 96, 112–28
Blair Witch Project, The (film), 25
Blake, Samantha, 133
Blankenhorn, Stewart, 86–87
Blom, Thomas, 9
Bogle, Kathleen A., 8
Borden, Lizzie, 18
"Boyfriend's Death, The," 65
bridges, haunted, 13, 22, 63, 70
Bronner, Simon J., 8, 87, 194–95
Brown, Alan, 181, 184
Brown, Gary E., 31–32
Bruner, Edward M., 114
Brunvand, Jan Harold, 7, 119–20

Carey Tombstone (Ohio), 71
cars, 3, 68, 85–86, 139, 163, 172–73
cell phone. *See* smartphone
Chas McGee's Grave (Colorado), 15
children, sanctity of, 161–63
Christiansen, Reidar Th., 6
Clements, William M., 10, 47, 48, 51–52, 54, 58, 61, 75
Coffin Factory (Canada), 18
Cropsey Maniac (New York), 17
Cry Baby Bridge, 63, 69–70, 209

death, fear of, 89–90
DeBolt, Margaret Wayt, 150
DeFeo, Ronald, 25
Dégh, Linda, 4, 5–6, 8–9, 11, 13, 31–46, 54–56, 62, 87, 94–95, 97, 131, 141, 143–45, 148, 153–55, 167, 173–74, 194–96, 207, 209
digital legend trips, 26–30
disbelief, 179–91
Doctor Crow's House (Ohio), 70
Dolezal, Edward, 115
Dorson, Richard M., 9
dowsing rods, 181, 185
drugs, 64, 86
Dundes, Alan, 29

ecotypification, 7
Eigenmann Hall (Indiana University), 59–60
Einarsson-Mullarky, Magnús, 37, 42
Eisenbud, Jule, 184
electronic voice phenomena (EVPs), 26, 179, 182, 189
Ellis, Bill, 8, 10–13, 23, 61–62, 75, 86, 90, 94, 123, 131–32, 136, 138–40, 142, 146–48, 153–54, 194, 208
epics, 20–21

Feldevert, Nicholas, 116
Feldevert, Teresa, 113
FitzHugh, Osbert (knight), 22
folktales, 5
Fox, Kate, 19, 197
Fox, Margaret, 19, 197
frame analysis, 12, 123–24, 129–52

gender, 36, 64, 86, 88–89, 112–13, 121–24, 128
Georgia Southern University, 132–33
Gervase of Tilbury, 22
Gesar, King, 21
Ghost Adventures (TV show), 26
Ghost Asylum (TV show), 26
Ghost Hunters (TV show), 26
ghost hunting, 17, 178–91
Ghost Lab (TV show), 26

ghost photography, 29, 179, 182, 185
Ghost Road (Georgia), 129–52
ghosts, 4, 34, 51, 156, 178–206
Ghost Tracks (San Antonio), 12, 153–74
Gilgamesh, 20
Glazer, Mark, 172
Goffman, Erving, 129, 146–47
Goldstein, Diane E., 9, 197
Gordon, Avery, 195
Gore Orphanage (Ohio), 70
graffiti, 98
gravity hill, 153, 156, 174
Green Man (Ohio), 63, 71
Grider, Sylvia Ann, 9, 54–55
Grimm, Jacob, 4–5
Grimm, Wilhelm, 5

Hall, Gary, 10, 52, 62
Halloween, 12, 25, 35, 113
harassment trip, 75
Haug's Road (Pennsylvania), 72, 78, 80–83, 86, 88
Haunting, The (film), 24
Hawthorne, Nathaniel, 23, 52
healing, 166–71
Hearn, Lafcadio, 22
Hecate, 207
Hills and Dales Park (Ohio), 70–71
Hinson, Glenn, 143–44
Homer, 21
Honko, Lauri, 5, 123
"Hook, The," 33, 66, 71
House of Blue Lights (Indiana), 9, 36–45
House of the Troll (Pennsylvania), 78
houses, haunted, 22, 24
Houston, University of, 155
Hufford, David, 130, 132, 149
Hunnicutt, Robert, 191

initiation, 51, 64, 82, 85
International Society for Contemporary Legend Research, 7–8, 29
internet, 26–29

Jackson, Shirley, 24, 52
James, Henry, 24
Johnson, Donald F., 96, 114
Jones, Jack, 196

Kalmre, Eda, 8
Kearney, Matt, 138
Kearney, Ralph, 138

Kearney, Ryan, 138
Kimball, Solon, 85
King, Stephen, 15
Kinsella, Michael, 13, 26–27, 193
Kitta, Andrea, 8, 28
Koven, Michael J., 25

La Llorona, 154, 207
Lassen, Henrik, 8
LaVey, Anton, 105
Lee, BarBara, 54–60
legend conduits, 144
legend dialectics, 4, 167–71
legend quests, 8
legends: contemporary, 8; migratory, 6. 63; saint's, 5; urban, 7
Leija, Juana, 154
Lewis, C.S., 16
Lightfoot, William E., 10, 47, 48, 51, 54, 58, 61
Lily Dale (New York), 19
liminality, 16–19
Lindahl, Carl, 12, 153–54, 209
Lizzie Borden Bed and Breakfast (Massachusetts), 18
Lowney, Kathleen S., 110
Lüthi, Max, 5

Märchen, 5, 156
Mary Jane's Grave (Ohio), 67, 70, 102
Mary Stuckum's Grave (Ohio), 70
McNeill, Lynne S., 13–17, 178–79, 207–10
Meley, Patricia M., 10, 72–73
Midget House (Pennsylvania), 78
Mikkelson, Barbara, 7
Mikkelson, David, 7
miracles, 164–65
mobile phone. *See* smartphone
Moonville Tunnel (Ohio), 68
moral panic, 11, 94
Morgan-Monroe State Forest (Indiana), 47
Morris, Robert L., 184
Morse, Ella Mae, 45
Most Haunted (TV show), 25, 187
Mud Man (Indiana), 33
Mullen, Patrick, 116, 120

numinous, 5, 30, 190–91

O'Bryan, Ronald "Candy Man," 154
Oester, Dave, 185–86, 188
Old Rafuse (Binghamton University), 199–205

Index

Omvedt, Gail, 123
orbs, ghost 185
ostension, 94; criminal, 12; hypermodern, 195–96; proto-, 11, 195–96; performative, 146; pseudo-, 11–12, 97, 100–102, 195; quasi-, 11, 98–100, 195; reverse, 29, 195
Otto, Rudolph, 190

Page, Truman, 133
Page, Vivinea, 133
parties, 52, 64
Pentikaïnen, Juha, 6
Peter Ghoul (Ohio), 65
Peuckert, Will-Erich, 6
pilgrimage, 8–9, 13, 155, 174
Poe, Edgar Allan, 23
prank, 12
Preston, Cathy, 14
Price, Harry, 181
Prizer, Tim, 12, 129–30, 209
Puglia, David, 7

railroad, 52–53, 61, 134–39, 142–52, 155, 159–60, 174
Raines, Sharon, 188, 190
Raphael, Ray, 85
Real Ghostbusters (TV show), 187
rebellion, rituals of, 75
rites of passage, 64, 85, 89, 91
rituals, 74, 79, 87, 102–11, 172
Röhrich, Lutz, 7
Roll, Todd, 179, 184, 190
rumor panics, 94

Saint Ann's Retreat (Utah), 207–9
Samuelson, Sue, 36, 62
Satanism, 94–111
Scotch Ridge Cemetery (Ohio), 71
Screaming Mimi Bridge (Ohio), 70
sexuality, 16, 64–65, 89, 112, 128
Shotgun Lady (Ohio), 105
Slack, Freddie, 45
Slender Man, 28–29
smartphone, 3, 13, 17, 26, 28, 192–206
Snow White (Disney film), 45
Spiritualist Church, 17, 197–98
Spook Hill (Florida), 153
Spook Light (Ohio), 70
Stepp Cemetery (Indiana), 9–10, 47–52, 54–58, 61

Stick Lady (Ohio), 63, 105
Sweet Hollow Road (New York), 153
Sydow, Carl Wilhelm von, 6

Test, Skiles E., 37–43
Thigpen, Kenneth A., 10, 45–46, 62, 74, 87, 96–97, 146, 194
Thomas, Jeannie Banks, 9, 112, 195–96
Thouless, Robert, 183
Tolbert, Jeffrey A., 195
Toledo Dig (Ohio), 104–9
tourism, 8–9
tricksters, 20
Tucker, Elizabeth, 7–8, 13–18, 54–60, 94, 192–93, 209
Tucker, Margaret, 15
Turner, Victor, 8–9
Tyson, Alvis, 133
Tyson, Joann, 133

University of Colorado, 184
Utah State University, 14

vandalism, 102–3
Van Gennep, Arnold, 85
"Vanishing Hitchhiker, The," 8, 66
Vázsonyi, Andrew, 4–5, 11, 94, 97, 141, 143–45, 148, 153–55, 167, 195–96
Victor, Jeffrey, 94
Virgil, 20
vortex, ghost 182

Walhalla Drive (Ohio), 70
Wall, The (Pennsylvania), 72, 78–80, 83, 86, 88
Walpole, Horace, 23
warlocks, 68
water babies, 209
Weeping Woman (statue in Utah), 14, 18
Weidner, Stephen, 180
werewolves, 64–65
Wise, Eleanor, 133
Wise, Jesse, 133
Wiseman, Richard, 184
witches, 49–51, 63–64, 66, 70, 119
Woman in White (Indiana), 33
wonder, sense of, 12, 157–58

Zombieland (Ohio), 105

www.ingramcontent.com/pod-product-compliance
Ingram Content Group UK Ltd.
Pitfield, Milton Keynes, MK11 3LW, UK
UKHW041941140426
5217IPUK00014B/591